IN THE RED CORNER

IN THE RED CORNER

A Journey into Cuban Boxing

John Duncan

YELLOW JERSEY PRESS
LONDON

Published by Yellow Jersey 2000

2 4 6 8 10 9 7 5 3 1

First published in Great Britain in 2000 by Yellow Jersey Press
Random House, 20 Vauxhall Bridge Road, London SW1V 2SA

Random House Australia (Pty) Limited
20 Alfred Street, Milsons Point, Sydney,
New South Wales 2061, Australia

Random House New Zealand Limited
18 Poland Road, Glenfield,
Auckland 10, New Zealand

Random House South Africa (Pty) Limited
Endulini, 5A Jubilee Road, Parktown 2193, South Africa

The Random House Group Limited Reg. No. 954009
www.randomhouse.co.uk

A CIP catalogue record for this book
is available from the British Library

ISBN 0-224-05147-4

Papers used by The Random House Group Limited are natural,
recyclable products made from wood grown in sustainable forests;
the manufacturing processes conform to the environmental
regulations of the country of origin

Typeset by Deltatype Ltd, Birkenhead, Merseyside
Printed and bound in Great Britain by
Biddles Ltd, Guildford and King's Lynn

To Mariela. Mi vida.

Contents

Acknowledgements | ix
1 You Don King, Me Don Quixote | 1
2 Should I Stay or Should I Go? | 7
3 Communism, Pugilism and Montecristianity | 13
4 Jack Johnson v. Jess Willard | 25
5 The Italian Restaurant Job | 35
6 Kid Chocolate | 44
7 Frankly Terrified | 64
8 Teofilo Stevenson | 77
9 Welcome to the Hotel Pernik | 96
10 Angel Espinosa | 108
11 Running with the Hack Pack | 130
12 Joel Casamayor | 149
13 Introducing Señor Yon Doooncan | 177
14 El Gallego Alvarez | 188
15 Go Away and Don't Come Back | 195
16 Felix Savon | 206
17 Behind Enemy Lines | 224
18 A Love Story with an Unhappy Ending:
Kid Gavilan | 234
19 How Much Is That Lada Tyre in the Window?:
The 1997 World Championships | 256
20 The Total Boxer: Adolfo Horta | 290
21 Close but no Sagarra:
To the Heart of the Cuban Team | 305
22 Houston, 1999 | 317

Acknowledgements

Above all I would like to thank Rachel Cugnoni, my editor, for spotting the possibility, keeping me enthused and not losing patience. This is her book as well as mine; Frank Warren, for backing my quixotic dream at the start; Kevin Mitchell for encouraging me and not laughing at my lack of boxing knowledge; Alan Rusbridger, the editor of the *Guardian*, for not letting me pack in journalism completely and taking me back after thirteen months; Mike Collett, for being the next best thing to a big brother; Shekhar Bhatia and the other Rotters for seeing me all right when I got back to England; Mike Ellison and Lucy Cavendish, for lending me their floor when I needed it and letting me stay there far too long; Guillem Balague for being a friend and picking up where we left off; Steve Bunce, for sharing two world championships and his taste in loud shirts; Brian Oliver, my sports editor at the *Observer*, for being the Gaffer; Caroline Cleary for helping with Miami arrangements and generally looking after me; the Havana rugby team, Ramon and the boys, for treating me like a Cuban; the Cuban press pack, Modesto, Pacheco, Robertico, Miguel, for letting me into the gang. And other Cubans who helped me but who I wouldn't wish to risk embarrassing by naming. You know who you are. Thanks.

In terms of content I am grateful to everyone who spoke to me, boxers, coaches, journalists, blokes on buses, librarians and friends of friends. In a country where no two people have the same version of the same incident, I am also grateful to several reliable published sources. Elio Menendez and I had many long conversations about Kid Chocolate and the chapter on Chocolate draws heavily on the information in his excellent book, *El Boxeo Soy Yo*, as well as those chats in Pinar del Rio at the 1997 Copa Cardin. I am also lucky to have got one of the few existing copies of Manolo Cabale Ruiz's book on Teofilo Stevenson to confirm the story of his early life in Cuba. Jorge Alfonso's work as a journalist for *Bohemia* and his book *Punos Dorados* were also a huge help. Sadly none of these books are published outside Cuba. I would also like to acknowledge the work of Jess Losada, whose published journalism in every major Cuban publication of the Thirties, Forties, and Fifties, was inspirational and also helped tie down a few facts.

I would like to thank my family; my mum for giving me a sense of adventure and gently pushing me to the left and my dad for teaching me to hate conformity and trying to drag me back to the right. On a practical level I am grateful to my mother-in-law, Martha, for transcribing the parts of the interviews with boxers that I couldn't decipher and for introducing me to the joys of Jerry Springer; my father-in-law, René Snr, for trusting me; my brothers-in-law, Rafael and René, for putting up with me in Havana; Tio Ruly, Tia Marie Elena, Tio Carlos, Tia Leisy, Tio Eddie and Abuelo Ruben for help in Miami when I was there. And Peregrina for the use of her phone and for helping Mariela and me get together in the end.

1 *You Don King, Me Don Quixote*

It was October, I think. Definitely a Monday morning, cold and grey outside, stiflingly hot in the *Guardian*'s concrete offices in Clerkenwell. I picked up the white envelope that had been sitting on top of my computer terminal for a week and walked past the news desk along what is supposed to be the longest news floor in world journalism and into the office of the editor, Alan Rusbridger. I sat down at a plain round table as he looked at me wearily. Rusbridger's technique involves saying little and looking at you plaintively, letting you fill in the gaps out of guilt. My voice wobbled and my hands were shaking. I resigned. Not to work for another paper, not for a bit more money, a company car, a set of brackets after my name, but to go to a foreign country where I didn't speak the language, didn't know anyone and where I was going to try and arrange a world heavyweight title fight between Felix Savon and Mike Tyson. Don King had failed to do it with a $25 million contract in his pocket at the Cuban training camp before the Mexico Olympics. I had a credit limit (recently raised to £2,500) and £2,000 in travellers' cheques. At least Don Quixote had Sancho Panza to talk to on his trip.

I didn't even have an obsession with the country, or with Cuban boxing, or with any particular Cuban boxer. I wish I could say that I had dedicated my spare time to clipping out articles about Savon or Teofilo Stevenson, but my only scrapbook contains Everton's full results, teams and match reports between 1978 and 1981, perhaps the least interesting and most unsuccessful era in the club's post-war history. Communism leaves me cold, though I did have that red and black Che Guevara poster above my bed when I was in the Harrogate branch of the Workers Socialist League back in the early Eighties. No, if I take the chain of events back before that Monday morning, I ended up spending a year in Cuba because I needed some serious time off work. And, I wrote this book because I spent the most beautiful, fucked-up year of my life there.

It all started when I went on holiday for the first time in a long while. January 1996 was freezing, that damp, in-your-nose sort of cold London specialises in. The Northern line wasn't working, the coffee machine at work was empty, my love life was in a deep coma, I was having a bad day and I decided I needed a holiday. I hadn't had a break from my job as sports news correspondent of the *Guardian* – drugs, hooligans, bungs, court cases – for two years, for the same reasons that most journalists are reluctant to take holidays. I was terrified that something would happen while I was away and I would be blamed for not anticipating it. Or worse, that someone would stand in for me and do the job better: more honourable to die of exhaustion at your terminal than be exposed as a fraud.

Besides, I reckoned that if I didn't get a holiday soon then two years without a break would become three. The European football championships were taking place in England in June 1996 and there was no question of a holiday close to them.

Euro '96 would involve me running around London, Manchester and Leeds after football hooligans. Then there were the Atlanta Olympics, and after them nine weeks in a Winchester courthouse listening to three footballers and a Malaysian businessman defend themselves against allegations of matchfixing.

Why Cuba? Well, like all decisions that change your life, I can't claim that I thought very hard about it at the time. Guilt maybe? Two years earlier I had split up with my Spanish girlfriend Beatriz, whom I had been living with for nearly four years. Basically I kicked her out a week before the start of the 1994 World Cup because everything seemed to be going wrong in my life. A house deal collapsed after three months, I was made redundant two days before I could even start a new job at the *Sunday Times*, my Grandma died and my relationship with Beatriz wasn't exactly idyllic.

One night Beatriz said perhaps I shouldn't be coming in from work at one in the morning and watching satellite highlights of Germany's greatest World Cup games for an hour before coming to bed. Perhaps I might try and talk to her sometimes, an act requiring some effort on my part because she worked from six in the morning to four in the afternoon and I worked three-fifteen in the afternoon to eleven-thirty. To justify myself, in the awful conversations that precede such whirlwind splits I remember making a crass remark about how I needed to be with someone who understood the subtleties of the English language, who could get my jokes about *Star Trek* or *Starsky and Hutch*. I was someone who worked with words – that was my excuse.

I said this to a woman who had turned up in England five years earlier without a word of English and who now spoke the language at a pretty normal pace and without an accent. When I decided to go to Cuba for a holiday that crass remark kept banging around my head. I had to make some amends to Beatriz, to scratch a two-year-old itch and ease my conscience.

I would go on holiday for the first time in two years to a Latin country, where no one would understand me and certainly not my jokes, because I wanted to punish myself for what I did to a beautiful woman from Madrid. I can remember suggesting to Beatriz that we might go somewhere like Cuba, where she would have the upper hand. She laughed because she knew I would never do it. But it was just a holiday, it wasn't a life-changing decision, or so I thought at the time. It was a butterfly flapping its wings in one corner of my life.

I landed in Havana on 20 February 1996, thirty-six hours after arriving at Stansted airport for a theoretically nine-hour flight. Cubana, the national airline, had to put me and 167 passengers up in the Stansted Hilton (no, I didn't know there was one either) for the first night of my penance because a tyre had burst on the plane and no one in the airport would allow Cubana credit or lend them another one. Apparently no one believed that they would get their money back.

We eventually took off and after nine hours of drinking and smoking at the back of the plane stepped out into the humid night air of Cuba, which felt like walking into a badly ventilated launderette.

I stayed with a Cuban family, who were well-to-do and terrified of everything. Allergic to any activity other than staying at home and watching television, they kept their son off school (about 300 yards away) if it was raining. Every time I asked them how I could arrange to do something, Miguel, the head of the house, would shake his head in awe at my stupidity. 'Let me explain you something about Cuba . . .' he would say and a sad diatribe about the inadvisability of leaving the house would follow. I asked him once if I could get a ticket for a baseball match. 'Let me explain you,' he said. 'Now is

4

very bad time with planes being shot down and the atmosphere is very, very tense, the crowd will be bad, everyone is very nervous, and you will probably not get a ticket and transport here in Cuba is very, very difficult. Why not watch it on the TV?'

Even that wasn't easy as the family's monosyllabic teenage son had first call on the small set to play with his elderly Nintendo, of which his parents were incomprehensibly proud – 'We prepare him for the Western life, we will make any sacrifice for our Miguelito.'

Miguel was scared because the Cubans had just shot down two planes flown over Havana by the Brothers to the Rescue, anti-Castro dissidents from among the million or so in Miami. Miguel was afraid the police would be jumpy and bombs might be planted in reprisal. Fortunately, for a Brit like me, the politics of Northern Ireland make you reasonably sanguine.

I went to the baseball anyway, figuring that having survived riots during the miners' strike, Italia 90, Sweden 92, and a variety of other foreign and domestic football-related skirmishes I could cope with a bit of bad 'atmosphere' in Havana. And I could get a ticket from a tout. I knew what Miguel did not want to admit – that you can buy anything for dollars in Havana.

When I got to the Estadio Latinoamericano, a functional but characterless stadium built for the baseball at the Pan-American games in the Sixties, there were no touts for the simple reason that entry cost three pesos (about 8p). The atmosphere in the 40,000-seat stadium was considerably less tense than bingo night at Walton Women's Institute because there were at most 900 people there. And transport home? Well, compared to shuffling along inch by inch up Wembley Way after an England football international, through half-eaten burgers borne along on a reservoir of piss, it was a cakewalk. I stood looking confused at a road junction for a second and a bloke stopped and gave me a lift for the price of a one-zone London bus ride.

On top of the baseball I discovered the Buleria, a small nightclub in which women paw you as you walk to the bar, prostitutes most of them, but not something that had happened to me before. I found the Café Cantante, a higher-class nightclub. I found respite from the attentions of prostitutes in the Sunday afternoon Cubans-only disco at the otherwise hooker-infested Hotel Commodoro, and I found a soccer team to play with. I travelled in old American cars; was hassled by men and women alike ('Hey, you, my friend, where you from!'); had the worst steak and chips of my life in the best surroundings, at the top of a tower in central Havana; drank too much rum; smoked too many filterless black-tobacco Populars (less of a cigarette, more a state-assisted suicide scheme); walked for miles around the city, awed by its beaten-up buildings and bleached beauty, and at the range of women from supermodel, drop-dead gorgeous, to the overweight with an inexplicable fondness for lurid Lycra catsuits, the most popular of which was crafted fraternally out of the stars and stripes. It was a fantastic time and I fell in love with Havana. I even started to be understood in Spanish. I began to wonder what it would be like to live there, but before I knew it I was back in London. Which is what happens at the end of great holidays, but somehow this didn't just feel like a great holiday.

2 Should I Stay or Should I Go?

Once I was back in London, in lifeless, nondescript March, I couldn't stop thinking about Havana. The idle thought of living in Cuba, in Havana, sprouted in the barren soil that was poor, overworked me and began to grow. I felt as if something was missing, that I ought to go back. Why, I wasn't sure, but I could guess. My life, like many people's when they get to their thirties, was OK but not as great as we'd imagined when we were sixteen. And at thirty-odd, maybe it's too late to do much about it.

How to live in Cuba and what to do while I lived there were problems too, but I could probably get round them. However, I couldn't help wondering if, after a crap couple of years without a holiday, I would have felt like living in Chernobyl if I had taken a fortnight's holiday there instead. Maybe it was all just day-dreaming. So, I decided to go back only two months later, in April, with what I thought would be a more critical eye.

On this occasion the plane left on time. And I arrived on schedule in Havana airport's Terminal Two. There were only about fifteen flights a day from the José Marti International

Airport, but they reckoned they needed three terminals (one international, one Caribbean, one internal).

Everyone piled off the plane and walked across the tarmac to a well-appointed Soviet-style concrete shed which housed Immigration, a row of booths in front of which you queue. They are chest-high, flimsy wooden constructions with a glass pane from waist to head height and a wooden shelf on the inside so you can't see what the man behind the counter is doing with his hands. Next to each booth is a chest-high wooden door, which swings open once you are deemed worthy of entry. There were twelve of them, each staffed by a uniformed officer, with Ministerio del Interior sewn untidily onto his bright green crumpled combat shirt. Imagine the least 'customer-oriented' dole officer you have ever signed on for, the one who looks at you as if the only thing he hates more than his job is you. Add the sort of nightclub bouncer who you sense would rather be at home dismembering small woodland creatures, slowly, with a blunt knife, than assisting in your enjoyment of the evening. Then multiply by the most authoritarian, cane-happy PE and geography teacher and throw in a doctor's waiting room full of traffic wardens and park attendants. Stick on a black moustache. That's him.

His is the first face seen by visitors to Cuba, who are a generally affable lot, oozing with good will towards the slightly risqué holiday destination they have chosen but jolly happy to be here, and, at least there won't be any Americans, not like in Florida last year – the place was bloody full of them. Above all, you are left with the impression, once you have been stamped and approved and the wooden door swings open, that you are entering a country which considers you an enemy.

It feels as if you've walked into a Second World War escape film, straight into the scene near the end just before everyone gets rounded up and shot, in which documents made out of potato peelings and congealed goat's piss ('a trick I learned in

India, sir') are scanned and checked and the stupid, hard-faced young Nazi lets two of our gallant lads into Switzerland.

If, as a first-time visitor to Cuba, you can get out of the airport terminal without mumbling 'fucking', with the word Cubans in close proximity, then you probably have what it takes to enjoy yourself. If not, you are in trouble.

Me, I was fine again. The flat I was staying in was pleasant enough, hottish water, clean, but penned in by other blocks. Next door was so close that it would have been easier to ask my new neighbour for the salt than go to my own kitchen. And I discovered one of the negative sides of Cuba, that the invention of volume control has totally passed the nation by. A Cuban TV set is either on or off and the same principle applies to the volume: with no carpets and the windows open, if the programme can't be heard in the next postcode the set needs adjusting. The same is true of hi-fis, which must be played just above the point where the music is distorted. There was a song by a relative of Julio Iglesias, a standard Latin Euro rock number called 'Es Un Esperienza Religiosa', which I had to endure a painful number of times a day under these conditions. Through repetition it grew on me like some nasty flesh-eating virus. And, because there are only two channels, and Cuban TV shows two blockbuster films stolen off the US satellite channels on Saturday nights (*Speed* was on Cuban TV before it was released in the UK), you can walk to the shop to get a can of Coke without missing a second of the dialogue.

Cuban friends say the top-volume trick is a habit from the more paranoid days of the revolution when people wanted to talk politics and didn't want the neighbours to hear. But Cubans are noisy in pretty much everything that they do. There is a gaggle of men in the Parque Central every day, shouting at each other as if they have all just discovered simultaneously that everyone else in the group has slept with his wife. All they are in fact doing is discussing baseball, the supposed national obsession which so few people in Havana bother to go and watch. It says something about Cubans that they consider it more fun to shout and argue with each other than actually to go and do anything. It may even explain why the government survives.

Certainly, their lack of action as a people, their passivity in the face of anything requiring commitment or sacrifice, would help to explain why Cuba has never been a truly independent country. It was ruled by Spain until 1898, when the United States intervened at the last stages of a war of independence to claim victory and the ownership of Cuba and the Philippines (the tactic worked so well that they tried it in a couple of world wars too). While theoretically independent for the first half of the twentieth century, Cuba's presidents were dependent on US good will regarding their sugar, which gave the United States a huge say in what happened.

Then in the aftermath of the revolution of 1 January 1959 the United States abolished their sugar quota. The Cubans sold their sugar and themselves to the Soviet Union instead for twenty-eight years, until the USSR's sweet tooth was pulled with the collapse of Communism, and what the Cubans euphemistically call 'the special period' began. Special in the way that Waterloo was special for Napoleon or the Blitz was special for Londoners. A lot of Cubans came close to starving. They are still not sure if the special period is over. One barometer trusted by many is that when the one-way systems of Havana's grid-designed suburbs are actually enforced the special period will be over – Cubans were told they should take the quickest route home to save petrol and they should ignore the street signs, a patriotic gesture for which little encouragement was required.

This was what first drew me to the country, its chaos, disorganisation and love of futile defiant gestures. It was intoxicating to find somewhere I felt I belonged. Cuba defies logic with the same two-fingered zeal with which it has defied the United States for thirty-five years. I loved it.

When you get into Havana and see the buildings, their peeling glory hanging on by a forty-year-old coat of paint, when you watch the people going about their business and surviving, and when you see the old American cars bumping and clunking along potholed streets that, in places, would challenge an armoured vehicle, let alone a 1959 Chevrolet with a 1300 Lada engine, it's impossible not to wonder how it all works, what makes the city and its people survive. The joke locally was that the Pope, who came in January 1998, was keen to visit Cuba to see for himself the only country in the world that survives purely by the grace of God.

And there's the rest of Cuba. History and mystery: the revolution and the myth of the heroic guerrillas, big fat cigars, baseball, rum, Che Guevara, Castro, the Bay of Pigs, the Cuban missile crisis. And, like most people in Europe who saw the Berlin Wall come down in 1989, it seemed only a matter of time before Cuba followed and there would be nowhere left to stand outside the norm.

On this second trip I found that I could get a good apartment by the sea in safe, middle-class Miramar, just to the west of Havana, where most of the embassies and foreign companies are based, for around 300 dollars a month. And that I liked the sunshine and the time I had to read and write. That the odd bit of journalism would go a long way. That it didn't take long to adapt to a slower pace of life. That calm and introspection could replace the fear and exhaustion which seemed to be part of the deal of living in London. That I could be happy being alone.

And a voice kept saying that if I didn't do this now then I never would. That I was thirty-one, single and at a point in my career where a year away wouldn't be fatal if I needed to come back. I had enough friends and contacts to survive if it all went belly up. When I looked around me I saw people who had spent their whole lives in journalism, who needed a break even more than I did, but who had no chance of getting one because you can't put the wife and kids and the whole smortgagebord in storage and go away. I could.

3 *Communism, Pugilism and Montecristianity*

There are three things which everybody thinks they know about Cuba. The first is that the island produces excellent cigars rolled on the thighs of beautiful maidens. They are indeed excellent (though if you get conned into buying a ten-dollar box of fake Montecristos on the street you may not think so when you try to smoke them). Having been round a few cigar factories, I now know that they are rolled on a wooden table by hand, and the people who roll them are men and women of widely varying ages and degrees of desirability. They're about as romantic as a fish-processing plant in Grimsby, only with more sunshine.

The second is that Cuba is the last bastion of Communism, the embers of the greatest social experiment in human history, but one which still has great education and health systems. In Latin American terms the education's not bad at all, compulsory, well-organised and free. All Cuban kids wear the same school uniforms with yellowy brown shorts or long trousers depending on how old they are – no school has its own identity – and almost every kid attends. There is no child labour in Cuba. But the quality of the education has been ravaged by a lack of resources, teachers and textbooks, which has devalued the system dramatically from what it was in the Seventies and it wasn't that well supplied then. Kids can miss whole years of certain subjects because of the shortage of teachers. Despite that, literacy levels are high and everyone has a chance to go to university for free providing they can put up with the pre-university requirements that they work for a period of time in the countryside and pass the course in Marxism-Leninism which will be the paradigm for their undergraduate education. The problem is that jobs after university attract nothing more than the national maximum wage of about twenty dollars a month, so many bright kids have started to wonder whether it is worth the effort. The health system is also a shadow of what it was intended to be. The hospitals are there, in greater numbers than in many Latin countries, the doctors are well trained and of high calibre and they are free. But they have little in the way of modern equipment and only their diagnostic skills prevent the system from collapsing completely. You have to bring your own lightbulbs, clean sheets and food if you want to give birth in hospital. A friend of mine who worked in a Cuban hospital as part of his English medical training was amazed at what they achieved with so little, finding out with a physical examination and a few simple questions what a million-pound machine in the UK would struggle to diagnose.

But to talk about Communism is to talk about Fidel Castro. Everything about him seems mythical and this aura is fed by the myriad failures to kill or replace him. Castro is the anti-Christ to the American government, the last cockroach of world Communism, impossible to neutralise or eliminate. Because of that he is hero to revolutionaries and anti-Americans everywhere. The stories about the CIA's attempts to topple him are endless: how they concocted a boot polish which they thought would make his trademark beard fall out and therefore cause him to lose his magical hold over the population (someone in Langley had been reading the Old Testament that weekend). The attempt to slip him an exploding cigar is celebrated along with the rest of these pitiful schemes in the Interior Ministry's museum in Miramar, where the cigar in question, successfully defused, now resides. Less well-known stories add to the myth. It is said that the CIA discovered a weakness in his elaborate security procedures, that he would visit the same ice-cream stall every day at the same time. They paid off the woman who worked there to poison him. When Castro turned up as expected, the woman took the phial of poison out of the fridge only for her hand to shake so violently that she dropped the phial on the floor, where it smashed. These stories, and his longevity, add to the sense on the streets of Havana as much as in Washington that Castro has a pact with the devil.

It is still hard to get Cubans to criticise him with much enthusiasm – most people prefer to blame the people around him for the country's ills – and many prefer the devil they know to the foaming lunatics who dominate politics in Miami and who would like to dominate Cuba once again. It is they who orchestrated some random terror plots, such as fire-bombing tourist hotels while I was there. In one attack an unlucky Italian was killed when glass from a ceiling panel fell and cut his throat. But it was pretty amateur stuff. The intention – to scare away tourists and create terror in Havana – was not even close to being accomplished because the campaign was so half-hearted.

Few Cubans on the island passionately want to see Castro dead, but they aren't in love with him like they used to be, which is probably his own fault. Castro has let himself fall into the role of vain dictator surrounded by weak men, who protect him from the truth. One of his former aides told me that in the early days Castro employed a man whose sole duty was to report to Fidel himself all the Castro jokes that were doing the rounds in Havana. He lost his job years ago. The jokes still go round, but Castro doesn't share them any more.

The third thing people know is that Cuba is good at sport: baseball, athletics and, of course, boxing. Most people remember Alberto Juantorena (his middle name was Danger, well, his second surname). His performance at the 1976 Montreal Olympics, breaking the world record in the 800 metres, an event which he had barely practised, on top of winning the 400 metres for which he was widely tipped, made him the first non-English-speaking winner of those events and the first man to win them both at the same Olympics. A few can even remember Ana Fidelia Quirot, a bronze medallist in the 800 metres in Barcelona, whose recovery from horrific burns to the face made a touching sight in Atlanta, where she won silver. Javier Sotomayor, the world-record-holding high jumper, is another athlete whom most people know of. He dominated his event for years and won the gold in Barcelona, but he had a disappointing Atlanta and late in 1998 completed his fall from grace when a drugs test revealed traces of cocaine. The Cubans, perhaps out of habit, blamed the CIA.

Even if you don't remember these athletes, you've surely heard of the boxer, Teofilo Stevenson, the treble Olympic champion robbed of a fourth title by the pointless boycott of the Los Angeles games. Cuba has produced some great boxers. Kid Chocolate, the little fighter in the Twenties who could stop traffic in Broadway. World champions like Ultiminio Ramos, who tragically killed two men in the ring; José Mantequilla Napoles, who left after the revolution and fought out of Mexico to become a longstanding WBC middleweight champion; Luis Rodriguez, another boxer who left after the revolution, who had the misfortune to be on a plane which was hijacked and flown to Havana while he was allegedly on a Cuban death list – he survived and died a couple of years ago. Kid Gavilan, whose world championship welterweight bouts in the Fifties were massive events. Black Bill, the Cuban featherweight who became a star in New York until, penniless and half-blind, he killed himself when his girlfriend left him. Kid Charol, the brightest Cuban young hope of the Twenties, who left for Argentina to box and star in music hall, before dying of tuberculosis two weeks after getting in the ring with a future world champion and scraping a draw. Benny Paret, briefly world middleweight champion before he was killed in the ring after a brutal fight with Emile Griffith. Emilio Correa, Adolfo Horta, Angel Espinosa – and the heavyweight everyone was talking about now, Felix Savon.

All this was in my mind when I came to think about how I could make a life in Cuba pay. I had considered starting a cultural centre, organising events to encourage friendly relations with Britain, teaching English cheaply, holding an annual festival maybe, a Beatles exhibition (the Beatles were banned in the Sixties and the Cubans are just catching up on them). But I didn't know anything about organising exhibitions or teaching English and anyway all of that would have relied on the generosity and desire for self-promotion of British companies, which were sensibly keeping their heads down as the United States sought to tighten the noose around Cuba and its trading partners. Maybe a bike race, a football match, a boxing match. Rubbish, really. Strictly beer-mat stuff. Except for the last. That might actually have some mileage in it.

And when I got home this was the idea I chose to look at more closely. I spoke to the chief sports writer and boxing correspondent of the *Observer*, Kevin Mitchell. We went to the *Guardian*'s local pub, the Coach and Horses, and sank a few Guinnesses. Our enthusiasm got stronger with every passing pint. He told me more about Felix Savon, the Olympic heavyweight champion in 1992 and unbeatable according to those who claim to know about these things. I knew the name from the last Olympics, but not much more. Kevin told me about Teofilo Stevenson in the Seventies, who was so frightening that opponents sometimes didn't turn up for Olympic finals, so assured were they of a bad beating. Savon was his heir, said Kevin. And there would be big money on the table for a fight between Savon and Mike Tyson, then re-establishing himself as the king of the heavyweight division after a stint in Indiana's Youth Correctional Institute for rape. The thinking at the time was that once Tyson had reunified the division, it would become as dull as ditchwater within a year, as the bum-a-month club lined up to give Tyson a yawn, a stretch and a few million dollars in ever-decreasing amounts as the fights became less and less interesting and pay-per-viewable. Something fresh would be needed. By the end of the conversation Kevin and I had decided we were the men to save heavyweight boxing. And then the minicab came.

Unlike the usual pub-inspired rubbish, this idea had something to say for itself. OK, it wasn't exactly my line of work, but it wasn't a million miles away. I knew people, I knew how it worked, sort of. I knew that most sport deals are fuelled and sustained by bullshit and bluster. And after all I was a hustler at heart. I could take on Don King. I could do deals with cable companies, merchandising, books, films. The world would take notice. Maybe the Guinness hadn't quite worn off.

Savon versus Tyson had mystery and political edge. It wouldn't be hard to hype in the States or among Latin fight fans. And Savon was good enough for it to be a real fight, with no one sure what would happen. There was, as Kevin had pointed out, a historical parallel too. Stevenson had been due to fight Muhammad Ali in the Seventies, but the fight never came off because of disagreement over the rules. Stevenson refused to turn professional completely, but was prepared to fight under rules agreed with the amateur governing body. Castro even gave his consent publicly. But it never happened. Cuban journalists blame the Americans and, guess what, the Americans blame the Cubans. In the end Ali came to Havana for the first time in 1995 to deliver medical supplies – Havana has the world's leading research facility for Parkinson's disease – and was asked how it might have turned out. 'A draw,' he said and smiled.

So on my second trip I had some work to do. These were nice ideas and the boxing possibilities sounded fine, but what on earth could I actually do that might be useful to someone? The only fight I'd ever had involved a kid called McGregor at school and a teacher walking into the room just as I was banging his head against a locker. The answer came from two meetings: one was at a restaurant in the centre of Havana with an ex-boxer called Henry; the other was a beautiful meal in the Hertfordshire countryside with Frank Warren.

Henry was the owner of the restaurant, the Three Musketeers. It wasn't officially a restaurant – that was a word the Cuban state kept for themselves – but a *paladar*, a private establishment run by families in their own homes with a maximum of twelve chairs, taxed ten times the monthly maximum wage, forbidden to serve lobster or beef and unable to advertise. I had discovered the Three Musketeers by accident on my first visit.

Henry's *paladar* was on the first floor of a colonial building on one of Havana's main streets, which runs from central Havana to Miramar in the west through Vedado. All the buses and cars travelling across town have to go that way. To get to the first floor you go up a path along the side of the building past an open door, where two unshaven old men sit with the radio at full volume mending shoes in a room full of rusting Chinese bikes.

They always listened to Radio Reloj, a Cuban institution since before the revolution and possibly the worst radio station in the world. Basically Radio Reloj is rolling news, twenty-four hours a day of it, read out from sheets of paper, copied from the newspaper, stolen off agencies. No colour, no interviews, no recipes, no celebs, no sporting events. Just two people reading deadpan news bulletins twenty-four hours a day. Its place in broadcasting ignominy, however, is secured by the fact that under these bulletins is the sound of a clock ticking, which sets off an electronic buzzer, an annoying beep like the first hand-held space invader machines used to make, at the top of every minute. At that point the bulletin is interrupted for the newsreader to give the station a name check – like you might have thought this was Kiss FM accidentally – and tell the time. The only trouble is that sometimes the newsreaders go too fast and finish their bulletins ahead of time, which means that Radio Reloj broadcasts the sound of a clock ticking for ten seconds and nothing else. It was spooky enough listening to it in the house alone, but coming out of a cobblers' shed at full volume with two old blokes staring out at you it was scary.

Past the cobblers was a narrow dark staircase, which looked as if it had been carved into the house. It was wide enough to climb but claustrophobic, which forced you to mind your head as you rose towards the *paladar*. Inside were three areas: a sitting room, where the owners and family could be found shouting at each other over the sound of one of the two reggae tapes the management owned; the kitchen, where another elderly bloke in a filthy, once-white apron smoked over a stove as he boiled up some lobster (illegal can be a theoretical concept in Havana); and the eating area, a balcony with a beautiful view of the white church opposite and the building site next to it, from which the management were negotiating the theft of a few materials to build an extension to their own establishment. They also rented out a few rooms, very cheaply, sometimes by the hour to couples who had tired of having sex in cars and wanted a bed. The mattress in one room was deformed and uneven, rippled as if someone had frozen a waterbed in mid-wave. I only ever met one person staying there, a Palestinian political activist who seemed to have no money and who would disappear for a few days at a time without much in the way of a sensible explanation. It wasn't paranoid to imagine what he was probably up to, though he might well have suspected the same of me because he kept asking not very subtle questions about Ireland which I answered with a smile. He must have thought I was well trained. He scared me.

Henry, a thick-set bald black man, with a round Congolese-shaped face like the black baddies in Sixties' James Bond films, was nice enough and turned out to be a former boxer of quite high calibre. Apparently he had reached a decent level nationally as a welterweight and had a crumpled black and white photo to back it up. He looked pretty hard and the shadow-boxing he did out on the patio was impressive, so I believed him. In Cuba there is so little information about anything that believing someone is a personal choice based on how much you want what they say to be true. I wanted to believe Henry, he was going to be my way into Cuban boxing.

'I'll teach you if you want, John,' he said. 'It's very good for your protection. In the street.' Looking at his meat-cleaver hands, muscled upper body and bollard thick neck, I reckoned it would be safer to take my chance with muggers than with him in a gym. 'No thanks, Henry,' I said as politely as I could.

'I know them very well. The team, the trainers, the big chief Alcides Sagarra, they are all friends of mine.' He went to a back room and returned with a book, a well-worn paperback the size of an school exercise book with a red and blue cover and a picture of Sagarra, who had been the national coach of the boxing team since 1964, on the front. It was called *Charlas Entre Cuerdas* (Tales from the Ring) and was Sagarra's portrait of Cuban boxing past, present and future. I borrowed it and went back to the flat to find out what my chances were.

Sagarra's importance in what I was going to do cannot be overestimated and Henry's apparent inside knowledge was a huge boost. I needed to convince Sagarra that I had a good and feasible idea, or at least I had to be sure I wouldn't get thrown out of the country for asking him about it. Sagarra has been on the central committee of the Cuban Communist Party for many years. A severe, grandfatherly figure, with expressive full lips and hangdog eyes, he is to be found wherever Cuba's boxers are, wearing his trademark well-worn tracksuit and a pair of round spectacles. At tournaments he sits alone at a small Formica table in a corner of the arena making notes, ignoring the action for minutes on end before looking up and fixing his stare intently on the ring. There is an empty seat next to him because someone always needs to talk to him. Trainers, team managers, former boxers, politicians – some get a smile, others get polite but grim-faced attention. Few leave with the sound of his gravelly old man's laugh in their ears. It takes a few rums to warm him up and he rarely relaxes.

Sagarra entered the newly formed Escuela de Boxeo Cubano in 1963 at its formation, a young trainer who had been part of a gym in Havana where some of the better professionals had trained. He took up boxing himself at a youngish age because he was told it would be a good cure for his asthma. But he was only moderately successful and as a young trainer, politically committed to the revolution, he was eager to be a part of the new era in Cuban boxing. In truth, though, his role in the early years was to learn as much as teach. The Soviet Union and East Germany sent over coaches to help in the new school, as part of their belief that the superiority of Communism could be demonstrated through sport. The key figure in this was Andrei Chervorenko, a very Soviet-looking chap, all cheap tracksuit and wrinkled-tobacco skin, tall and broad like a bear. He brought with him the ideas of science and preparation and the importance of what they always called physical culture. There is no evidence that he also brought with him the drugs technology that had been introduced to give Communism the chemical as well as the moral high ground. However it was done, the Soviets brought the Cubans their techniques and attitudes to preparation. And when Chervorenko, who had picked out and personally trained Teofilo Stevenson when no one else in the camp saw his potential, was called back to Moscow in 1980, unwillingly by all accounts, Sagarra, who was his deputy, took control.

What Sagarra had nurtured and developed alongside the governing bodies of sport on the island was a national vacuum cleaner for athletic ability, which no one with talent could, or would have wanted to, escape. At local level promising athletes are reported by schools to local sports coaches. After testing, many of them are selected at an early age – how early depends on the sport, but boxers are nurtured from the age of eleven – to attend special sports schools, where their ability is encouraged still further. These places are popular among parents too, in that they are residential, a bonus in often overcrowded homes, and the food is better than normal. Not all make it and a number drop out each year as they fail to come up to scratch. From here successful athletes go to regional centres of sports excellence. And, in time, the best from the regions are summoned to Havana to be part of either the national youth centre of sports training or of one of the elite national squads – what the Cubans call the 'Preseleccion'. The youth teams are put up in an ugly Sixties housing estate built for the Pan-American Games of 1991 and close to the national stadium. If you are physically fit and show some aptitude for sport, a space will be found for you. Felix Savon, for example, had hoped to get into school as a rower, but failed. He took up a place as a boxer as his second prize. When a coach turned up at his school he had never boxed before. Four years later he was world champion heavyweight. That is how good the Cuban system is.

And Henry seemed to be saying that I had found a point of access to it. What if they were looking for a way to enter the professional world? What if they wanted someone to introduce them to a way of turning professional en masse? This could be the biggest thing that ever happened in boxing and I could be the catalyst. Henry and I sat and talked more. Sometimes he sounded like a drunk man on speed, incomprehensibly slurred but blurrily fast. His wife, an attractive plumpish woman of about twenty-eight, came and joined us. She was calm and quiet, with a sad, thoughtful smile permanently on the edges of her lips. I wondered how she managed to keep up with Henry. After a few glasses of Bucanero I failed my first test as an undercover operator and spilled my guts.

'What it is, Henry, is whether the government here could be persuaded to sanction a fight between Mike Tyson and Felix Savon. The plan would be to stage the fight here in Havana, maybe at the baseball stadium, American TV, lots of money. The Cuban government would act as his agent and take a cut of the fee and use the event as a massive propaganda coup against the United States. Don King is no friend of the US government so he wouldn't care about an embargo and for boxing fans it would be irresistible. A chance to see, by proxy, the Stevenson versus Ali fight that never happened, a rerun of Johnson against Willard. But I need to get to important people, like Sagarra, to ask them if it's possible. Can you help me, do you know them?'

'Yes,' said Henry. 'I know them all.'

4 *Jack Johnson v. Jess Willard*

The idea of a heavyweight world title bout in Havana laced with political undertones was not without precedent, though you had to go back to 5 April 1915 to find it. Cuba's one and only world heavyweight title fight took place in the Hipodromo Oriental Park, a long-since vanished racetrack in the countryside of the Marianao area of the city, a part of town which now plays host to the world-famous cabaret, the Tropicana, and is one of Havana's roughest working-class districts. The fight was between the greatest and most controversial black heavyweight champion of all time, Jack Johnson, and the man who was burdened with carrying the great white hopes of the still segregated United States, Jess Willard, the Pottawotamie Giant, a 6ft 5in rancher who emerged at the head of a list of possible men to take the title from the upstart negro. The fight was scheduled for forty-five rounds in the open air, in a city where April spews a damp, sapping 35°C heat.

Cuba in those days had little tradition of organised boxing aside from street brawls and fist fights with a few side bets, the sort of rough and tumble of every major city over any number

25

of centuries. At the turn of the century the major sports clubs were run and patronised by colonial aristocrats with little interest in the sport. The first official boxing association was formed in 1910 not by a Cuban but by a visiting Chilean, John Budinich. He had been a journeyman pro in the United States and came to Cuba to eke out a living as a self-defence and boxing instructor. He found work almost immediately at the Vedado Tennis Club. In order to interest more people in the sport he organised some exhibitions, the first of which took place on the stage at the Teatro Payret in Vedado in August 1912 against an American, Jack Ryan. Budinich, watched by the kids he was trying to attract to the sport, was knocked out in two rounds.

Budinich's group stifled their sniggers and carried on honing their skills with fights staged, at first, in each other's homes. Later that year prize-fighting of any kind was banned by the government, a regular hazard that was to hinder professional boxing in Cuba many times over the next forty years. Happily, in time-honoured Cuban style, the ban was largely ignored and boxing carried on, barely even bothering to go underground. Budinich himself hung around until 1915, the year of the Johnson–Willard fight. He was last heard of fighting for the Foreign Legion in the First World War.

The first official national title fight was a flyweight bout between Victor Achan and Florentino Llano in April 1913, a fight which took place in the front room of another fighter, Mike Febles. It was hardly pay-per-view. The only way spectators could be tempted in was to offer free drinks. After Achan defended his title (knocking out poor old Llano in the first round), on home turf in his own front room this time, there was an exhibition of ju-jitsu between two other boxers. When Achan defended his title a fortnight later his opponent was knocked unconscious for an hour in the second round when a punch knocked his head back against the living-room wall.

Cuba's first heavyweight champion was declared in 1914, a guy called Anastasio Peñalver. He had never actually boxed but was the only person around the scene at the time who was heavy enough. In his first fight against a touring American his corner threw in the towel after two minutes of the first round.

While domestic boxing wasn't big, interest was growing in higher-quality American boxers on the island and one American entrepreneur, publisher of the English-language *Havana Post*, opened a boxing stadium in the centre of town. It attracted good crowds, the best of them for a fight in March 1915 when Battling Jim Johnson took on an ageing Sam McVey, two world title contenders of that era, in front of 15,000 people. Typically in the cocked-up history of Cuban boxing the fight was declared a draw, the crowd demanded five more rounds to decide it and a riot broke out. The arena was shut down months later.

But Johnson versus Willard was the real thing, especially for a Havana that was growing rapidly into a playground for America's prosperous south-east. Jack Johnson was a great defensive heavyweight who first won the title in 1908. He exacerbated that particular crime by enjoying the company of white women and showing no desire to pander to white sensibilities about how a black man should conduct himself. He liked fast cars and fine living and by relentlessly doing whatever he felt like made himself white America's most hated black fighter of all time, until Muhammad Ali came along and claimed the title in the Sixties. Johnson was a quiet kid from a small town in Texas, whose more physical sister was regularly called upon to protect his honour in the playground. He ran away from home in 1890 and ended up in Massachusetts cadging an existence on urban streets before cheekily asking Joe Walcott, a well-known welterweight, for work as a sparring partner. Walcott took to him and Johnson worked his way up the ranks in Walcott's gym. The better he got, the harder doors were slammed in his face. He was left to fight inferior black fighters in meaningless contests because the white American world champions of the time refused to fight blacks. Only when the title left the United States with the Australian Tommy Burns was the door ajar to black fighters. Johnson's manager pursued Burns relentlessly for a fight, but Burns turned him down again and again, actively encouraging gossip that he was running from Johnson and thus whipping up the pressure for the fight (with a large purse, naturally) to be organised. Finally the money was put up by an Australian promoter and Burns defended against Johnson in Sydney in 1908. Burns was easy meat – he was a stone and a half lighter than his opponent – and totally outboxed by Johnson. Pictures of the fight show Johnson practically bending over to hit his dwarfed opponent. Police ordered the fight to be stopped in the fourteenth with Burns taking heavy punishment. The heavyweight champion of the world was black.

Which, of course, white America wasn't going to stomach for long. When news of the fight reached the United States there were race riots and lynchings. Johnson defended successfully in Pittsburgh, Philadelphia and California before he was set up to face Stanley Ketchel, a middleweight, but the best challenger white boxing could find. It's said that the fight was deliberately extended by the boxers, who recognised the dangerous difference in their weights, through a tacit agreement that neither would get too aggressive. Ketchel, who was giving away an impossible amount of weight to Johnson, got over-excited, however, and knocked Johnson down in the twelfth. The error of his ways was demonstrated to him moments later when Johnson bounced up with an uppercut which removed five of Ketchel's teeth at their roots. Two of Ketchel's teeth were later found embedded in Johnson's glove.

In July 1910 Jim Jeffries, a great former champion who had retired unbeaten, was talked out of retirement on an alfalfa farm by those who thought he could wallop the cocky black boy. When they met in Reno, Johnson knocked him down in fifteen, a fight result which ruined Jeffries's reputation and is the only one for which he is now remembered.

Unable to humiliate Johnson in the ring – he defended successfully against Fireman Jim Flynn in Las Vegas in April 1912 – the white establishment tried to nab him in court. First he was indicted on a charge of illegally importing jewellery. Then he was taken to court under America's Mann Act, which prevented transport between states for 'immoral purposes' and was ostensibly designed to stop organised prostitution. Johnson's crime was to pay for a white 'girlfriend' to travel from Pittsburgh to Chicago and he was sentenced to a year and a day in prison and a $1,000 fine. Johnson admitted in court that he was 'technically guilty', but he ignored the verdict, skipped bail and headed for Europe.

Johnson made two defences in nearly three years in Paris – a definite change of pace: he had made four in six months in 1909 – and threw himself into European life with vigour. He spent some time as a spy in Spain, challenged Rasputin to a vodka-drinking contest in pre-revolutionary Russia and 'starred' as a spear carrier in a production of *Aida*. The high life must have started to wear thin and the money run low by the time he was offered a fight in Havana against Jess Willard. They tried to make the fight in Mexico, but it didn't pan out. They settled on Havana, which was about as close as Johnson could get to the United States without being arrested. White America had bankrupted him, now they had to knock him down.

Jess Willard was born on 29 December 1881 in a small town in Kansas. Two months before he was born his father had died, at the age of thirty-seven, from wounds received in the

Civil War. Willard would probably have become a cowboy, but his unusually large stature made him unsuitable. He was, however, an enthusiastic ranch hand and trader, sometimes buying the horses from the Pottawotamie Indians (from whom he later got his nickname) and selling them on to locals. His grandson says that he probably started boxing in December 1910 in Oklahoma City.

Jess Willard's first exhibition bouts were in 1911, though no one considered the fights important enough to record the names of the opponents. In 1912 Willard had thirteen bouts and exhibitions. In 1913 he fought thirteen more. The names were getting bigger and the results better: 'Gunboat' Smith and 'Bull' Young both died as a result of Willard's punches. Willard fought only three bouts in 1914, but middle America saw in him the whitest hope yet of winning back the world heavyweight title.

The capacity for the Havana fight, held in front of the race track's grandstand, was not massive, but interest was large enough for a full-scale feature-film crew to record it with three cameras, a massive operation for the time. While the main bulk of the crowd sat in the shade of the stand, a few hundred Panama-hatted men sat sweltering in suits around three sides of the ring, about forty deep. Behind them was a makeshift gantry that announced the fight in handpainted letters next to the name of the venue written out in English 'Oriente Race Track Havana, Cuba'. This was an American event and it was Americans who had come to see it. President Menocal of Cuba looked down on proceedings from the upper tier of the stand, surrounded by senior army officers. As did the mayor of Havana, Pedro Bustillo, a man with a huge bushy white moustache and formal collar, the very picture of a frontier administrator. The MC, Fred Mace, introduced the fighters and read out the receipt of the purses. Johnson was to receive

29,000 dollars, he announced to the grandstand through a handheld cardboard loudhailer. The timekeepers were named: Pommery Bob Vernon and Ben Harris. Then the referee, Jack Welsh. Johnson was first into the ring, ambling up in a full-length heavy dressing gown that covered his shoes and with decorative brocade around thigh level. He kept his hands tucked into its pockets throughout the long preamble to the fight. His corner were all dressed in white turtle-necked pullovers with full-length sleeves, two black men and one white. Johnson moved to the edge of the ring and leaned over as a cornerman pointed to where his white wife, Lucille Cameron, was sitting at ringside in the paddock next to the press. The incident was followed faithfully by the cameras, a reminder perhaps to anyone back home who wasn't sure why America wanted Johnson beaten.

The fighters were weighed in the ring, Johnson still had his dressing gown on, its collar turned up as if against an imaginary cold breeze as he strolled across the ring aimlessly, no shadow-boxing, no movement at all, for all the world a man who had popped out to collect the milk from his doorstep on a Sunday morning.

Willard wore only a light black cape over his shoulders, which he held in place with his left hand as he shook Johnson's hand, perfunctorily, without smiles, and dropped it. The pair had their gloves put on, Johnson still with his gown on, Willard's white skin shining in the sun.

Referee Welsh calls for the start of the fight and finally the dressing gown comes off. Johnson wipes his feet in the white resin deposited in the corners to avoid slipperiness. He is wearing grey shorts, thigh length, slightly loose. Willard is huge, three or four inches taller than Johnson, in small black shorts that are tight enough to pass as oversized swimming trunks.

They start the first of a scheduled forty-five rounds. The

two square up, left feet planted in front of each other, feinting, both leaning slightly back, their hands in front moving at waist height in circles, waiting. Johnson occasionally sees chances and launches himself through Willard's long reach with his left. He charges after it and follows with his right, running headlong at Willard. Willard retreats and looks for his chance to do the same. He picks Johnson off with the occasional right hand. Both know that there are forty-four rounds to go. Johnson knows that Willard probably is the stronger. It isn't much to watch.

And that basically is how the fight goes. Johnson lands a few and has a few good rounds. Willard takes the punches and retreats. Johnson has a good 14th, a good 17th, a good 20th, violent flurries of action when he catches his opponent and tries to follow up. But no knockdown. Little by little Willard is coming more into the fight, catching Johnson, whose sweating back is glinting in the sun. The referee Welsh has to shield his eyes from the glare as the fight goes on. Now it is Willard who is probing and charging, and Johnson, whose legs are looking more sluggish than before and, who is fending him off. At the end of the 25th Johnson gestures to his wife and sends her away from the heat at ringside. In the 26th Johnson is caught by Willard's swinging left. He staggers and falls. Welsh is above him as Johnson lies on the floor, motionless, but with his arms raised, his gloves in front of his face. He makes no attempt to get up. Welsh counts to ten and then having counted him out simply walks away from Johnson on the floor. The ring fills up. Johnson still doesn't move. The press and ringside hangers-on clamber into the ring. Cuban soldiers and police make their way to fetch the winner, Willard, and accompany him through the lines of cheering fans. Panama hats sail into the air, the air is white hot with American pleasure. Poor Jack Johnson.

Even at the time of the fight there were commentators who

smelled a rat. They pointed out that the blow which felled Johnson was of little consequence and should not have troubled him. The rumour went around that he had dived in exchange for cash and the right to go home to Texas, but the theory never held much water. Johnson certainly looks to be trying for most of the fight and was obviously tired when the final blows came in. A photo was published which showed him knocked out, apparently trying to keep the sun out of his eyes as he lay on the canvas. Why would a knocked-out fighter do that, it was asked? Why, countered Willard's supporters, would a man wait twenty-six punishing rounds in the heat of Havana to take a dive?

Johnson himself stoked the flames several years later when he sold a story to *Ring* magazine in which he 'admitted' to throwing the fight. He claimed that his wife had been waiting at ringside to receive the money, but that it had not arrived (which certainly might explain why he wanted to see where his wife was before the fight), that the money didn't turn up (which might explain why she left) and that a deal had been done for him to go back to the United States without trouble. He sold this story to *Ring* for a few thousand dollars, but even the editor who bought it said he didn't give it much credibility, since it came at a time when Johnson needed money and would have done pretty much anything to get it.

Willard's decline post-Havana was spectacular. He wasn't a great or even a particularly enthusiastic fighter. After falling out with his manager he spurned a series of big-money offers and joined the circus. He did a stint in vaudeville at Hammersteins' Victoria Theatre in New York, but the biggest deal was with Buffalo Bill's Wild West Show, and later the 101 Ranch Wild West Show. He even starred in a film, *The Challenge of Chance.*

Willard did fight again: six times in 1916, four in 1918, and then in 1919 he took on Jack Dempsey. Dempsey, twenty-four at the time, beat Willard black and blue over three rounds. Willard was knocked down seven times in the first round, and by the end of the third his jaw was broken in two places, he had two fractured ribs, five missing teeth and an ear so badly damaged that he never regained his full hearing. Willard maintained for the rest of his life that Dempsey's gloves were loaded and the severity of the beating handed out to him does nothing to diminish that possibility. Willard's job in boxing was done. He had lived to the age of almost eighty-seven, when he died on 15 December 1968. By the time of his death, black civil rights had made only fitful progress and Martin Luther King Jr had been murdered five months before.

Johnson left Havana and went to Spain, where he fought a few times in Madrid and Barcelona, and got mixed up in spying for the Americans, seeking out possible submarine bases on the west coast of Spain, a most generous gesture given the treatment he had received at the hands of the American establishment. He moved on to Mexico, opened a café and kept boxing on a small scale before, homesick, he handed himself in at the US–Mexican border at San Diego and was sent to Leavenworth prison (where he carried on boxing) for a year and a day after a trial heavily influenced by stories that he had cut a deal and was not concerned at what the court might dish out to him. His first two engagements after his release were back in Havana in May 1923 against Francis Lodge and Jack Thompson. No fanfares this time, no racial superiority at stake, a few bucks nothing more. He carried on fighting until he was fifty. He was killed in a car accident in Raleigh, North Carolina, on 10 June 1946.

5 The Italian Restaurant Job

Although I didn't know it at the time, I met Frank Warren to discuss going to Cuba on the fiftieth anniversary of Johnson's death. One Christmas, two years earlier, Warren had taken Kevin Mitchell and me to an Italian restaurant just outside Hertford. Kevin talked boxing because he could, and I sat and listened and tried not to make too much of an idiot of myself. I thought Warren was awesome, a man of personality and intelligence, though he hadn't got into boxing via an Oxbridge graduate entry scheme. After that first lunch we staggered back to Warren's offices in Hertford late. Warren said he had a few phone calls to make, but if we waited in the boardroom we could all go on for a Christmas drink – the girls from the office were going out for their Christmas party and Warren was feeling left out. He deposited a bottle of champagne on the table, which Kevin and I dutifully drank. Then his secretary brought another. And we drank that. And when, two hours later, Warren emerged to take us out we were both roaring drunk. We had a Guinness in the pub with Warren and then went our separate ways. Back in London Kevin headed for a pub and I lost him. He woke up the next morning with a sore back he couldn't explain and vague memories of betting locals he could beat them at pool. I got a taxi home and woke up with a headache. From then on Warren had recognised me at press conferences and we became nodding acquaintances.

Warren was different from the duckers and divers who inhabited his world. He had always seemed like a man up for a grand gesture, fascinated by left-field things. Warren collects art, for example, and has commissioned a boxing artist to produce dark portraits in which it is easy to see a knowing reference to the ugliness of the business he happens to be very good at. The paintings glare down from the walls of his office, dislocated, painful-looking portraits of menacing strength that demand your attention. My feeling was that Warren might be imaginative and mischievous enough to see the possibilities in what I was going to offer him. The money involved in the Cuban adventure would mean little or nothing to him. Like all big boxing promoters, he dealt in the winning – and losing – of hundreds of thousands and occasionally millions. If he could be convinced that this was a gamble, but one which might pay off handsomely, then there wouldn't seem to be anything to stop it happening.

We met in May, a fortnight after I came back from my second trip to Cuba. Warren's offices in Hertford are not the premises of a flash Harry who feels the need to show off (he saves his massive country house, beautifully decorated and maintained with gardens measured in acres, for that). They nestle on a corner of a one-way street opposite a run-down, grubby-looking shopping centre. Warren's car (or his jeep), parked round the back in a scruffy loading-bay area, is neither genteel nor flash. The door to the building has only a small sign to let you know it's there, though the taxi drivers all know where to go. You buzz the intercom and the door admits you automatically. You climb carpeted stairs to a landing, where a television is endlessly rerunning promotional videos for Warren's fighters. You wait two minutes on the chair on the small landing because the next door is security locked as well. Eventually one of Warren's assistants comes to let you in. Inside, the reception area feels a bit like a doctor's waiting room, apart from the giant posters of Warren-promoted fights on the wall with their classic old-school designs all screaming colours and loud slogans – 'Simply the Best', 'This Time It's Personal', 'Unfinished Business' – and the small print a list of outlets and minor promoters, corner shops and hustlers, boxing's small fry who swim in the ample slipstream of the professional game's sharks. It's hard to imagine that Warren was ever one of them. You sit and wait as coffee is brought, as ticket sales people wander in and out, as Jean on reception cheerily answers the phone, singing out her employer's name with tireless enthusiasm each time. 'Hello, Sports Network.'

I was sitting there in my best interview suit with my rarely used briefcase, a present from my mother for my sixteenth birthday, wondering what on earth I was going to say. This was the first time I had met Warren without Kevin Mitchell. He would undoubtedly find out that I knew little more than the basics about boxing. He might test me and I would fail and be humiliated. It felt like a school exam. I had even done some revision on the train with a list of his boxers and their most recent fights. I'd read up on Naseem Hamed so I wouldn't make an idiot of myself.

'Hello, John,' said Warren as he walked in. He looked at me with a smile, his head tilted slightly to one side, the sort of look you give an old friend or a brother. He was totally disarming. We walked to the end of a corridor of three offices from which everyone could see who was coming and going and entered his office, a huge room with a large old-fashioned desk expertly placed to dominate the room and intimidate visitors. Next to the desk was an American-style big TV screen in a cabinet and a couple of comfortable chairs, leather, I think. Next to the chairs was a Fifties' American jukebox in perfect condition. We sat down.

'So how are you?' he said.

'Fine,' I replied, smiling unconvincingly. Christ, how was I going to get through this?

'Do you want a coffee?'

'Yes.'

When the coffee came I realised it was the last thing in the world I wanted because every time I picked the cup up I was shaking so much that I spilled it. I had to lift it with both hands so as not to appear like a terrified child, which might have been acceptable if we had been outside a kebab shop in winter but was odd in a heated office in May in Hertford. I had to make the pitch now or he would think I was hopeless.

'Frank, I want to put a business proposition to you,' I said. God, he's good, I thought. He didn't bat an eyelid. A hack from the *Guardian* he barely knows has a business proposition for him, a major boxing promoter whose name and face everyone in Britain knows. He tucked in his chin and shrugged his shoulders, all the time smiling. He was taking me seriously.

'I'm packing in my job and going to Cuba. I want to take some time away from journalism. Anyway, I don't really see myself working for other people for ever and now is a good time to make a break. The proposition I have is this. Cuba produces loads of boxers at a variety of weights and there are plenty of promoters in the United States who are trying to get hold of them, but they can't because they don't get on with the regime. They have to wait for boxers to defect and the ones that defect are often the last ones you would want to have on your side.

'To leave they have to abandon family and friends and country and most of them think that just getting out is winning the lottery. They leave Cuba and they lose their anchor, they party, they get into trouble, they drink, they stop training, they're never heard of again. That route is discredited and anyway the US promoters are the ones in the best position to exploit those people. What I want to do is go and talk to the people who run things in Cuba and find out if they would legally allow certain boxers to turn professional under their supervision and for their profit. Politically they can't deal with any of the sharks in Miami and Don King is not the sort of person they respect. But if a promoter from Britain, one of their key trading partners and no enemy of the revolution, came along and offered to help them, maybe they would listen.

'The first deal would be to try and get them to arrange Felix Savon versus Mike Tyson, possibly in Havana, and show them how much money they might be able to make. The beauty of this is that in dealing through the government you work the way the country works and at the same time make it impossible for anyone else to muscle in. What you would get is not just the odd defecting fighter but a ready-built production line and a way into the American market.'

I was warming to this now. That was a killer point, a touch of the top salesman. I knew, because people had told me, that Warren was desperate to get into the United States and mix it with the top promoters there, none of whom he had a good word for. Especially those who would be most hurt by a deal of this sort, Luis de Cubas and his tackily titled Team Freedom in Miami, where a lot of the boxing defectors ended up. Warren had done a deal with Don King and was officially King's partner which many saw as Warren being groomed for the succession should King end up in jail, as most of his enemies at that time confidently expected. Warren was warm about King, but the rest he dismissed. The sort of money I was talking was probably worth it just to wind them up.

Warren listened and then took a phone call. When he got back he leapt over to the giant TV screen and switched it on.

'Have a look at this.' It was a promotional video for a US army assault vehicle called a Hummer. 'I was in New York last week with Don and a few people. We went into a restaurant and Don was on the mobile. Suddenly he shouts over to me and says, "Hey, Frank, you want a Hummer?" I thought he was asking if I wanted hummus with my food, but it wasn't a Greek restaurant so I didn't really get what he was saying. He explains and tells me he was getting four already for Tyson and himself. So he gets on the phone to some guy and says, "And add another Hummer for my good friend Frank Warren to be delivered to Hertford, London, England." It's supposed to arrive next month.' The video showed a vehicle capable of going over walls and through rivers and with a powerful hi-fi system. It cost over $150,000.

'Let's go to lunch,' he said.

So we went. Into the jeep out back. We talked a little about Naseem Hamed. Warren's respect for King was obvious. 'It's like Don says he's in the Mike Tyson business,' said Warren, 'I'm in the Naz business.' We chatted about Naz and kids and how boxing writers hated him and older folk didn't like his cockiness.

'But the kids love him,' said Frank. 'They don't want any of this shrinking violet stuff any more. They respect a kid who says, "I'm the best."'

In fact, on the boxing front Warren was diplomatically not testing me too much. The only excruciating moment in the jeep came out of the blue when he confessed to liking the Prodigy. 'The *Firestarter* video is fantastic. Fantastic. Isn't it?' I hadn't seen it, but mumbled approvingly.

The restaurant Frank chose was as far from Henry and Havana and the Three Musketeers as you could possibly imagine. It was on a country road with fields on three sides and big windows all round, which gave you the impression of eating in an air-conditioned conservatory. From what I recall the menu didn't have prices. We were greeted at the door by the classic Italian family restaurateur, charming, who'd obviously lived a little, English not perfect but wasn't going to get any better now. The restaurant was spotless, the service perfect and the wine list excellent. We talked about loads of stuff, with Cuba something of a minor topic, and I tried not to drink too much. I was sure he was just being nice. I was a journalist, he needed friends in newspapers, he didn't want to make me feel a prick for thinking I could be a player of any sort in his world. He would find a gentle way to let me down. Maybe just a quiet phone call. And I would smile and we would carry on nodding at each other at press conferences.

Then unnervingly Warren turned the conversation again. When we got back to the office he paused at the door. 'This Cuba deal sounds good. But what do you want out of it? If we got Savon out, you would want to be joint manager, right? We could do that.' I had only really thought about him paying me to go and check it out, but now I was being mentioned as an equal in the boxing promoter's game by Frank Warren. Fuck.

'Errrrm. Well, I don't know anything about managing boxers, it's not really my area, Frank, but, errr, we could certainly factor that in.'

'OK. Get me some costings and we'll talk about them.'

He stood up and smiled and tilted his head again. We went our separate ways.

The process of working out costings on a project that I so obviously knew nothing about was embarrassingly simplistic. I worked out what you needed to survive in Havana for a year and doubled it to come up with £30,000. I figured that might seem a rip-off so I suggested he pay £10,000 up front before I left, £10,000 three months in and £10,000 six months further down the line. It seemed fair to me that if it was obvious nothing was going to happen he should have the chance to pull the plug. Which, of course, is why I'm not a boxing promoter. I should have screwed the thirty grand out of him while he was enthused. Instead I was worried about saving Frank Warren £20,000.

It had all seemed rather too easy, though. He hadn't even wanted to think it through, even though he didn't know much about Cuban boxing. Maybe I was a tax loss. Maybe he didn't care how much he spent on my adventure. Maybe, as he saw it, thirty grand wasn't so much to spend to have a journalist in your pocket.

When I sent in the costings I offered him the chance of two projects, one the thirty grand bijou, comfortable but economical; another a £150,000 de-luxe, fuel-injected plan which involved setting up the cultural centre I'd originally thought of as a cover for what we were really doing. I faxed them and arranged a meeting.

Arranging to see Frank Warren is a complicated process. He has a diary like anyone else, but undoubtedly there is an A list of people who are accommodated within it at the expense of alphabetically inferior creatures like me. Every time I arranged an appointment he cancelled the first time. I got used to this and never really expected to see him on the date initially arranged. Two cancellations were my average in the time I dealt with Frank. In fact, I was never really sure that he would be there until he was shaking my hand. Once I got all the way to his office in Hertford to be greeted by an embarrassed assistant telling me that Frank had just had to go out and could he see me next week. You couldn't blame him. Who was I, really?

When I did get to him the process of agreement was shockingly brief. I sat among the fight posters for five minutes clutching my briefcase and tried to imagine the one that would promote Savon versus Tyson. What about 'The Day of Pigs'? No. It would be at night and what had pigs got to do with it? 'Rumba in the Jungle'? Nice, but there was no jungle in Cuba.

I tried to think of a word that rhymed with Havana but all I could come up with were Savannah and Hosanna and Bandana. None of which were any use at all. Then I thought of that *Frankie Goes to Hollywood* video in which actors who look like Gorbachev and Reagan wrestle in a ring, Communism versus capitalism personified and personalised. What was the song? 'Two Tribes'. 'When Two Tribes Go to War'. Yes. Two Tribes. I had the poster and I hadn't even done the deal yet.

Warren entered. Handshake. 'I've looked at the proposals and I'll go for the thirty grand option. It's a done deal.' No discussion, no arguing, no grilling, just a handshake and it was on. Now there was no going back. I was going to Cuba to set up a world heavyweight title fight.

6 *Kid Chocolate*

Kid Chocolate, Cuba's first world boxing champion, is buried in the Christopher Columbus Cemetery in Vedado. The woman at the reception just isn't quite sure where.

His grave isn't marked on the tourist map of the Necropolis Cristobal Colon, a giant rectangular encampment of Cuba's great and good (deceased). The cemetery is a marble and concrete crop circle disrupting the orderly grid pattern of west-central Havana. There's an arrow for Jesus Menendez (a sugar union leader: died 1948) and Victor Munoz (the inventor of Mother's Day: died 1922), for Cecilia Valdes (who inspired a character in a Cuban novel: died 1893) and for other nationalist and revolutionary heroes of the past hundred years. But nothing for the Kid. Where are his fifteen cubic metres of fame?

She consults a splintering wooden filing cabinet and pulls out a dog-eared card. 'I don't think he's here, you know. Oh no, you're right, here he is.' She shuffles across the bare, roughly painted office at the gates of the cemetery and points to the map of the necropolis, which is organised on an

American town grid pattern with the odd sepulchral flourish at the major intersections on its central boulevard.

'Eligio Sardinas, common ground, block 15, up to the sort of roundabout thing, turn right and ask a gravedigger. Have you paid your entrance fee?'

Five dollars and a five-minute walk later and there, one sitting on a tomb, the other leaning against a tree, are Raul and Acosta. Raul, in brown trousers and a blue shirt open to the waist, hasn't shaved for a couple of days and scratches his crotch. Acosta, burly, 6ft 2in, white in dungarees but no T-shirt, points the way.

'There,' said Raul, gesturing half-heartedly at 1,000 square metres of waist-high marble tombs. 'He must be in there somewhere.'

The tombs in common ground 15 are not exactly fancy. Most are of a similar simple design, flat, two metres long, with the name of the family carved at shin level on the front. Occasional plaques for additional occupants break the marbled horizon. The only other difference is the varying states of disrepair; some even have the giant top slab slid to one side like a hastily exited bed. In the narrow gaps between them are weeds and reeds and lizards and old plastic bottles. Though the tombs are arranged in relatively orderly fashion around the edges, they lose most of their symmetry as you get away from the sides. By the middle of a block some of them are so small that you can only assume the person inside has been buried standing up.

After an hour of tramping through the graves checking each individual inscription, Chocolate has still not revealed himself. Most of the tombs are from the Twenties, worn down by the sun and with a hard crust of white dirt. The name plate has to be rubbed with a stone to give up the identity of who is buried there (Acosta demonstrated the art to me). Tired and annoyed,

I sit in the shade under a tree on top of Mr Gainzas and his family and pick the plant life off my trousers.

Eligio Sardinas was born on 28 October 1910 in a tough, industrial neighbourhood on what was then the fringes of Havana. It was a tight-knit community where everyone either recognised you on the street or knew you weren't from around those parts. The *barrio* of Cerro had been the informal focus of Cuban boxing since its earliest days. The national boxing commission wasn't formed until the early Twenties and boxing's rules and etiquette were only brought to the island in 1910 by John Budinich. But Cerro was where it took root.

In the aftermath of the Johnson–Willard fight on 5 April 1915, boxing took off in Cuba. Promoters sprung up in the neon bars and back-street dives of Old Havana and it was to neighbourhoods like Marianao and Cerro that they looked for the raw material to fill the rings and arenas. Chocolate was growing up just as the sport was finding its feet. Many older record books list his birth date as 6 January 1907, a date Chocolate put on an official form in June 1928 just before he went to the United States. He had been told that you had to be twenty-one to fight in New York. He later admitted he was born in 1910.

Chocolate's father, a labourer, died when he was a young child and the family had to move down the Cerro social scale, from their reasonably comfortable house to a cramped flat in the less desirable inner section of an apartment block. There were six children – four boys and two girls – of whom Chocolate was the youngest boy. The oldest child, Domingo, brought the money in, Chocolate's mother, Encarnacion Montalvo, washed and took in ironing and his sisters went into domestic service, where they earned nothing but at least didn't need to be fed at home. Chocolate did his bit selling newspapers on the street and occasionally shining the shoes of

Havana's wealthy men. He later became known as a soft touch among the shoeshine boys of New York. According to one story, which is almost certainly apocryphal, he made a lasting impact on one particular boy, Sugar Ray Robinson, who, Chocolate claims, had shone his shoes in New York and asked his advice on how to become a boxer. The incident is not recorded in Robinson's biography.

Chocolate's own interest in the sport came from his brother Domingo, who was a mediocre small-time boxer in Havana. Chocolate went to see his brother fight at the Arena Colon, and occasionally trained with him at the El Manguito gym, where the only equipment was a punchbag full of sawdust. His brother fought under the ring name Kid Chocolate. When Eligio picked up the gloves put aside by Domingo, he picked up the family ring name too.

He got his first fight at the age of ten when, weighing in at 55lb, he tried to enter the regular boxing tournament organised by *La Noche*, the newspaper he was selling at the time. The Havana papers all held competitions among the paperboys to attract new vendors and the prize for the winners was usually the same: a free bag of newspapers to sell. The organisers laughed at him. He was too small, they said. But he came back to the office every week to enter until the organisers got tired of him and set up a filler fight one competition evening between him and a youngster calling himself Kid Wititio, who was bigger and older but the nearest they could find. Chocolate won.

He kept his interest going by holding the round numbers up at the Arena Fronton, one of Havana's most prestigious venues. While he worked there he became the unofficial mascot of a fighter called Chico Wallace. There is a picture from those days, the classic wannabe kid's boxing shot, with a twelve-year-old Chocolate being held back by a referee in the ring at the Colon. The stands are half-full behind him, the youngster's left is outstretched and Wallace is kneeling on the floor as if knocked down, a warm smile on his face as the referee, grinning too, counts him out. But you can see Chocolate has something. His legs are planted like a pro and his right is waiting to follow up in an uppercut from his waist.

Chocolate finally got his first official paperboy's fight against Kid Viejita, who was fifteen years old but had almost a man's physique. Chocolate won on points. And won the free newspapers. He then rose through the ranks of junior boxing with ease and by the time he was eleven he had won the 75lb title and confronted his first piece of incomprehensible refereeing – a feature that was to dog his career. He fought and beat a young kid fighting under the name 'Jimmy Kelly', but the decision was given to Kelly until the crowd threatened to destroy the arena and the promoters backpedalled and reversed the decision.

At the age of fifteen in 1925 his semi-pro career began with a win over Joe Castillo. Chocolate wasn't a stylish boxer at the time. According to Elio Menendez, his biographer and Cuba's most respected boxing journalist, he had the quick feet and rapid jab which he used throughout his career, but he wasn't technically adept. He liked to get involved in rapid exchanges, jabbing permanently and using his instinct and foot speed to come off the better.

He won his shot at boxing as a career through sheer unadulterated cheek. In 1927 Pincho Gutierrez brought back a boxer, Johnny Cruz, from New York. Cruz was a hardened pro, the New York title holder. Chocolate approached Gutierrez to let him fight Cruz. Gutierrez ignored him. But months later Gutierrez needed a late replacement to take on Cruz after his man had pulled out due to injury. He offered Chocolate $40 – a pitiful sum for a fight of this calibre even then – but Chocolate took his break.

Against huge odds he beat Cruz strongly on points. Then in

a rematch organised at four days' notice and designed to give Chocolate no time to prepare, he beat him again, knocking him out in the seventh. 'The last time', said Cruz, 'they made up a whole load of excuses as to why I lost, like that I wasn't prepared, but this time there aren't any. I trained hard and well and look at the result. I'd like to see the Cuban who can beat this guy.'

On 22 June 1928 Chocolate set off for New York with Pincho's latest crop of Cuban hopefuls, whose names would never quite echo round the world like his. The Cubans took lodgings in a cheap boarding house in Harlem and earned enough for the rent but not much more, sparring here and there, and training at the St Nicholas gym. Pincho couldn't find a fight for any of his team. He became a fixture in the offices of the New York promoters, none of whom were interested in his untried Cubans, whom no one knew or cared about. Desperate, he used to hang around the weigh-ins in the city, hoping to find fighters who didn't make the weight and offer his own fighters as replacements.

And one day, for the second time in a career that had barely started, Chocolate got a lucky break and a fight he had no right to. It was a hot August morning in New York and the other Cubans were sweating at St Nicholas. Pincho trudged to yet another weigh-in.

This time he got lucky. A fighter due to face the local boy Eddie Enos was ill and the promoter was desperate for a replacement. Pincho offered Chocolate even though the kid was a couple of weight classes below Enos, a potentially dangerous disparity. But the promoter grudgingly accepted the offer and Pincho raced off to find Chocolate and get him to the weigh-in. The fight was on.

Thursday at the Necropolis Colon was hotter than Wednesday. A taxi driver, or more precisely a bloke in a Lada with a cardboard sign saying TAXI wedged against the cracked windscreen, had told me the day before to go back and ask for an old man called Alberto. 'He's fat and has grey hair. You can't miss him. He's worked there all his life, he knows everything. The rest of them are ignorant and don't care.'

The man in the boiler suit guarding the bicycle parking had never heard of him. Neither had Acosta. Eventually another old man – thin, this one, but with grey hair – told me to go to the Archive Office. The Archive Office was a small window at the far end of a colonnade in a grand Spanish-style pavilion that had inexplicably been painted bright yellow. Behind the window was a large room, the size of a tennis court, which was unfurnished apart from a giant oak table in the centre. A wooden card-filing cabinet ran along one wall to a height of about eight feet. A set of metal stepladders reached up the side of the filing cabinet to a dusty row of giant ledgers, which were twice the size of a full-size atlas. A sign on the window outlined the terms and conditions under which the staff would help you. 'You must have the full name and date of burial or we will not help you. We can find nothing with other data.' The woman in front of me was chatting to a man behind the glass about a mutual friend.

When I reached the front, I was confronted by a man of about sixty, with Steptoe-ish stubble and toothless smile, in a dirty sleeveless blue shirt and lived-in, worn-out white shoes that looked as if he had borrowed them from a golf museum. He consulted some cards on the oak table and smiled. He glanced back at me behind the glass from ten feet away and smiled, banging his fist against the table and miming the act of rubber-stamping a document, presumably as exuberant and international a victory salute as you will ever see from a bureaucrat. It appeared that this didn't happen very often. He took a pen and scribbled furiously on a scrap of paper, which he then brought to me. 'This is where you will find Kid Chocolate,' he said.

Chocolate, despite the weight difference and a hostile crowd, won his first fight in the United States, against Enos, in three rounds. The referee had to stop the bout with Enos's face bloodied and bruised by Chocolate's constant jabbing. The Kid himself was unmarked. Now the offers flowed in. Pincho didn't dare say no. Chocolate fought six times in August after the first match, then four times in the space of eleven days in November, culminating in his first appearance at Madison Square Garden on 30 November against Joe Scalfaro.

There were 19,000 people in the audience and Chocolate was fancied to win quite comfortably on the back of a reputation built incredibly over only the previous three months. He left his corner for the start of the fight, maybe thinking of how he used to dream of even seeing a fight in the Garden let alone appearing in one. And before he had time to even throw a blow Scalfaro had caught him cold with a big right and Chocolate was down.

In the first seconds of the first round of his first fight at Madison Square Garden. An unlit cigar fell from the mouth of Pincho Gutierrez.

Chocolate struggled to his feet and held off Scalfaro until the bell. He came back in the second and settled down, ducking, swaying, moving his feet, jabbing, jabbing, retreating. He wasn't hurting Scalfaro, but at least his opponent was hardly touching him now. By the time the bell went for the end of the seventh round, though, Chocolate was clearly concussed. He sat in his corner and turned to Pincho to ask when the fight was going to start. Pincho told him the good news – that he was seven rounds in – and sent him back into the ring. The night ended in an honourable draw.

His last fight of 1928 was the 23 December defeat of

Pancho Denico. Since 1 August, his debut in the United States, he had fought fifteen times: ten KOs, four ten-round decisions and a draw.

The pace scarcely let up in 1929. He fought twenty-two times in ten months, but of all the fights that year only one mattered. This was the contest which set Chocolate up for life. Al Singer. 29 August. The Polo Grounds. With 37,000 people paying to watch it. Singer had been a paperboy in the Bronx when Chocolate was selling *La Noche* on the streets of Havana. He was adored by Jewish fight fans in New York and was coached by Benny Leonard. His record of 48 fights, 42 wins, 14 KOs, 2 draws and 4 defeats, was scary.

And Chocolate? This is what Nat Fleischer of the *Ring* said before the fight. 'I've seen Kid Chocolate's last three fights and I feel the same as most of my colleagues that Kid Chocolate is an exceptional boxer, and his range of skills are better even than those possessed by George Dixon [feather-weight world champion at the turn of the century]. Some of us feel Chocolate is in fact the most complete boxer of all time. He hits hard with both hands and his superb footwork is inimitable.'

And he lived up to it. Singer wanted a slugging match, wanted to bring Chocolate in close. But the referee Lou Magnolia broke the clinches up quickly and Chocolate danced and jabbed around Singer, who never gave up his attack. When the decision was announced the Polo Grounds went wild and fights broke out. Magnolia, who as a Jew himself was above attacks about racial bias, was lambasted by Jewish fight fans for weeks after for his part in Singer's defeat, for not letting the clinches last.

The referee in Chocolate's next big fight didn't make the same 'unpopular' mistake. This was against the Englishman Jack Kid Berg, from Whitechapel in the East End of London. Berg had earned his name the Whitechapel Whirlwind for his ceaseless aggression. He was a tireless fighter, less technical than Chocolate but with a bigger punch than anyone Chocolate had fought so far. He was also Jewish. And New York's Jewish fight fans felt there was a score to be settled. There was an argument before the fight over whether the weights had been fixed to let Berg come in at 135lb (he would have lost a $5,000 deposit if he hadn't). The Chocolate camp certainly complained, but of more interest was the 123lb Chocolate weighed in at. He was way under his fighting weight. There were rumours circulating that he was enjoying New York life a little too much and was looking weak in training.

The fight went as expected. Berg launched himself at Chocolate without apparent regard for the punishment he was taking. He got a few shots in, worked on Chocolate's body. Chocolate moved away. Berg followed him and increasingly was finding him. Chocolate moved on to the ropes to rest his legs and waited for his chance to catch Berg. Or let Berg come at him, swerving away from his blows. Chocolate didn't look anything like at his best, but many spectators at ringside thought he had done enough by the end. Berg was aggressive, but hadn't landed much. The split decision, though, went for Berg. Chocolate sat in his corner and cried.

There were cries of a fix the day after the fight. Pincho said that the board had deliberately forced the fighters to wear heavier gloves (6oz) than normal, which would hinder a jabbing Chocolate. And they argued that Berg had fought dirty in the clinches with the referee doing nothing about it. Like all press conference storms, it blew over in a day and the result stood.

There were enough other voices to give Chocolate comfort and protect his reputation. Singer's trainer, Benny Leonard, who might have been expected to hold a grudge after his fighter's defeat, came into Chocolate's dressing room and told him he had won 'by a mile'. The judge who had voted for Chocolate said, 'I was as surprised as anyone when Berg got the decision. But maybe they had a better view of it than me.'

So Chocolate didn't worry too much and continued to indulge his prodigious appetites. But Pincho was starting to worry. Chocolate was a socialiser. He loved women and he liked to drink. When he was in Cuba he was incorrigibly generous and kind-spirited. You won't find many Havana residents of his generation who haven't got a story about Chocolate in a bar buying drinks for everyone. When he visited Cuba for New Year he used to dish out cash and drinks until he had no money left. While there are a thousand tales of boxers who lose their money on their managers and are hoodwinked by their own ignorance, Chocolate's cash seems to have gone on drink, his friends and fine clothes – he once claimed to own 150 suits and in 1931 was voted New York's best-dressed man. He beat the Prince at Wales into second place. Another possibly apocryphal street story runs that his New York hotel suite was once robbed and some of his clothes were stolen. He telephoned Pincho, screaming in a panic. 'I'm in a terrible mess,' he said. 'I just don't know how someone could do this to me. For God's sake the bastard has left me with only twenty suits.'

And because of his flamboyance and the warmth with which he embraced New York, the public embraced him. Elio Menendez told me a story once of how a few days after the Singer fight Chocolate went for a walk near Gutierrez's office on Broadway. A traffic policeman recognised him and abandoned his post to ask for an autograph. A crowd gathered and the traffic quickly snarled up as drivers got out of their cars to see what the fuss was all about. The swarm spilled on to the street. The traffic stayed blocked on Broadway until he had gone.

The man from the Archive Office banged on the window and shouted past me to a shrivelled old gent in a greyish vest wheeling a bike past the window. 'Oy, Humberto. Look after this gentleman, will you? The map reference is on this bit of paper.' Humberto leaned his old Chinese bike – a Flying Pigeon – against a tomb and and waved me over. He looked at the piece of paper as if it meant something to him: 'VNE 93850 NY 386VE: Sergio Eligio Sardinas Montalvo; Cartel M0; Cuadro 15CC; Apt 17367; Encarnacion Montalvo.'

Apart from his full name, the name of his mother and Cuadro 15CC (CC stands for *campo commun*, which means common ground) the references meant nothing. I was in the hands of the man with the Flying Pigeon.

'I worked here for fifty-two years, you know,' he told me as we wheeled his bike to 15CC. 'I'm retired now of course, but I still come down to help out.'

'Why doesn't Chocolate have a monument?'

'Well, his funeral was held over by the sports' stars monument, I think, but then they would have moved him straight after down here. It's normal if there is a family plot.'

'But why isn't Cuba's most famous boxer even on the tourist map of the cemetery?'

'He's not political, is he, so they wouldn't have bothered.'

We reached the crossroads that marked the start of common ground 15 and Humberto suddenly shifted pace from the lazy amble befitting a man who has worked in a graveyard for fifty-two years to a measured stride that was way too big for him, as if he was measuring a distance in paces. The archive man had given him a map reference which, he said, called for thirty-six paces east.

'Uno, dos, tres . . .'

'I suppose X marks the spot, Humberto?'

'What do you mean?'

'You know, like in pirates and buried treasure.'

'I'm sorry, I don't know what you are talking about.'

Life lesson number 364: Never try to make small talk with retired gravediggers.

'Thirty-four . . . thirty-five . . . thirty-six . . .'

'This,' he announced, his hands extended in a gesture of welcome and triumph, 'is the tomb of Kid Chocolate.' Except that the relatively well-kept plaque on the very plain tomb said Carol y Casanova and there was no mention of Eligio Sardinas or Encarnacion Montalvo.

'It's not,' I said.

'It is,' he replied.

'Then why don't any of the names on the paper match any of the names on the tomb?'

The logic of this took a while to sink in, but eventually he gave in to it. 'In which case this one is the tomb you are looking for,' pointing to the plot immediately next to Carol and Casanova, which was more of a grave than a tomb, a patch of bare earth surrounded by a knee-high wall, with a small black doll in a pink pinafore propped up in one corner. 'Perhaps my paces are not long enough any more.'

'So who do you reckon Don Pepe was, Humberto?'

'What?'

'It says, "To Don Pepe – Pablito". It doesn't mention Kid Chocolate.'

Humberto eased himself over the wall and tramped over the grave to see if he could find another plaque. He couldn't.

'This is it.'

'No, it isn't.'

'The instructions say it is here.'

'But it isn't, Humberto, is it?'

'Well, no, my friend. I suppose it isn't.'

After the Berg defeat Chocolate was exhausted. He took a couple of months off and had a couple of simple first-round

KOs before losing an unquestionable decision to Fidel La Barba, whom he had trounced a year earlier. He didn't just lose, he stank. No movement, no punch. Rumours about his nocturnal activities grew and it was being said in the Parque Central, a square outside the Hotel Inglaterra in old Havana where Cuban men gather in groups to shout at each other about sport, that he would never be as good again.

The test of that would come against Battling Battalino for the featherweight championship of the world and yet again the arguments would last longer than the fifteen rounds. Chocolate put Battalino down for a *slow* count of seven in the first round. He never wavered in his claim that a generous referee gave Battalino a few crucial extra seconds to recover.

Chocolate couldn't finish Battalino off. The Kid jabbed and sidestepped his way expertly through the next fourteen rounds and looked to have won, by press consent, about ten rounds to five. But the decision once again went against him. The heavy rectangular radio announcer's microphone descended on a cable above the ring, the expressionless announcer rattled off the verdict and the referee lifted a surprised Battalino's arm. The crowd booed for almost five minutes

Chocolate's next title shot was against Benny Bass in Philadelphia. Bass was the junior lightweight champion of the world, a short tricky fighter – he was only 5ft 3in – and aggressive like Berg. Chocolate fought him in July 1931 in Philadelphia, his home town, and destroyed him. Bass took so much punishment that the crowd were yelling for the referee to stop the fight in the seventh after Chocolate had pulverised the champion almost without reply for four rounds. Eventually, with blood seeping down Bass's beaten face, the referee stopped the fight. Kid Chocolate was Cuba's first world champion. He was twenty years old.

Chocolate went back to Havana and was offered $1,000 a day to appear in vaudeville for fifteen minutes every night.

Pincho wouldn't let him. He would only have spent the money on more suits. The Cuban fight magazine *Nocaut* reported in an interview that he didn't look like a boxer at all, 'More like an Abyssinian prince just back from a London tailor with enough clobber for a world tour.'

This time, though, he seemed to be keeping in shape, and there was one good reason. The next time he fought it would be for the lightweight world title, which was held by Tony Canzoneri. He had a few months' rest and then he was back in New York, building up to a 20 November battle.

Canzoneri versus Chocolate could hardly have been a more exciting prospect. Canzoneri's trademark was that he barely bothered with a guard and took his punishment while he waited for the chance to let off his big punch. 'Canzoneri will be the easiest of the lot,' Chocolate told Jess Losada at Carteles. 'How I love those guys that just want to come rushing in. No one has ever knocked him out and I am the one to do it.'

He wasn't. Canzoneri chased Chocolate from the start of the fight, but Chocolate hardly seemed ruffled and had bloodied Canzoneri's nose by the second.

Canzoneri keeps working on Chocolate's body, Chocolate keeps veering away from him and jabbing and draws blood from Canzoneri's eye. In the sixth Chocolate gets in an uppercut and Canzoneri's legs wobble. As Chocolate goes in to finish the job Canzoneri smashes him with his big right. It goes on. Canzoneri standing there exposed, half-smiling, half-grimacing, staring through Chocolate's jabs, working to the body and waiting for the chance to hit him with the right. Chocolate, swerving and sidestepping, jabbing with the left as Canzoneri pounds his body. The late rounds are Canzoneri's. The last is Chocolate's. It was one of the toughest, most courageous fights Madison Square Garden had ever seen among lighter weights.

Chocolate lost the verdict again. Again it was a split decision. Again the crowd booed. Again Pincho screamed the day after that the referee was bent. And again it made no difference.

'It seems to me that to win the title I am going to have to kill my opponent,' said Chocolate, angry more than disconsolate this time. 'There are times when I think it is almost impossible to win in New York when I am fighting a local favourite. I was so sure that I had won the fight that I couldn't believe that this time there was any doubt in anyone's heart.'

In the public's heart he remained a favourite whatever the result. That night Chocolate was mobbed in Harlem and carried through the streets at shoulder height by the crowd.

The Canzoneri decision was harsh but within the elastic boundaries of boxing justice. It had been a fairly even fight. It would have been cruel whichever way the decision went. But when, eight months after the Canzoneri reverse, Chocolate lost his rematch with Jack Kid Berg, it seemed as if his faith in boxing was broken for ever and he never had the same enthusiasm for the sport again. He annihilated Berg, who himself had faded somewhat as a fighter, in the second meeting. He was so far ahead after eight rounds that he rested himself. Berg, his eyes almost closed, came back with a hugely courageous flurry in the final two rounds, but no way did he win the fight. Except, that is, on two of the judge's score cards.

Chocolate still had it in him to fight Lew Feldman and win the New York version of the world featherweight title. But Feldman wasn't in Chocolate's class, even a Chocolate enjoying all he could of New York life. The Kid had already beaten Feldman twice and had used him for warm-up bouts. It should have been easy. Except that Chocolate spent most of the nights leading up to the fight chasing women and sneaking out of the training camp. He won the title against Feldman, eventually knocking him out in the twelfth, but it was a sluggish display. Feldman made him work hard for his victory. Too hard. A weary Chocolate had to knock his opponent down twice to win the fight and he, Pincho and everyone who saw the fight knew that it shouldn't have been so close.

Humberto returned from the Archive Office with renewed enthusiasm. When he got back to Carol and Casanova, where I was waiting under a tree, he was apologetic. 'I'm sorry,' he said, 'I made a mistake. It is thirty-six paces north, not east. Come on.' At last. 'This is the one,' he said with no less pride than previously, though if he had looked up before speaking he would have seen that he had stopped next to an overgrown patch of long grass waving in a gentle breeze rather than a tomb. In fact he had stopped next to almost the only vacant space in common ground 15. No one was buried there.

And as Humberto leaned backwards to see who was next door he could see as well as I could that it belonged to Angela Pedroso, whose middle-class white Latin name didn't make her a likely candidate as relative of a black kid from Cerro. Humberto went back to the crossroads and paced himself inevitably and pointlessly back to exactly the same spot. As he strode back there was a metallic banging noise, repeated but irregular, from one of the tombs nearer to the centre of the block, like a stone on a tin can. Perhaps it was Chocolate. Perhaps he was getting upset with all this fuss and wanted to be found by his English admirer. I was doing my best. I started looking for the source of the banging and it stopped. 'Let me have a look at the instructions again,' said Humberto.

The sensible thing for Chocolate to do after his good fortune in the Feldman fight and as the holder of a world title of sorts was to earn a few bob in the United States. Chocolate decided that he would rather go to Europe. Which he did. There he fought a series of very average Europeans, the French champion, the Belgian champion, on which he lost money because pig-headed Pincho decided to promote the fights himself rather than let locals do it for him. By now Chocolate's reputation for leading a pleasant but unhealthy life was reaching the papers, which were starting to lament that he could not hope to keep his skills intact if he carried on the way he was.

Why should he care? He was hanging out in Montmartre with film stars and cabaret artists, and he would have chased women if they had been running away. If he was a bad boy in the Big Apple, he was wicked in Europe and Pincho was tearing his hair out. He came back from Europe in even worse shape than when he had arrived. So bad that when the New York board insisted he defend the title he had won from Feldman within the next thirty days, the man who used to be able to prepare for a fight in a few hours gave up his title rather than submit to it. He was in a terrible state.

That much was confirmed in stark, unpleasant detail in his rematch with Canzoneri in November 1933. This time it wasn't close at all. Chocolate's legs didn't move and Canzoneri was battering him senseless as the bell sounded to end the first round. In the second Canzoneri pummelled a helpless-looking Chocolate again and he went down, knocked out for the first time in his career, flat on his face, his arms limp by his side as Canzoneri jogged to a neutral corner, practically leaping over Chocolate's motionless body. He was knocked out again a month later on Boxing Day by Frankie Klick, another less than world-class performer. He boxed for five years more, but his career was effectively ended that night. He was twenty-three.

Those five years were not distinguished and he was moving increasingly to the fringes of boxing – San Francisco, San José, Los Angeles, New Haven, Long Beach, Jersey City and finally back to Havana, where he imposed himself on a young protégé, Fillo Etcheverria, and earned a lucky draw against Nick Jerome, a decision given more out of respect for his position in Cuban boxing than what happened in the ring. 'I'd thought about retiring before that but Pincho helped me make my mind up after the Jerome fight,' said Chocolate. Pincho, who was no longer his manager, called him up after the fight and told him that if he kept on taking punishment in the ring he would pay the price, that he was ruining his reputation by carrying on, that he should retire straight away.

Chocolate quickly trod the well-worn boxer's path right back to where he had started. As fast as his suits went out of fashion, Chocolate's money disappeared, until all he was left with was the house he had bought his mother in 1930. His son and grandchildren still live there.

One day in October 1956 he was arrested for drunkenness. He was asked for 100 pesos bail at the police station and didn't have it. Neither did his family. He was given six months in prison, which was later repealed when the press launched a campaign against it. He was seen around over the years that followed. He was always applauded when he turned up at boxing events. And afterwards he went back to his small house in the south-west of Havana, living off the pension granted him by the Cuban revolution. He sat with his son and grandchildren, surrounded by his mementoes, his photos, his old gloves hanging on the wall darkening with age, still greeted in the street, still remembered by everyone, still loved. He died in 1988.

Humberto came back from the Archive again. 'It's this way,' he said, striding purposefully into the middle of common ground 15. His ability to measure paces was obstructed by inconveniently placed tombs. He was up to twenty when we passed a mother with her son and daughter standing grimly at the side of a grave laying flowers in silence. Ten yards past them and Humberto stopped once again to pick out a burial spot that wasn't Chocolate's. He didn't need to be told this time and without a word stood on the top of the tomb to look at the adjoining monuments. The mourning family hardly batted an eyelid as he shouted, 'Can you see it?' And I could. About five paces further on was a tomb like all the others, a small stone plaque with a tin can resting on top of it which had old tobacco leaves and water inside. I cleaned the plaque with a handkerchief and stared at it. 'Encarnacion Montalvo, Eligio Sardinas.' No dates, no fanfare, no little stone boxing gloves. Just two names smaller than the size of a newspaper headline, one after the other. A mother and her son. A paperboy from Cerro, Cuba's first world boxing champion, buried almost anonymously in common ground 15. Dust to dust.

7 *Frankly Terrified*

The journey back from my final meeting with Frank Warren was a confusing mix of elation and terror. Dreams and theories and imagined adventures are fine and dandy, full of drama and possibilities. Up close it scared the shit out of me. The reality of changing your life is not so much fun; the fantastic starts to become obscured by the mundane. Who will rent the flat? (After a succession of people coming to look round and deciding against it, my sister moved in.) Who will look after the cat? How will you get cash over there to live on? What will it be like moving to a country where you don't speak the language? How will you feel knowing that 90 per cent of the people you meet will look at you as someone who is impossibly rich and fair game for their rip-offs and the other 10 per cent are spying on you for the government.

It's a bit like death – you know it's going to happen but the thought of that actual moment when you can't take anything back terrifies you none the less. You try, of course, to be superior, calm, cocky. You develop a mantra. 'Yes, Cuba. Well, I suppose it is quite brave but I really don't see what I have to lose. I'm thirty-one, I have no family, no girlfriend. If there is ever a time to do it, this is it. I suppose I am lucky, yes, thank you. Thank you. Thank you.' All the time just wanting to scream at people and let them know how scared you are, that you are in the middle of possibly ruining your life, but you got yourself in this position and now there is no way out. The admiration of others keeps you going for a while. But the riskiness of it all keeps you awake at night. You've got a nice job, it's well paid, and you are going to a country where you don't know anyone, where they are poor and where you don't speak the language and can't earn any money. You are insane. Please, God, offer me a way out of this. Let something happen that means I can get out of this with some dignity. I don't want to do this any more. But at the same time I kept digging myself in deeper, committing myself in small subtle ways that would involve humiliation to back out of.

There was one main reason why I couldn't back out and that was Frank Warren. Somehow I felt it was better to face misery in Cuba and the end of my career as a journalist than risk his disdain. I looked up to him, I suppose. I wanted his respect. And if I talked the talk and then blew it, it would be a huge blow for my self-image. I just had to do it. But I kept putting off the moment when I walked into the editor's office and burnt the biggest bridge of all. Somehow I never quite got round to it.

And then something very bad happened. When I got back from the Olympics in Atlanta, another fake deadline was about to pass – I swore I would resign after Atlanta, but I had been back a week and hadn't done anything. I went into work full of doubt my first day back. The telephone rang. It was Chris Nawrat, the former sports editor of the *Sunday Times*. Before he left the paper he had tried to make me the football correspondent, a move that alienated a lot of people there and hastened his departure. After that experience we had spent a year trying to start a Sunday sports newspaper and were good friends. Chris, a heavy-drinking former Communist expelled for going to Wapping with Rupert Murdoch, was the longest-serving executive at the *Sunday Times* bar Andrew Neil, and was a fiercely bright and dominating man who had a theory for everything. He was married to a quiet, intelligent woman called Christine, who took part in everything he did in some form. You could hear her in the background of Nawrat's hours-long telephone calls putting in her halfpennyworth. During the newspaper project they had adopted me and we used to meet every Wednesday night to discuss and develop the business plan. The failure of the project – I had split up with Beatriz in the middle, partly because of the commitment it involved – the collapse of another dream, was certainly part of the reason for wanting this one so badly.

'Are you sitting down?' he said. He could be melodramatic at times, so I didn't think much of it. 'Christine's dead.' I leaned forward in my chair, the words hanging on the line, echoing. Nawrat was still in Spain. 'She's had a brain haemorrhage. It's OK, she didn't suffer. She still thinks she's sleeping.' He told me that one day she had had a headache. She fell into a coma, the doctors couldn't revive her and in a matter of hours she was dead and he had to agree for her machine to be switched off. And everything that Nawrat had assumed about his own life was in a raggedy mess. In a matter of hours the most self-assured person I knew had seen his life fall apart. He didn't want to be alone and so he had organised for friends to come out in shifts. He had pencilled me in for the following week.

I arrived at his flat in Spain, a top-floor apartment in a modern block on the fringes of a small fishing village called Finisterre, which people have only heard of because it usually gets mentioned in the shipping forecasts. It was the hardest week of my life. And when I left I knew I was going to Cuba as

66

soon as I could. What did anything really matter? Nothing seemed cosy about life any more.

Frank's money didn't turn up before I went so I was forced to set off with my £2,000 savings and a £2,500 credit-card limit as my only comforts. The resignation from work – I walked in and Alan Rusbridger suggested I take a year's sabbatical rather than resign – and the leaving do in the Coach and Horses, a pub at the back of the *Guardian*, passed by in a blur of frantic mundane activity. The *Guardian*, in a typically bizarre and complimentary way, decided to give me the Diary column to look after in my final week. It was one of the prestige jobs on the paper and impossible to turn down, but it was nothing to do with sport, which meant a lot of work and was the last thing I needed as I tried to beat an organised retreat from my life and country.

Actually, that's not true. The very last thing you need when you are about to leave the country for a year to organise a world title fight for Mike Tyson, based on the theory of the division being boring because Mike Tyson was unbeatable, is for Mike Tyson to get beaten. Which is what happened on 10 November, a mere thirteen days before I was scheduled to set off. Tyson's fight with Evander Holyfield was not supposed to be tough. At the beginning of the week in Las Vegas Holyfield had been a 22–1 shot to beat the WBA champion, which, while plainly ridiculous, reflected how the fight was supposed to go.

Tyson's game plan was a mess. He didn't jab and kept swinging amateurishly at Holyfield in the hope of landing a winning blow. With Holyfield keeping close to him to minimise his speed and, according to Tyson, headbutting him throughout the fight, Tyson found himself in trouble. He went down in the sixth, a round in which he was badly cut by Holyfield's head. Tyson ran out of gas and in the tenth was being beaten up. He was saved from a knockout by the bell, but the fight lasted only one more round when a seven-punch flurry put Tyson helplessly on the floor. The picture of him bewildered and heading bum first for the canvas made every paper the next day. I knew how he felt.

I rang Warren, but couldn't get hold of him. So I rang Kevin Mitchell and like a real friend he told me exactly what I wanted to hear. That Tyson would win back the title in a rematch without any trouble at all. That everything would be back to normal in the six months that the mess took to sort out. That it was in fact a good thing because it had stirred up interest in the heavyweights again and that anyway if it wasn't Tyson then it didn't matter. It would be someone else and it would still be a big fight. I doubt he believed any of it, but I wasn't in a position to argue. I just had to pack my bags and hope he was right. It was too late to back out now.

I had already put together a mental safety net for all this in my mind. The risk was not so great. I could go to Cuba, have a look, find out if I had made a terrible mistake and come back one way or another in three months if I had to. I could justify the return as an opportunity to report to Frank on what was going on, assess what I was doing and to eat something other than pork, rice or beans for a couple of weeks. If it had all fallen apart by then, I could just come back and blame circumstances, couldn't I?

It was a cold early morning when I finally set off and I hadn't had much sleep for the past four days. The night before I had driven up to Yorkshire to leave my cat with my mother. This had unfortunate echoes of the last time I was in a car with a cat. Soon after we moved to Harrogate my sister, my mother and I were driving along North Yorkshire's deserted stone-walled roads when the cat got diarrhoea in its basket. The stench hit us, the windows were opened and my mum attempted to stem the odour by opening up a bottle of Chanel

No. 19 that one of her brothers had bought her for Christmas and putting it on tissues for us to hold against our noses. The cat basket was abandoned in a hedge to cut off the problem at source, but it seemed that the smell had bonded with the car at molecular level and we endured forty miles of beautiful wintery countryside retching all the way.

Happily, this time was a less testing experience. I set off from Crouch End at nine p.m., having kept the cat on dry food for a day and urged her to have a crap before we set off, a pointless waste of energy as anyone who has ever had a cat will know. She wailed as if she was about to be abandoned, but the odd stroke when we strayed into the slow lane kept her bowels in check. We arrived at midnight, the cat hid somewhere where my mother couldn't find her for two days and I grabbed four hours' sleep and then set off back to London.

The final day was a pre-holiday round of 'tickets, passport, credit card' panic. Every time the to-do list came out to have something ticked off, something else was added. Every binliner of junk left outside seemed to have precisely no impact on the stuff I had to clear out of the flat to leave it habitable for my sister and her husband. 'Tickets, credit card, passport, insurance, computer, power lead, modem, CD player, CDs, heavyweight power converter, books for a year, clothes.'

I would recommend the process of putting all your belongings in storage to anyone who feels their life is a little cluttered – after ten years I finally threw away my notes on European integration from the LSE – but I would warn against actually looking at the result before you lock up the metal broom cupboard that now contains all your worldly goods. How can you be thirty-three and have everything you own squeezed relatively comfortably into thirty cardboard boxes and a 4ft by 4ft by 15ft storage cell on the Holloway Road? But finally the tennis rackets were stuffed in down the sides, the jumper I was wearing to keep out the cold was taken off and chucked on top of the pile and the door was locked.

Now I was sitting in an empty flat with a few remaining boxes of junk and dust everywhere, nothing personal in sight, my suitcases by the door. A bloke came in a battered Nissan at five-thirty a.m. and I was on my way out of my old life and into a new one. Off with little more than half-baked dreams to Havana, a place I had been to twice, with nowhere permanent to live, no idea how much money I would end up with and relying on the Venezuelan national airline to transport me there. But it was too late to worry about that now.

'Stansted, please, mate.'

The flight took fourteen hours, with a delay at Caracas – the only airline that would give me a six-month open return ticket to Cuba was Viasa, which meant flying to Venezuela first and then on to Cuba, the geographical equivalent of flying from New York to London via Moscow.

There was the usual long wait at Havana airport, except this time it wasn't a few holiday clothes that could go astray but everything I owned. As each bag came through on the carousel I got more and more panicked. Eventually the two giant sports bags arrived practically bursting open. I had only arranged a tourist visa. It seemed easier to get in the country and then argue about my status rather than spend weeks at the Cuban embassy in London, which was not noted for rapid expedition of anything involving foreign journalists. But there was something very exciting this time about waiting in the queue knowing I was not what I appeared. I was effectively a sort of spy, an envoy sent to arrange something illegal. It was a childish thought, but beguiling. It was exciting. It was the feeling which had led Graham Greene to write *Our Man in Havana*. I had worried that customs might query a tourist who was bringing an electricity transformer, thirty compact discs and a portable computer on holiday, but they were only interested in a magazine I had bought at Stansted, *Men's Health*. It had some sort of sex guide on the front and they were worried in case it was porn. They immediately confiscated it for further inspection and sent me on my way.

The family I was staying with for the first few weeks were the same timid folks I had lodged with before, Miguel and Susanna. They had sent an elderly man in a Fiat 126 to collect me and my luggage for a year. For those not familiar with the Fiat 126 it is significantly smaller than a Mini, has an engine in the boot that struggles up any incline and is most certainly not intended for use as a taxi. Add to that the fact that every three miles or so the driver was forced to get out of the car, fiddle with the carburettor and suck petrol through a plastic pipe to get it going again and it is safe to say that any doubts about the wisdom of my decision to move abroad were not immediately eased. Like all things in Cuba, however, the taxi driver was not what he seemed. As we lurched from one lane to another in clouds of diesel fumes from Cuba's fleet of overworked eco-enemy lorries and buses, he reached into his glove compartment and said something in very quick Spanish. I only recognised the words – well, names actually – Malcolm and Castro. He handed me a picture stamped with an agency credit on the back. The picture showed Malcolm X (pronounced 'eccies' in Spanish, which is why I didn't clock the full name first time) earnestly listening to another wiry thin black man on a sofa. The thin wiry man was my driver. He had been a journalist for many years and had gone to New York with the Castro party in the early days of the revolution to visit the United Nations. Now he was an old man, his pension was worth nothing and he was working with what he had left, failing eyesight and a failing car that needed his kiss of life every few miles, to earn something to supplement his valueless savings.

Miguel and Susanna had moved their son out to his

Grandma's for the first week I was there because my old room was being decorated. I unpacked the two giant sports bags I had brought with me and slept.

I had booked in for a couple of weeks with them because I didn't know anyone else. While I knew that I couldn't bear the idea of staying there any longer, they didn't. The process of getting out was none the less a heartbreaking insight into Cuba. They were a middle-class couple, both professionals, nice people in a nice house in a nice area. But the accidental egalitarianism of Cuba's economic plight meant that they were as much in need of dollars as anyone else. So for the whole time I was with them they thwarted every attempt I made to find a new place to live. I went to see the BBC's man in Havana, Tom, to find out what the score was on apartments. He had found a pleasant house with two old ladies in a quiet area of town for not much money. The old ladies gave me the number of a friend of theirs who had a place to rent nearby. Not speaking Spanish, I made the mistake of asking Susanna to ring on my behalf. She rang while I was out one day and said that they had already rented it. Never mind.

As the time for me to find somewhere ran out, odd things started to happen. Whenever I was alone in the house they would take the phone in their bedroom off the hook and lock the door so I could not replace it and make telephone calls from the extension in the living room. I thought at first it was caution, to stop me making expensive calls, but the telephone is virtually free in Cuba and international calls can only be made reverse charge from normal lines. Then I thought maybe it was to stop neighbours or friends ringing up and finding I was staying there. But it would have been easier just to tell me not to answer the phone – I couldn't say anything, so it wouldn't have been a burden. A couple of weeks later I found out why. Tom, the BBC man, told me that the old ladies wanted to know why I hadn't rung their friends. I said that Susanna had done it and they had said it was rented already. She hadn't and it wasn't. Middle-class or not, they wanted to hang on to me and my dollars and weren't going to let anyone else have them. The phone was off the hook to stop anyone poaching me from them. Desperation makes even nice people do strange things.

Their desperation worked in my favour on one occasion. Susanna was a journalist on *Bohemia*, an official magazine with a rich and long history dating back to the late nineteenth century. It had survived the revolutionary purge of the press because it had printed photos and articles in support of Castro while he was fighting in the hills against the government. In the Sixties and Seventies, when there was still paper for it to be printed on, it had carried sections on the arts, history and architecture alongside the predictable political polemics of the new Communist government. But it quickly became a very dull read, pictures of fields and peasants and factories and slogans. And that awful, Soviet-style, modernist typeface. Now, after the special period, with no money in the kitty it was a tired, barely fanzine quality, magazine of few pages but with a huge staff. The offices were on a main highway near the government buildings of Havana and close to the Marti monument, a giant concrete Cleopatra's needle with a huge bust of the national poet outside, which leans towards you at an alarming angle. Below is the banking on which Fidel and the central committee stand to salute the annual pass-by of the army and workers on 1 May.

Susanna, in the short time that I stayed with her, arranged for me to see the head of the international press centre, who was responsible for issuing visas to foreign journalists. You could stay in Cuba as a tourist for a maximum of three months and I thought it might be better, given that this was after all a Communist country with paranoia about foreigners, to put everything on a semi-official footing. Susanna knew the man in charge from her days studying journalism. He was friendly, took my passport, my card and the letter I had squeezed from the *Guardian* news desk in London. After I paid him 100 dollars for administration he processed my application and gave me a temporary journalist's visa. I was in.

I wasn't having much joy escaping from the family house, though, and my lack of Spanish made me fairly easy to control. My salvation came when I delivered a letter to a woman called Martha Gonzalez, which I had been asked to take by someone at the *Guardian*. The same wiry old man who had brought me from the airport drove me to Martha's house, though the address was difficult to find. By coincidence, he said, he had delivered another journalist to this address recently and took me to where he thought it was. She lived in a block of flats on the seafront in Miramar, which had been a grand area of boat moorings and great houses from the Twenties onwards. The government had since created a tenement block by the sea called the Sierra Maestra, after the area where the rebels won their major victories in the mountains. It was close to the site of the old yacht club (now a posh restaurant and nightclub) and had housed Eastern Europeans who came to Havana as advisers and trainers. The big houses along Miramar's rocky seafront had either been taken over by the state or by large numbers of families crammed into too little space. The best places now were the more modern apartment blocks (modern as in built just before the revolution) which housed the Cuban middle classes, flats given as rewards or perks to party people. Martha lived in one of them. To reach her flat, however, you had to use a side entrance because she had divided it in two to rent out the nicer part of it.

She didn't open the door when I knocked. 'Who is it?'

'It's John Duncan. I'm from the *Guardian*. I have a letter for you from a colleague of mine.' The door was unbolted and there she was, a small, wrinkled, heavily tanned, white woman in an ill-fitting vest. She spoke perfect English with the occasional Americanised slur thrown in.

'Any friend of Maaeerggie's is a friend of mine,' she said. 'Sit down.'

I sat in a rocking chair by the wooden slatted window looking across a concreted beach area over the Atlantic towards Miami.

Martha had fixed for Maggie O'Kane when she had been in Havana doing a story when thousands of Cubans took to rafts and clambered on to boats sent from Miami while the Cuban government turned a blind eye. Many of them had died on the way. Martha herself had been a spy for Cuba in the United States. She had been a supporter of the revolution and because her husband was a wealthy exile who had left Cuba in its aftermath, under the pretext of following him she was sent to keep an eye on the activities of Cuban exiles in the States. Eventually she had to come back to Cuba when her role was about to be exposed. She wrote a book, became famous for a time and was given this flat in addition to the house she already owned. Now she worked in television as a subtitler of the Saturday night films, but had a lucrative sideline as the best fixer you could find in the whole of Havana. She was almost certainly still working for the security services – it isn't a profession that you ever leave completely. She said that the flat she was letting, which was in fact the other half of her own flat, would be available in a few weeks and would I like to move in. I accepted. I paid 350 dollars a month, quite a lot at the time, but foreigner inflation made it look pretty good a few months down the line.

Martha also provided me with my first official boxing contact. Henry from the restaurant, it turned out, knew practically no one, though he wanted me to rent a room at the Three Musketeers and wondered if I could help him start an ex-boxers' association in Havana. This was the first of several disappointments, people who promised much but in fact had little to offer. It was a blow at first, but quickly forgotten when Martha said she had a friend called Masjuan who was a sports broadcaster. I asked if I could meet him. A week later I was sitting at his house as he explained to me how the Cuban sports system works. He also told me that the national boxing championships were being held in Holguin in the east of Cuba in only a few weeks' time at the beginning of January and he gave me the names of two people who would be there. He told me where they would be staying – the Hotel Pernik, which didn't sound very Cuban – and suggested I get out there as soon as I could. It was my first assignment in my new life.

8 *Teofilo Stevenson*

But for the collapse in 1923 of the economy of St Vincent, a bittersweet Caribbean outpost of the British empire, the greatest Cuban boxer of all time might have been the greatest British boxer of all time.

Teofilo Stevenson Patterson boarded a boat in St Vincent, driven out by unemployment, in search of the riches that were said to be found in Cuba at the time. The deal on the boat was simple. You could pay the thirty-five dollar fare and work wherever you wanted or you could travel for free and be obliged to work in the sugar fields. Teofilo Senior paid. Ignoring advice, his brother and two cousins decided to go for free. They landed in February 1923 in the east of the island and went straight to work, where they quickly realised the grim reality of their situation. Their employers were ruthless in their pursuit of cheap labour; they were barely paid enough to eat. Cuba wasn't the promised land after all but there was no way back now.

Teofilo Senior stayed with his family to see how things were working out for them in the sugar fields, but when it was obvious they had been sold into semi-slavery he got out as quickly as he could, showing his ticket to a confused supervisor and scarpering. He found work in a place called Delicias, roadbuilding, navvying, whatever, until because of his huge size and strength he found regular employment as a stevedore. The money was still bad, so he moved to Camaguey, where he gave English classes to top up his meagre earnings. His route home took him past a gym and one day he went in. When the trainer saw his size he asked him if he wanted a go. He handed his new pupil some gloves and then hit him hard. Two weeks later Stevenson was back. He'd spent the fortnight putting in some practice and this time it was the trainer's turn to take the hits. After that he became a regular.

Stevenson Senior made a brilliant start to what was to be a very short boxing career, winning his first six fights impressively, but earning ten pesos for his efforts. His reputation spread enough for his seventh fight to be sold out. It was to be Stevenson against a local unbeaten heavyweight, with the biggest punch, so they said, in the region. Stevenson won after an epic battle, but when he met his brother, who was in charge of getting hold of the purse, he found he was only getting ten pesos. Stevenson gave up boxing on the spot as a bad job.

Dolores Stevenson, Teofilo Senior's wife, had lost her first two babies in childbirth because of pre-eclampsia and there was a great deal of nervousness before she gave birth to a son in 1952: Teofilo Stevenson Lawrence.

As a kid Teofilo was restless and difficult. At school, while he was considered bright, he was always seeking out mischief in one form or another. He had boundless energy and it wasn't long before he found an outlet for it in the gym. Like so many of Cuba's champions, Teofilo Stevenson started out training in secret, this time directed by John Herrera. He was terrified that his parents would find out and when the time came to tell his mother he ducked out. His father later told his biographer, 'He came in one day saying in a whisper that he was going to Las Tunas with John Herrera because he was going to make his debut as a middleweight. I told him that was fine, but he would have to go and tell his mother so that she could prepare his clothes. "You tell her," he said, and sneaked out. Well, when I did tell Dolores I was lucky that I had been a boxer because I knew how to avoid a punch. She hit the roof and told me it was my fault. When she calmed down she agreed to let the boy box but only if I went with him.'

They went and Teofilo lost to Luis Enriquez, a boxer with twenty fights under his belt. It was a respectable defeat, however, and Teofilo Senior was just relieved that his son had not taken a beating.

'I liked the way he fought that night,' said Herrera, at whose makeshift open-air gym Teofilo had had his only training. 'You could see that he had something, even against this guy who was much more experienced than him. I knew then that he had what it takes.' Herrera was no village enthusiast either. He had been national champion as light heavyweight and the work he did with Teofilo was an excellent grounding.

Teofilo's career took the normal post-revolutionary Cuban path, eventually coming under the Cuban sports system. He fought a few more times for Herrera, then won the junior title in the eastern part of Cuba and went to Havana for further tuition. In 1968 he went back east again and in Camaguey won the national youth title. At seventeen he went to the national senior championships, the Playa Giron, which were held in December 1969 in the province of Havana, the countryside stretching from Havana in the north for sixty miles all around. Teofilo made it to the heavyweight final against Gabriel Garcia. It wasn't a great contest. He lost, although he should have won, but it was less the result than one man in the audience who was to be the key for Teofilo Stevenson. In the crowd was the Soviet coach who had been sent to help Cuban boxing get on its feet, Andrei Chervorenko, who from that day was to champion Stevenson's cause in the Cuban national team. Stevenson was brought into the senior national set-up on the insistence of the Russian. After that defeat against Garcia his career never looked back.

It was in 1970, however, that the reputation and stature of Teofilo really started to grow, with a knockout victory over Nancio Carrillo. Carrillo had gone to the Mexico Olympics in 1968 with the Cuban team. That and another victory over one of Cuba's more experienced heavyweights, Juan Perez, won him a surprise inclusion in the team for the Central American Championships in Havana in September. He knocked out his first opponent within seconds of the start and his second, a Bermudan, Earl McClay, received a thorough working over and was beaten by unanimous decision. He showed how much he had improved when he walloped Garcia, the man who had beaten him in the national championships the previous year, inside two rounds. In the final he was beaten by Bernd Andern, a tricky and experienced southpaw, and losing was no shame. He was now firmly established as Cuba's number one in his weight.

Perhaps it was a useful reminder of the work remaining to be done that the following year was the worst in his life as a boxer, with three defeats ten in twelve months. Two were close fights against the Czech Peter Sonmer in a friendly tournament between the two countries, and caused little concern to the Cuban team. After a series of victories in Cuba he headed off to the Pan-Americans. First came victory against an Argentinian they called the Monster, Pablo Sarmientos, who had won eighty-three fights without defeat up to that point. Then Stevenson lost to Duane Bobick, a moderately talented white heavyweight who had high hopes of turning professional and cleaning up as a white challenger. It was a fairly even fight with a 3–2 decision against the Cuban.

Chervorenko again was unconcerned and according to newspaper reports said that Bobick would never beat Stevenson again even if the pair fought a hundred times. Back in Havana, they worked even harder on Stevenson's jab, the weapon that was to ensure few ever got close enough to beat him again. He fought the East German Bernd Andern once more, this time on his home territory in Berlin in a tournament at which Cuban boxing suffered a number of defeats. And against a supportive home crowd Stevenson survived a difficult first round before downing Andern, East Germany's most fearsome boxer, in the second round under a hail of punches to the body and face. Andern crawled back to his feet, but Stevenson kept coming and the referee stopped the fight. The German public were stunned. This fight made the Eastern Europeans take Teofilo seriously and arguably made Teofilo himself realise the potential he had.

Stevenson now was being thought of as the man who would lead Cuba into a new sporting era at the Olympics in Munich in 1972. Cuba had not won a gold medal in an Olympics since the fencer Ramon Fonst in 1904, who had won both foil and épée and repeated his achievement in the épée. Boxing now looked to be Cuba's best hope. Enrique Figuerola just missed out on gold in the 1964 100 metres, coming second to Bob Hayes, who equalled the world record to beat him. With professional sport banned in 1961 and with the government committed from then on to mass participation and improvement of facilities, which was allied to a massive injection of help from other Communist-bloc countries, the success of the regime's sports policy was now to be proved at the Olympics. In 1968, only nine years after the revolution, two boxers, Enrique Regueiferos at light welter and Rolando Garbey at light middle, reached Olympic finals and lost. In 1972 it was to be a different story.

For Stevenson the year began with the national championships in Santiago de Cuba. In the final he knocked out his training partner, the southpaw Luis Valier, in the first round after hitting him twice. Stevenson, still only twenty years old, spent the year unbeaten in tournaments in Cuba and abroad, until September 1972 saw the beginning of the Munich Olympics which would make his name. Ludwik Denderys was an experienced twenty-eight-year-old Pole, a huge man with a reputation for being able to take a punch. Stevenson knocked him down within thirty seconds, opened a massive cut later in the first and forced the fight to be stopped later on that round. This was the division that the Americans considered their own. In 1964 the title had been won by Joe Frazier and in 1968 by George Foreman. According to Cubans who were there, they had a special desire to rob the Americans of something they believed to be theirs by right. The American entrant was Duane Bobick, the Great White Hope, who was about to be fanfared into a black-dominated world much as Willard had been against Jack Johnson in Havana two generations before.

The Cuban and the American were now set to fight only 48 hours later, with Bobick favourite, having won their only previous meeting the previous year. As the early part of the fight unfolded, Stevenson caught the American with a left and sent him stumbling backwards. He kept up the attack and won the round. The second was Bobick's as Stevenson's corner warned him not to finish the fight on an empty tank. Bobick meanwhile attacked at full pelt and had Stevenson on the ropes covering up. The American won the round, but at a price – his face was marked and he looked exhausted. Stevenson was unmarked and breathing normally. It was time. At the start of the third, after taking relentless sapping jabs, a body shot sent Bobick reeling to the floor. Bobick, his vision now severely restricted, tried to battle on but was caught flush with one of Stevenson's big rights and went down again. He staggered to his feet, but was barely able to defend himself. One more left and he was back on the canvas and the referee stopped the contest. It was a beautiful moment for Cuban sport, one in which you could sense a whole century of inferiority complexes melting away. Stevenson beat better opponents than Bobick, he beat better Americans, but this is the fight that every Cuban boxer talks about. Though Cubans will occasionally try to deny that the politics of relations between Cuba and the United States have anything to do with sport, others admit they go to tournaments praying they will meet an American. The rivalry has occasionally been given an extra vicious *frisson* by vulgar American attempts to wind up the Cubans. In one Olympics the Cubans offered their opponents a gift before each fight and one surly American boxer threw it on the floor. He joined it there inside two rounds. But another part of the reason for the particularly enthusiastic approach to beating Americans is the mental list that all Cuban boxers keep of the world professional champions whom they have beaten as amateurs. For a country where information on professional boxers is limited their ability to keep up with boxing's promotional bodies, the WBA, WBC, WBO, IBF, whatever, is remarkable. They love to look through the rankings and tick off vanquished pros.

The Bobick fight has achieved such importance that few Cubans remember it was merely a quarter final. In his next battle Stevenson brushed aside Peter Hussing, the home nation's favourite, in two rounds. He was in the final. In the end Stevenson won gold without having to throw another punch and knew that he was Olympic champion on the morning of the last day, when it was announced that the Romanian Ion Alexe was injured and could not compete. Orlando Martinez and Emilio Correa are always credited as the first Cubans to win boxing golds in the post-revolutionary era, but in fact Stevenson had won his before their contests even started. There remained only the formality of him getting changed and turning up in the ring to stare across at an empty corner opposite. Stevenson was also awarded the Val Barker Trophy for the best boxer of the Olympics.

But now it was back to the run of the mill and there were a few old scores to be settled. He faced Peter Sonmer in the 1973 Cordoba Cardin, the boxer who had beaten him twice in a tournament in Czechoslovakia. (The Cordoba Cardin, or to give it its full title the Torneo Internacional Giraldo Cordoba Cardin In Memoriam, is an international tournament named after a young boxer killed in the revolution.) Stevenson, now a far more experienced and wily boxer, weathered an early flurry and then knocked Sonmer down twice in the first round to win the fight. But in the final, having rid himself of one nemesis, he was to find himself another when he faced the short and tricky Russian Igor Visotsky. It was a fairly even fight, with Visotsky trying to fight close in and weaken Stevenson with body shots and Stevenson trying to keep Visotsky at a distance where he could hit him. This fight too came down to the third round, in which Stevenson seemed drained of energy and conceded the initiative to the Russian, who edged it and won the fight 3–2. Few observers complained about the result.

Towards the end of the year Stevenson got the opportunity to get in the ring with Alexe, the Romanian who had not turned up for the Olympic final. Nothing in the mullering which Stevenson dished out suggested that his gold medal would have come much harder if he had actually had to take on Alexe in the final.

In 1974 the first amateur world championships were held in Havana and, two years after Munich, Cuba's boxers had the chance to show how much they had progressed in front of their own fans. Stevenson's first-round opponent failed to turn up, a sensible man given the mismatches that often occur at this stage of international competitions. The second was poor old Peter Hussing again, who lasted a mere two minutes before he was flattened by a right. The third, duly warned, concentrated his energy on simply trying to keep out of range of Stevenson's right, either by moving around or holding on. It wasn't pretty. What no one knew until after the tournament was over was that Stevenson had injured himself in the fight, and had developed a problem in his foot. A few Cuban journalists had spotted it, but were asked to keep quiet in order not to boost the morale of Stevenson's opponent in the final. That was to be Marvin Stinson, a twenty-two-year-old American who had spent the majority of the tournament talking up his chances of beating the Cuban. Stevenson made no comment.

The night of the finals provided a hint of what was to come for amateur boxing. Jorge Hernandez started it off with a points victory over the Kenyan Stephen Mushoki. Victories followed for Douglas Rodriguez, then Emilio Correa, who took gold by knocking out the American Clinton Jackson, and then Rolando Garbey, who won narrowly by 3–2. It was turning into a stunning night for Cuban boxing. The Stevenson fight was, as the heavyweights always are, the last bout of the evening. As the warm night of Havana closed in, the pair entered the ring at about ten-thirty. Poor old Stinson. Not a bad boxer, agile, tall and thin with stick legs like Stevenson's but somehow not quite as long, he had not realised what he was getting into. He tried to feint and duck to make room to attack Stevenson, but the Cuban seemed to read everything and slammed counterpunches into his body and jaw whenever Stinson made a move. The American stayed on the back foot for most of the first round. And the second. In the third, tired, Stinson was caught with Stevenson's right, the shot he had been running from all night, and only managed to avoid going down by hanging on to the Cuban. The verdict at the end was inevitable, unanimous for Stevenson.

After the fight Stevenson was surrounded by Cuban journalists in the dressing room. The Cuban grimaced as he removed his boots and revealed a hugely swollen foot, the result, he said, of a basketball accident.

Stevenson had been approached by professional promoters at the Olympics. They kept sniffing around him for a few years after and were still trying to snap him up in the Central American Games of 1974 in the Dominican Republic. He was happy to talk to them, but sent them all away disappointed. The offer at Munich and Santo Domingo was the same. One million dollars to turn professional and leave Cuba, where professional boxing was illegal. 'No, I won't abandon my country for a million dollars nor even for much more money than that. What is a million dollars compared to the love of eleven million Cubans? I've seen the pros on the television and I reckon Muhammed Ali is the best. But there are plenty of pros I could beat right now. What's that Canadian guy called ... Chuvalo? I'd beat him. And Oscar Bonavena and Floyd Patterson. As for the rest, I don't know.' Certainly few in the amateur world were able to keep up as Stevenson racked up a further sixteen victories without defeat in 1974, the over-whelming majority by knockouts in the first two rounds. Stevenson was too good for everyone.

In fact, the only man in the world at that time who could come close was a young Cuban called Angel Milian, a strong kid from Pinar del Rio who would have been the outstanding boxer of his generation if Teofilo Stevenson had not been his rival for Cuba's one allotted place in international competitions. Whenever Stevenson was asked at tournaments who he thought was the second best heavyweight in the world he usually smiled and said, 'Milian.' Milian's career came to very little, though, the odd outing abroad when Stevenson was injured, no Olympics, no world championships. When he retired he began to drink heavily and he was stabbed to death in a bar-room brawl in his home town of Pinar del Rio. No one I asked could remember exactly when. In February 1975 the pair fought for the first time in a special bout arranged in Havana. Milian had Stevenson against the ropes in the first, and even hurt him enough for the referee to give Stevenson a protection count. In the second he continued to attack and Stevenson was hardly able to reply. But Stevenson worked Milian's body with real ferocity in the last and Milian too got a protection count. He kept away from Stevenson after that to avoid a knockout, but he had lost the fight in the last round.

Stevenson's overpowering dominance of the division was starting to mean that few trainers actually wanted their boxers to get into the ring with him. He won two bouts, including the final, in the Golden Belt (Cinturon de Oro) in Romania because his opponents didn't turn up. It wasn't doing Stevenson any good that he was only getting a decent contest against other Cubans. A few at least had the good humour, if not good sense, to try and talk a good fight. At the Pan-American championships, the Bermudan Clarence Hill said he would beat Stevenson, but later failed to turn up after watching at ringside as Stevenson demolished a Costa Rican inside a few seconds of the first round in his first fight. Michael Dokes had strutted his stuff, declaring as the championship began that there was not room for two champions. He did at least turn up, if only to spend three rounds running away from Stevenson and offering little action. He was whistled mercilessly as he got out of the ring, but had got the best he could have hoped for from the fight. That was the limit of the ambitions of other heavyweights now.

Stevenson had to set his own standards and meet his own targets. Apart from Milian no one in Cuba could last the three rounds with him and in the 1976 Playa Giron he saw off four opponents without going the distance. They were all knocked out except for the one who didn't turn up. When the team was invited to Jamaica for a tournament there wasn't a local good enough, so he faced another Cuban instead (the only Jamaican who won in the match was Mike McCallum). In many ways it was a worrying set of events because the Montreal Olympics were on the horizon, where Stevenson was trying to become the only heavyweight in Olympic history to defend his crown successfully. While the Cuban athlete whom most people remember from Montreal is Alberto Juantorena, who won two gold medals on the track, Stevenson's achievement was probably the greater and the rarer.

The preparations in the early part of the year were too easy. And then came his nemesis, Igor Visotsky. The fight was in the final of a tournament in Minsk. Visotsky appeared to be the only fighter in the world not terrified of the big Cuban. In the first round he used his speed and lack of height to good effect, avoiding Stevenson, fighting him up close and winning the round easily. In the second Stevenson settled and fought well enough and far enough out of reach to get Visotsky a standing count. But in the third Stevenson was once again in trouble and Visotsky returned the compliment with a standing count before battering the dazed Cuban to the floor. The referee counted Stevenson out for one of the biggest shocks in amateur boxing of all time. In retrospect it was just what Stevenson needed and, according to those in the camp at the time, the defeat served to reinforce his training and attention to detail. His next preparation in Cuba was against Milian and 20,000 were there to see him in the final of that year's Copa Cardin. It was a tough fight. Level in the first, Milian attacked in the second and Stevenson's eye started to swell. In the third Stevenson regained control and won a unanimous verdict. And sparring for the next two months with Milian, himself worth a place in the top five boxers in the world, would see him set off for Montreal in what he himself said was the best condition of his career. Michael Draure of Senegal was seen off, knocked out in the second. Peter Ruokola of Finland lasted fifty-nine seconds before his corner threw in the towel. His next victim was the American fighter John Tate, a typically hard-as-nails former trucker, a black man with tree-trunk legs, a hard hitter, strong chin, who had beaten Peter Hussing in the previous round by a narrow decision. The fight went like this. Tate heard the bell and charged Stevenson. He missed and he overbalanced. Stevenson kept him off-balance with a left, a feint, another straight left and a destructive right and Tate was flat on his back in his own corner. Silence. As Stevenson left the ring the questions from journalists started.

'When are you going to turn professional?'

'Never. The revolution outlawed professional sport. And our commander-in-chief Fidel Castro knows all about professionalism. A professional sportsman stops being an athlete.'

'Why are Cuban boxers so good at the moment?'

'Because of the good work of the trainers and because of the help that the revolution has given to the sport because in Cuba sport is a right of the people.'

Stevenson was a 6ft 4in public relations weapon let loose on the world's press. This was free propaganda for Cuba, a worldwide dissemination of the Soviet-style slogans that adorned every wall in every stadium in the country, broadcast to the world by a boxer who seemed to offer living proof that it all seemed to work. But his message was always given added piquancy by his refusal to entertain the advantages of huge wealth, an unwavering insistence which added to his magic. While it might be possible to convince yourself that athletes could be bullied into saying the right thing for fear of the consequences, who could bully Teofilo Stevenson? He was for real, something that proved incomprehensible to those who listened to him and knew what riches he was turning down by saying all this.

The final was at least slightly longer, but no less of a challenge. Mircea Simon of Romania decided to hold on to Stevenson and when he wasn't holding he was simply covering his face and body with his gloves. In the third he came out of his shell once to launch a combination and when he missed with a jab Stevenson stuck a right flush on his jaw. He went down, struggled to his feet and as Stevenson's right wound up another time, the corner threw in the towel.

Beating the Americans on their own continent is something that Cuba has had a surprising number of chances to do. It is one of the myths about Cuban sport that sporting connections have been affected by the American blockade. The two countries have regularly competed at international tournaments and in boxing have even had a series of head-to-head matches. The real blockade for sportsmen came from the decision to make professional sport illegal and thus ensure that boxers (and baseball stars) could not maintain their links with the island and pursue a career as professionals. No one got near an international team if there was a hint they would try and turn pro, an act which, because of the law, involved defecting. And if you weren't on an international team who was interested in you anyway?

While the blockade may have had little direct impact on sport in Cuba, however, an understanding of it and how it makes Cubans see the world and their giant neighbour is important. There are two elements to the blockade. One is that goods with their origins in Cuba or using Cuban raw materials are not importable into the United States. Given that large chunks of the history of the island have geared its industry and agriculture to supply the United States with coffee and sugar, this is a huge blow. The United States has used this sort of blockade politically against its enemies throughout the world and still does against Libya, Iran and Iraq, for example. What few people know, however, is that there is a second, human blockade. As Cuba had been a natural holiday destination for Americans, the government wanted to close that source of revenue too, with the slight problem that the US constitution pretty much guarantees its citizens the right to go wherever they want. To avoid this awkward problem the blockade is enforced through the back door via the Treasury Department. It was made illegal by the Treasury for US citizens to spend any money in Cuba, with large fines for anyone who did. Given the impossibility of going to a country and not spending money, any returning citizen with evidence in their passport of a visit to Cuba could expect to be punished. Direct flights are also banned periodically, which has discouraged airlines from offering any official service to the island from the United States. Hush-hush charters have kept going from Miami for most of the dispute between the two countries, however. They generally have to touch down somewhere else before going on to the island, landing at a Caribbean strip, often on the Dominican Republic, before turning round, taxiing to the take-off runway and going on to Cuba. Other inquisitive Americans have travelled via Mexico and asked Cuban immigration not to stamp their passports. However, language barriers and Cuban regulations sometimes stymied this plan and it would be fascinating to know how many left-leaning US citizens have somehow lost or ruined their passports in Mexico. I met at least two in the first three months.

Sport, then, has become one of the few areas in which the United States has not found a way to deny Cuba what it craves. Competition between the nations has continued throughout this time, at the Pan-American Games, Central American Games and other major events. The first boxing world championships, held in Havana in 1974, were attended by a full complement of US boxers. But more surprisingly in 1977 Cuba and the United States started a series of bilateral boxing tournaments, the first of which was held in Houston in the Astrodome. Stevenson didn't box there, but turned up with the team and was mobbed wherever he went. Angel Milian fought in his place and beat Greg Page, a future, if short-lived and unheralded, world heavyweight champion, on points. In the return tournament in Havana a few months later Stevenson outpointed Jimmy Clark. He had never lost to an American in his career and by the time the second world championship came around in 1978 he had a record of 162 wins, 10 defeats, with 70 per cent of his wins coming by knockout.

The world championships were held in Belgrade and few believed the Cubans could do as well in Yugoslavia as they had done at home four years previously. Stevenson was boosted by Visotsky losing his first-round bout to a Frenchman, Dominique Nato, while the current American hope, Tony Tubbs, another who would flicker briefly as a professional contender in the post-Ali heavyweight confusion, hardly looked in exceptional form in his first-round fight. Stevenson won his inside two minutes. When Tubbs, who had claimed he would beat Teofilo, met Stevenson, he spent his time backpedalling and avoiding a fight. He lost on points by a very long way. In the semis came the mediocre Venezuelan Carlos Rivera, whom Stevenson knocked out cold in the first round. The day of the final built to a crescendo for the Cubans, who had won the team title with four golds by the time Stevenson climbed into the ring for the last bout of the night. The home supporters had a special interest in the battle. They had seen their hopes smashed by five straight defeats of all their finalists and now there was only the one left – Dragomir Vujkovic – who could save local pride only by beating Teofilo Stevenson. He lasted two rounds before his corner had to throw in the towel to save him from a beating. Boxing is not a romantic sport.

Stevenson won the Olympic gold in 1980, a games devalued by the non-attendance of the Americans and many of their political allies. He did it with two knockouts and two decisions over Istvan Levai of Hungary and Piotr Zaev of the Soviet Union. Then in 1984 he was unable to defend as the revenge boycott of the Los Angeles Games kicked in and the Cubans didn't go. A pity, because four successive Olympic golds in the same event would have made his place in the record books untouchable.

Stevenson got another wake-up call in the Munich world championships of 1982. Sagarra admits that Stevenson was starting to take his pre-eminence for granted at this stage. He told a Cuban journalist, 'I noticed that he was not giving 100 per cent in training, but I was relying on his capacity to up his fitness very quickly, something he had always been able to do. I guess I was being complacent too.' There should have been a warning when Stevenson lost in the final of the 1982 Cordoba Cardin to a young Italian called Francisco Damiani. When the pair met again in Munich, Damiani again won a 5–0 decision and Stevenson was out of the world championships in the first round.

Stevenson left Munich depressed and contemplating retirement, feeling that his career was on a downward spiral and he would never be truly great again. Then later that year he so thoroughly outclassed the Russian who was touted as his successor, Valeri Abadshiam, that he thought again. He confessed to Sagarra that he thought Abadshiam was the most difficult fighter he had ever faced. The Russian disappeared from the amateur boxing scene after a 1984 defeat by Stevenson, a fight in which the Russian showed how good a rival to Stevenson he might have been, wobbling the Cuban in the second round before wilting under a relentless exchange of blows in the third.

But somehow Stevenson was never the same. He lost to Alexander Krupkin in the Cordoba Cardin of 1984 and to a Cuban, Osvaldo Castillo, in 1986. 'A lot of people told him he should retire in 1986 after the Castillo defeat,' said Sagarra. 'But I felt that we had not heard everything from him and I thought a career as great as his deserved to go out on a high note. I had a feeling too that being beaten by a Cuban might have hurt his pride and left him something to prove to everyone.'

It had. A fortnight later, back at the Finca, the Havana-based training camp of the national team, while the pair were training together, Stevenson caught Castillo with such a hard right that he was unconscious for ten minutes. In sparring for the world championships of 1986 he was put in the ring with the eighteen-year-old Felix Savon. According to Sagarra, Savon was right on top until Stevenson let loose a massive quick right from nowhere and hit Savon hard enough to daze him. Savon, as you will learn later, tells the story slightly differently.

At Reno in the world championships Stevenson was unstoppable and in the semi-finals saw off the other Soviet fighter who had been touted as his nemesis, Viacheslav Yakolev (a 4–1 decision). But he made the decision to call it a day after that. He was thirty-four. For once the Cuban newspapers of the time offered a decent insight. 'The pressure of being at the top meant that he just couldn't keep getting back to the level at which he had operated for so long,' wrote Manolo Cabalé Ruiz in *Granma*. 'It had taken its toll. But he went out in a blaze of glory and in the certain knowledge that he is the greatest amateur boxer of all time.' The Cubans used his face and name for their own purposes by bringing him into the Boxing Commission and the official set-up as a figurehead.

He's neither an intellectual nor a politician, but his presence with the team at international events lifts them and brings awe from the crowd. You could feel it even in 1999 when he went to Houston for the disastrous world championships.

The question Stevenson must get tired of being asked again and again is why he turned down that million pounds and why he never fought Ali. He never answers the first question other than to repeat what he said at the time about the love of eleven million Cubans being worth more than a million pounds. For the second he just shrugs and smiles. But the encouraging thing for me was that I found out from one of the Cuban team that it was not through a lack of will on the Cubans' part that the fight had not taken place.

When the Cuban team got back to Havana late at night after a tournament in the mid-Seventies (no one can remember the exact date and the events are not recorded anywhere), they were greeted by an official party led by Fidel Castro himself, who joked and chatted with them about the world championships and offered his own thoughts on boxing.

Fidel was also asked about what the news was on the fight that was at the time being theoretically organised between Stevenson and Ali. 'People have been talking of this fight for some time', said Fidel, 'as some sort of test of strength between professional and amateur boxing. And we see it that way. Stevenson is the best boxer in the world, amateur or professional. He could fight with whatever pro you put in front of him and win. That is our belief. That is why we are prepared to sanction a contest of this sort in principle. I believe that everyone wants to see this battle, not just in Cuba but in the sporting world generally.' If he could believe it once, maybe he could be made to believe it again. Maybe I wasn't so mad after all?

9 *Welcome to the Hotel Pernik*

The airport at Holguin, where the national boxing championships were being held, is small and pretty much deserted, an unadorned concrete slab on a flat, dry expanse of brown-green land. It isn't here to be noticed because the people who come here don't stay long. On the charter route from Manchester, Frankfurt and other European cities there is nothing exciting about Holguin except that when you land here it means you are only a couple of hours away from your beach holiday.

Around this time Cuba was rapidly becoming a proper holiday destination and was building the trappings of proper holiday destinations as quickly as it could. New terminals were constantly being added to Havana airport and they were building a new road, designed to carry the Pope into town, they said. This tourism drive was a specific choice by the government, although they had shied away from it when they hadn't needed the cash. It had been illegal to have a dollar in your possession right up to the Eighties and people had gone to jail for it. Contact with foreigners was frowned on and tourism from non-socialist states discouraged. But when the Soviet collapse deflated the Cuban economy by about 50 per cent in twelve months it was quickly accepted that foreign currency to replace the Soviet subsidy had to come from somewhere. So the Cuban government developed tourism to bring in pesetas and liras and dollars and pounds. It was a tough call in some areas. The government had been told that there was oil off the coast of Varadero, a coastal resort about seventy miles from Havana, which was also home to the country's finest beaches and traditionally the resort of choice for rich Cubans. But exploiting the oil would ruin the potential of Varadero as a tourist resort. It was a question of policy. They went for tourism and have been running the resort and exploiting its possibilities like an open-cast mine ever since.

The thorny problem for the Cubans was that to attract Western hard-currency tourists you had to have all the trappings of the West too – proper food, plenty of beer and cocktails, decent clean facilities. None of these was available to local people, whose holiday resorts were cheap, cheerful, dirty and rundown. You could always pick them out if you went to the local beaches, lurking concrete monstrosities like disused multi-storey carparks lurking next door to the foreigners' resorts. They looked abandoned but they weren't. And winning the right to go to them was still the privilege of a few.

To bridge the gulf in standards between domestic and foreign standards of tourism, the Cuban tourist industry is based around a sort of apartheid, which frankly suits Western tourists as much as it does the Cuban government. Tourists are bussed in to stay in well-equipped hotels, where there are burgers and beers and cocktails and games and a TV in every room. If they ever leave their all-inclusive hotel, which plenty don't, they'll find a partially controlled environment where local riff-raff (which means every Cuban not in soldier's or waiter's uniform) are kept well away by police checkpoints. I once went out with a Cuban family and we were refused admission to the beaches because they didn't have their identity cards with them. In their own country on a day out, for Christ's sake. The security guard tried to shake me, the foreigner, down for ten bucks to let us all in.

The only locals who get near the best hotels are a number of prostitutes, who are what quite a few of the tourists come for anyway. Cubans cannot stay in the main tourist hotels, though the lower you go down the tourist food chain, the more the rules are relaxed and for a payment of 'commission' you can do pretty much what you want. But for the bigger all-inclusive places, run in partnership with foreign companies, it doesn't matter how much money a Cuban has, they don't get near. And you have to be well connected to get a job in one of them – the chance of access to dollar tips and leftover food was only offered to politically acceptable people. And, this being Latin America, their relatives.

Holguin has a separate problem all of its own. Which is that there is nothing very interesting about the place and there is no reason for tourists to want to go there. All it has is an international airport, which provides a landing point from where you can catch a bus to the beaches of Guardalavaca, which nestle against the north-eastern coast of the island. There is not much activity. The ubiquitous small, thin, leathery-skinned man in a blue or light brown shirt surfs slowly around the baggage carousel, which juts out of the wall like the jetty of a small rowing boat, picking bags off and dumping them in a random pile in the middle of the floor. The huge carpark is deserted and hot. Even the taxi hustlers seem taken by surprise that someone like me has come here on his own.

The taxi drivers know how to have fun, though. The modern roads, a corridor of well-kept concrete for the benefit of foreign eyes and the air-conditioned buses of Havanatur and Gaviota, a holiday company owned and financed by the Cuban air force, are deserted. The taxis have it pretty much to themselves and there are few Ladas waiting here. Mercedes, Citroens, Peugeots, all new and undented, with air-conditioning. It seemed like a chance to take a proper taxi for once, to lord it a little. After all, this was the first assignment of the mission proper, to infiltrate the press and through them get to the boxers.

When I arrived at the Hotel Pernik, the designated hotel for the press at the championships, there was no sign of the man I was supposed to meet and whose name I had been given by Martha Gonzalez. José Luis Salmeron was a fat man who worked for the Sports Ministry and who also had the luxury of writing for *Record*, the official – and, therefore, only – magazine of Cuban sport. *Record* came out whenever there was the will and the printing capacity to publish it, which wasn't very often, maybe a couple of times a year. The 1996 edition, published towards the end of the year, was still the most recent one available in October 1997. Writing for *Record* involved going to all the major sports events which Cubans were involved in throughout the country, and occasionally in other parts of the world, in the certain knowledge that you would only be required to trot out a series of uncritical, depersonalised, unexciting articles which would generally be of lower calibre than what you could have put together listening to it all on the radio. With the Cuban press discouraged – OK, pretty much forbidden – to print anything that might make their sportsmen look bad, or anything about their personality or upbringing, working for a sports magazine, which could only really thrive off these things, seemed a trifle pointless.

The Hotel Pernik had that familiar Eastern European, modernist feel to it, which felt quite cosy in sun-drenched Cuba, but which I can recall from stays at similarly styled hotels in Poland, Bulgaria and Albania as brutish and grim. A big, open, glassy lobby with plastic settees dotted around the edge hid a straight up-and-down tenement block. The hotel was on a deserted main road on the fringes of the town, with the large baseball stadium towering close by. The area had been landscaped and redeveloped and still had an untouched, scale-model feel, as if someone had put a giant tarpaulin over it in 1978 and then taken it off twenty years later. It was recognisably old but in disorientating good condition, like an antique Dinky toy or a mint-condition sheet of Penny Blacks. And it had that lingering smell of leatherette and cigarette smoke that most Eastern European hotels seem to have built into them.

I dumped my bags in the room, a reasonably clean and reasonably priced thirty-five bucks a night, film channel (American, pirated) included, and headed for the bar. It was empty except for two black men, one mid-thirties, good-looking, old red tracksuit bottoms, with a faintly Afro hairstyle that was as 1970s as the lobby's metal magazine racks and sculpted stand-alone push-to-stub ashtrays. The other was a smaller, wiry man, late twenties maybe, with a better tracksuit and a more neutral short-cropped hairstyle. They looked like hustlers.

I sat down to reread Sagarra's book, to familiarise myself with some of the bigger names and milestones of Cuban boxing, so when I finally met the Cuban hacks I would know a little more about my cover story – that I was writing a book about Cuban boxers. The two black men kept looking over. Ignore them. A few more beers and I started looking at the pictures at the back, in colour, a distinct rarity for any book published in this era. The hustlers kept looking. The older one came over.

He slurred something that was only decipherable by his hand movements – he reached over and picked up my lighter. He smiled at me and lit his cigarette. He said something else, which made no concession to the possibility that I might not speak Spanish – his accent was to his language what Falls Road slur is to English. It was all vowels and no consonants. I looked confused.

'Turista?' he said.

His friend looked across nervously. I shook my head and said as best I could that I was here for the boxing.

'Periodista?' he said.

'Si.'

To avoid trying to write up the conversation as it happened, which involved pointing, repeating, much shaking of heads, the smoking of a packet of cigarettes and eight beers, what roughly happened next is as follows.

'I'm in that book.'

Yeah, right, of course you are, I thought. But before the cynicism could burn itself into a look of disbelief he had leaned over and taken the book from the table. I looked at him. He was a good-looking man, his face moved economically, if at all, and he had a glazed, slightly punch-drunk look that lit up when he talked about himself. There was something childlike about him and even though his face was quite beautiful there was a menace about it, a sense that he could turn nasty if pushed. I didn't stop him taking the book.

'Here. That photograph is me.'

It was a picture of a young man training with Sarvelio Fuentes, one of the head coaches of the Cuban team.

'And this one too.'

He pointed to a photograph of a crouching boxer in the ring with a German fighter called Henry Maske in what the caption said was the World Cup in Belgrade in 1987. Maske has since gone on to make a good living as a professional. The young Cuban looked well on top.

His name was Angel Espinosa and he is one of the best boxers Cuba has ever produced, a middleweight and light-middleweight with a reputation as a trifle undisciplined, over-fond of women and drink. He had retired early, in his late twenties, because he was burnt out, didn't feel like training any more, couldn't be bothered. I felt childishly pleased with myself. Clearly I was very good at this subterfuge lark and Frank Warren's faith in me had been entirely justified. I'd been in Cuba for two months and already I was mixing it with the guys at the top. This was going to be easy.

'Give me the pen,' said Espinosa.

Laboriously and painstakingly he started to write on his photos in the book: 'Dedico mi hautografo [sic] al companero John, Angel Espinosa, campin [sic] de Reno 86, 87 Copa del Mundo y plata en Moscu.' Which means, 'I dedicate my autograph to comrade John Duncan, Angel Espinosa, world champion of Reno 1986, and the 1987 World Cup and silver in Moscow.' Moscow was another world championship. He had fought in Reno as a light middle and in Moscow as a middleweight.

He held the book roughly, the pages looking pitifully small in a pair of leathered chubby hands with a large ring bulging from his index finger.

'Sign the book,' he said to his friend, obviously a great deal more timid. 'Look. You're in here too.'

Espinosa flicked through the photos again. His friend looked on calmly and signed a couple. 'Dedico mi autografo de Julio Gonzalez, campeon mundial de Moscu 1989.' Gonzalez was another of Cuba's finest boxers of the Eighties, a lost era for the country with the boycotts of the Olympics of 1984 in Los Angeles and of 1988 in Seoul. By 1994 and the Barcelona Games both Gonzalez and Espinosa were past their best.

Gonzalez was a 'what you see is what you get' type of bloke. In the ring he was a technician, a jabber rather than a puncher, a slippery character who fights in the middle and long distance, jabbing into the face and then darting out of range. He was quite tall for a lightweight. We talked for a while as my packet of Populars disappeared and the tins of strong, black-label Bucanero beer piled up.

'Julio Gonzalez is a great champion,' said Espinosa. 'Tell him about Zulow, Julio, tell him about that fight with Zulow.'

Andreas Zulow was German, as were many of the Cubans' fiercest rivals. Because none of the Communist nations allowed professionalism, the East Germans and Cubans who made it in the amateurs were there for ten years, while the capitalist kids were in and out in a couple of years to make some money at their chosen profession. Gonzalez and Zulow were always ranked one and two in the lightweights, so it was little surprise when they met in the final in Moscow in 1989. Gonzalez had hardly broken sweat getting there. His US semi-finalist, whose name he couldn't remember – 'Maclaim, McLean, something like that' – had thrown in the towel and he went on to meet Zulow. It was just as well he had had a relatively easy ride. Amateur world championships are gruel-ling occasions with fights of consistently high standard in quick succession. The fights are not as intense as professional ones, but getting hit is getting hit and the pros can build up to forty-five minutes of pain for a few months. The amateurs get out there and do it every couple of days for a fortnight.

'The trainers had a lot of work to get me ready for Zulow,' Gonzalez said. 'We had fought a few times. He was a great technician and he had studied my style quite hard. There wasn't much that we didn't know about each other. We were both good all-round boxers, as good at defence as offence. Neither of us had any obvious weaknesses. Our fights were always pretty even. Sarvelio Fuentes spent a lot of time with me before we went to Moscow tying to work on the style of Zulow, who was the Olympic champion and had to be respected. Sarvelio spent hours studying Zulow and he eventually came up with the idea that instead of going for my usual straight shots I had to use combinations more. One, two.

Boof, boof, to get through his guard. That I wouldn't beat him if I didn't change the way I normally boxed.'

Espinosa butted in. He could barely control himself. 'It was a great contest. He started off jabbing, Zulow stood there and took it, nothing was getting past his guard, it was sealed absolutely fucking tight. Julio's left just bounced off. He knew he had to keep Julio away or the left would have had him. And Julio had to attack him without leaving himself open. It was like a fucking masterclass in boxing. At the end it was 14–14 in blows landed, which wasn't right, but there were a lot of dodgy decisions in Moscow. It went to the judges and they couldn't deny him. It was 4–1 and he'd won. It was a beautiful fight technically.'

It was hard at this point not to notice the enthusiasm the two men had for what they did. They were like kids talking about an adventure, a dare, a game. They carried on talking to each other as though they wanted to relive every moment. They spoke too fast for me to understand instantly, but their excitement was obvious.

The way they talked about the fight made it sound like chess, a technical, mental battle between two men, two approaches to what they saw as an art rather than an act of controlled violence. It struck me that I hadn't ever thought about boxing like this before, that I was a child of professional boxing, that I had been taught to admire the violence, to look for it, to find it exciting, especially as I wasn't someone who was equipped for it myself. I'd assumed that the pleasure boxers took in their sport was in humiliating or violating their opponents, which is after all what Western professional boxing seems to be all about, the fake hate, the cockiness, the fuck-you stuff. This didn't seem the same thing at all.

It was touching and I felt a little embarrassed. The problem with coming from one world into another is that you bring so many of your own values with you. For all the scorn I had poured on Costa Brava package types, the where's-the-fish-and-chip-shop mob, I was one of them really. I'd come here assuming that all these boxers would be intensely frustrated with their lot because they couldn't make any money out of what they did. And only now had the possibility that they did what they did because they enjoyed it dawned on me. Sneering at propaganda, I had blithely assumed that the only reason Savon had turned down ten million dollars, and Stevenson a million before him, was because he didn't know who was listening, or how to get out, or was afraid for his family. The idea that he might have meant exactly what he had said hadn't registered as a possibility.

'Why don't you come to my house, John?' said Espinosa. 'I live very close. You can come and meet my mother and have something to eat with us. If you could maybe bring some beer or some rum that would be nice.'

The three of us walked across the expanse of dusty grass in front of the Hotel Pernik towards the main road. The common reminded me of those bleak empty spaces in Leeds and other city centres, former bomb-sites or the end-results of the mass demolitions of back to backs, dog toilets with rusting, lopsided goalposts in the middle and a concrete shack in one corner with the initials of the football team writ large amid a host of scrawled tags. Nobody ever wanted to spend any time there, it was just a pointless, forgotten bit of land.

Down a grass bank and suddenly more concrete, a four-lane road, pristine. A large water tanker came lumbering past us, spewing out blue filth in our faces. I coughed. Espinosa and Gonzalez carried on talking. We crossed and reached a side-road with a garage on the corner. The local kids in their yellow school trousers raced around on bikes and hung out on corners, throwing things at each other and laughing. As we walked down the barely concreted road, everyone sneaked a glance. It didn't look like the sort of place foreigners visited much, lined by small concrete buildings, like stables or outhouses, done up as best they could be with gates and fences and planks of wood and the odd tree. On one corner was a trolley selling pizza, or an approximation to pizza. It looked like the cardboard base of a supermarket pizza with a thin layer of melted yellow rubber and a couple of squirts of tomato ketchup on it. (The rare times that I had been adventurous and hungry enough to try street pizza in Havana, that was what it tasted like too. The rumour was that some enterprising Cubans melted the condoms they got free from Médecins sans Frontières to make it look as if there was more cheese on their offerings.) This wasn't a time for pizza. I'd bought a bottle of seven-year-old Havana Club rum for $6.40, which is the price it was in every shop in every town that year. And we were going to drink it and talk about boxing.

We carried on walking towards his house and suddenly there wasn't any concrete on the road, just dust. And the mainly black women sat and stared out from their porches with dumb, worn faces, not saying anything or pretending not to look, just staring with their mouths slightly open. The men didn't catch our eye and I got the strong feeling that this was because of Espinosa. He swaggered down the street, not really one of them, with a tracksuit that was better than theirs, a glitter of gold from his bracelet. The looks subtly suggested fear but not respect. Other boxers I spent time with were greeted and touched and smiled at. Espinosa got a grudging glance and got what he wanted when he asked for it, but nothing more.

His house was near the end of the street. It was indistinguishable from the other shacks, a square concrete construction about fifteen foot wide with wooden slats on the window. There was a gate, metal and rusty, and a thin wooden door with pockmarked paint peeling away from it. Once through the door you were straight into the living room, bare concrete walls, an old Russian television, three cheap wooden chairs and a small side table. Behind the door (unpainted on the inside) was a bunch of dried branches, presumably to ward off evil spirits. And a small trophy cabinet with a selection of rusting, cheap-looking trophies and dull oxidised medals with foreign writing. Espinosa wasn't allowed to keep the best ones at his house in case they got stolen, they were in the local sports museum. There were also some certificates, the local Communist Party recognising him as a good citizen, and so on. But on the wall dominating everything was a picture of Espinosa as a young boxer, the now slightly cynical smile radiant and childlike – he looked like every naughty kid who knew he was pretty and knew he was hard, as if nothing would ever touch him, like the young Muhammad Ali. And this kid in the photo looked down on Espinosa like his little brother, all day, every day, the colours fading, the background now a bleached light blue, the once strong red a washed-out pink. But the face was as black and powerful as ever.

Espinosa got three glasses and dragged his mother from another room, which must have been her bedroom. She looked barely older than he was, a thin-framed timid black woman with a sad expressionless face in an oversized white nightie and pink curlers. She smiled and silently picked up the glasses that Espinosa had brought into the room. She returned a moment later with three cleaner ones as Espinosa went into his room and dug around for something. He came out with a book.

On the front of the book in chiselled lettering were the words, in Spanish, *Angel Espinosa: My Life in Boxing*. He laid it on my lap, roughly opened the first pages where a wide-eyed black kid in a scruffy red vest stared out at me, and started talking.

10 *Angel Espinosa*

'Tell me about this photo. It's beautiful,' I said. 'How old were you?'

'I was seventeen there. We were in a tournament in Czechoslovakia called the Tina Labe.'

Actually it's called the Usti Mad Laben or it could be the Ustin Laden. Czechoslovakia may have been a comradely country, but none of the Cubans I spoke to ever felt comradely enough about it to have got even a faint grip on the language.

'It was the last time I took part in the tournament. I won it four times, in '83, '85, '86 and, err, '87.'

'How did you start in boxing?'

'I started at ten years old, almost eleven. It pretty much all began when I was passing a boxing gym. I wasn't really bothered about boxing, but I went in to have a look and there were a couple of kids of about my size fighting. I looked at them and I said to myself that I could beat the pair of them, though they had spent a lot of time practising even by that age. But it seemed a daft sport to me. While I was watching these guys, I was thinking, 'What kind of sport is this where you get hit for fun? I'm not hanging around here.

'So I stopped going, but I kept on thinking about it. And quite soon I went back, really just with the intention of finding out a bit more, and I stopped and watched a few fights that they had that day. I went back a third time and as I arrived I saw Enrique Etcheverria, who you'll find in Peru right now training boxers there. He was giving some training and he saw me and said, "Come here, son".'

Espinosa laughs. It's a boyish, cheeky laugh and a gold flash glints from one of his teeth. But this is a rare moment. Espinosa doesn't seem a happy man. As he tells his story he stares down at the floor or looks away. Or he shows me a photo and then just stares at me while I look at it. As if he can't actually look the story of his life straight in the eye. He wants to tell me something important, but can't seem to get the words out. It's as if I'm just going to have to guess the (many, many) parts of his life that he is going to miss out and the (large, large) parts of his life that make him sad.

'I was an only child. It was a fairly normal upbringing.' This, I found out later, is not even half true. A friend of his told me that he had had a baby sister who died very young when his mother accidentally spilt hot fat on her in their tiny, cramped kitchen. His mother never forgave herself and had a nervous breakdown. His father left and took little interest in Angel (which you pronounce Ang-hell) until he had turned himself into a star. The absence of a wage-earner hit the Espinosa household hard and his mother took in odd bits of sewing to make ends meet. Angel was the only man in the house. All his mother's hopes were in him and he grew up too quickly. Like many people who have this kind of fast-track childhood, he never really had the chance to grow up properly at all.

'The trainer said to me, "Hey, hippy, get over here." I suppose my hair was quite long as a kid, I had an Afro. Anyway, he said to me, "What are you doing? What do you want?" And I said to him, "Can you show me how to box?"

"Have you brought shorts and a shirt?" "Yep." "So get changed." So I took my trousers off, put on some shorts. "Do three laps of the gym running first to warm up," he said. So I did three laps and when I finished he just looked at me and said, "Now get showered." And I thought, "Fucking hell." Because now, having got here, I really wanted to get in the ring. And put on some gloves. "Is this a fucking boxing gym or an athletics track?" I said to him. "I came here to box and all you want me to do is run three times round the gym and stop. Now I'm supposed to shower? Fuck that." I was really pissed off.

'I hung around a while and then I drifted off home. Anyway some time after that they put a different trainer, Orestes Salazar, in his place. When he got there they had competitions on Mondays and Fridays, yeah, Mondays and Fridays. There were a lot of bouts in those days and they publicised them quite widely.

'Orestes put us in two lines because he said he wanted a chance to see how good everyone was. One for those who had been around the gym for a while and another for the new boys, who were trained by Pepito Calixto. Seeing as he had no idea who anyone was, I put myself in the queue of those who had been around a bit, the older boys. I was a cocky little sod. So we started training and Orestes wanted to see all our starting positions. I started out as a rightie. No, no, I started as a southpaw, a left-hander. And he was telling us to move forward and backward and because I had no idea what I was doing I kept switching my stance from right to left-handed. I was totally confused. He had to call me over and say, "Look, son, are you southpaw or not? Because sometimes you step back with the left and sometimes with the right." "I'm not either. I'm both," I told him. "I'm ambidextrous." Which was a lie, just to hide the fact I didn't have a clue what I was doing. "Not any more you aren't," he said. "That last move you made was southpaw; stay that way and don't change again. You got that?"'

Southpaws, like left-handed batsmen in cricket and left-handed pitchers in baseball, have the distinct advantage of mucking up the style of opponents reared mainly on a diet of right-handers. Espinosa exploited this throughout his career.

'So from then on I learned everything in boxing as a southpaw. As I went further in the sport I tried to change back, but it was too late. When I tried to hit from a different stance it was like a gun without bullets, and when anyone had a go at me I just couldn't fend them off. So I stayed lefty and it was as a lefty that I won all my schoolboy prizes.

'It was there that it all started and about seven or eight days later I had my first fight. The coach used to come into the gym, look us up and down and say, you, you, you and you. There were some pretty big kids among them, but I was really desperate to box by now and I got my chance the next day. The trainer had some problems at home, I think, and didn't turn up for the weigh-in before the fights. So this guy was weighing everyone who was going to take part, but had no idea who he was supposed to be weighing. So he just sort of shouts out, "Anyone else need to be weighed?" Well, I hadn't actually been picked to fight, but seeing as the trainer wasn't there I just sort of got in the queue to be weighed. I never really thought anything would happen, I was sure they would realise that I shouldn't be there, but I got to the front and no one said anything. Anyway I remember that when it was my turn to get on to the scales I got on to it with my gown still on. The weighing guy said, "Terribly sorry, son, but you get on this in your birthday suit or you don't get on at all." I didn't know what he was on about. I just thought, "I'm not showing my bum in here with all these other kids looking." But in the end he gave me no choice, so I did it. I weighed 34 kg.

'Anyway, the competition was almost about to start when

our trainer finally arrives to check if all his boys are ready. He arrived and saw me ready with my hands bandaged up. "Hey, kid, who told you that you weighed enough to fight?" I just said, "Look, there was a queue for people who hadn't been weighed and I hadn't been weighed, had I? So I got in it." The trainer laughed. He said, "OK, kid, you win. Look, just throw jabs, nothing else. Don't swing, don't try uppercuts. And if you don't do exactly as I say you are out of here, OK?"

'Well, I just said, "Deal." I got in the ring for my first fight and I won. After winning I thanked the referee and I leaned out of the ring in each corner and thanked each of the judges who had marked the fight and I was just about to get out of the ring then when I heard people booing. How was I supposed to know any of the etiquette and stuff? It was only my first fight. Anyway the trainer who was waiting for me said, "Espinosa, you can't do that." And I said, "Why not?" And he said, "Espinosa, you only thank the people in the ring, the other fighter, the audience and the referee. Just touch gloves like this." "OK," I said. "I won't do it again." And that was the beginning of my career in boxing.

'I got to my forty-seventh fight before I lost. The forty-eighth was a fight I had in Cienfuegos and I'm telling you I was robbed blind. I cried a lot after that fight and I felt so bad that I almost packed in boxing. At thirteen and fourteen I was beating kids who were in the national junior team. At fifteen I was fighting men from the full team. But they wouldn't send me abroad, which is what I really wanted to do. Then I got picked for a national baseball team which was going on tour, but the boxing authorities told the baseball people that I belonged to them and I couldn't go. Anyway, when I found out I just thought, "Sod it, I'm not going to do sport if this is how they treat you." But then it just sort of kept nagging away at me and I had all this energy to burn so I ended up going back to boxing. I didn't really have anywhere else to go, did I?'

Corinna Chute left England to go to Cuba on an adventure early in 1988. She was in her early thirties, had no kids and no relationship. She never intended to spend ten years there, as a dancer and agent for Ronnie Scott's jazz club. She met Angel Espinosa for the first time when Espinosa was only twenty-one years old.

'Me and two friends went to Santa Maria beach one afternoon to get away from things and as we were sitting there these three guys started hopping around us in circles. They seemed like fun people, not dangerous. I remember they had an enormous dustbin of ice, which had loads of beers in. They offered us a couple. Angel was very quiet, it was the other two making all the noise. But I noticed this tall, dark, slightly oriental-looking bloke. He's got Chinesey eyes because of his Chinese grandmother. I thought he looked mysterious and fun and I also thought he was very good-looking. But the most exciting thing, I have to say, were these amazing shorts that he had on, with Cuba written across them. They were obviously causing a stir – they were there for exactly that purpose, a sort of trademark, so that people would know who he was.

'I think I said to one of the others, "I'd like to have your mate's shorts." I didn't even say it directly to him, but he promptly took them off and handed them to me. He had had quite a few beers by this stage. I was pretty happy with these shorts. He sat down and the others chatted and he sat there and lurked. He does a lot of lurking. He's very shy. I don't know if he believes in ESP or something, but he always stares very hard at you as if he's trying to send you mental messages. He never talks about his emotions. He uses his eyes. Anyway, I lost my watch in the sand and he gave me his, a really expensive one. I didn't think this was very fair, so I asked one of the others, his cousin, for a telephone number so that I could call him and give him the watch back when he sobered up. A few days later I rang up this number and apparently he had been sitting next to the phone for three days waiting for me to call.'

Espinosa stares at me hard as I look through his photos and cuttings. He sips his rum and carries on talking and turning the pages for me. 'I went to the national championships at Playa Girón in 1981 and I lost at 51kg to this guy called Leyva, from Santiago de Cuba. Another robbery. Anyway, after that I carried on winning tournaments: TV Cubana, Team Tournaments, the 5 September, the Paquito Espinosa. In 1982 I beat everyone in the 57kg apart from Adolfo Horta [one of the all-time greats of Cuban boxing] and Jesus Sollet [no mean fighter either]. Anyway I heard that Alcides Sagarra reckoned I was a decent prospect and he wanted to see a fight between me and Horta the next year at the Playa Giron. It didn't quite work out because I was a growing kid still and I just couldn't make the weight when next January came around and I had to move up to 60kg. Anyway, I had a couple of fights there and won them both, though I got a bad injury in the second one. In the third I came up against Angel Herrera. Herrera was a double Olympic champion, thirty-two years old, and I'm still only sixteen. I hit him hard in the first round and I had him. A double Olympic champion and me a kid of sixteen. He won on points in the end, 4–1, but it was a pretty close fight.'

His scalps up to that point and the victory against Herrera should have been enough to get him a plane ticket to a foreign tournament. But still nothing.

'I went back east to my home town that year, swearing that I would never box again. What was the point of putting all this energy into boxing if they were never going to let me leave the country? Anyway, I got a call from Havana about a month later telling me to get to the capital because I had been called up to replace José Miranda, who had been down to go to Czechoslovakia for a tournament called the Justine Lague [another phonetic version of Usti Mad Laben]. I won the best young fighter award as a sixteen-year-old and the gold medal. After Czechoslovakia we went to Romania for a tournament called the Cinturon de Oro [The Gold Belt], which is where I picked up this injury.'

Espinosa tilts his head to one side and points to a barely visible scar on his wrinkle-free face, which stretches from his eye to his ear like an old knife wound.

'I hardly ever got hurt in the ring except this once. I was fighting this Venezuelan and he took points off me on the inside and from a distance. Anyway, when I got out of the ring and into the dressing room, there was this big mirror and when I looked in it I nearly fainted. I was cut from my eye to my ear and if I rolled my eyes I could actually see my ear hanging off. When I saw it I thought, "Right, that's it, I'm not boxing any more."'

Corinna smiles and sips a glass of red wine in her clean Tooting flat, memories and mementoes of Cuba dotted around.

'We arranged to meet up and we had a little fling. I left to go back to Amsterdam and I thought that was the last I would ever see of this guy. I was setting up a travel agency with some other people and I was going to be the representative in Havana. While I was there I found out that I was "with child". I thought that was OK. I mean, I was thirty-two and, OK, I hadn't planned it, but it was cool. When I got back to Cuba I went looking for him and I managed to meet up with him at the Hotel Capri, where Orlando Reyes [another boxer] had been given a room for a few days because he had just got married. It was one of the perks they had. I took him up to the room and told him that I was going to have his child, that it was OK, that as far as I was concerned it was over and he needn't worry. He stared at his feet for a few minutes and just said, "Pa'lante" [onwards]. It was his way of saying that he wanted to carry on seeing me. Pa'lante.'

'Anyway, life got better when I got back from Europe in 1982,' said Espinosa. 'Alcides saw the results I had got and told me to go home to my family in the east for a week but to come back. I agreed, but, to be honest, inside I just wanted to get back to Holguin and stay there, because to me that was where I belonged. So I overstayed the seven days and Alcides was sending telegrams to the sports authorities here saying that I had to come back to Havana. I wasn't having any of it. One day my mum and the local boxing commissioner dragged me to the bus station and put me on a bus for Havana. I got there, joined the camp and started training and everything, but I didn't say a word to anyone. The group was quite close, Teofilo and Emilio Correa were there and here was me, this surly silent kid. When I training finished I just used to go straight to the dressing room without saying anything. I hated Havana, but it was the only place I could train.'

Espinosa was just a country boy. He preferred to sleep on the floor without pillows and despite his early desire to travel had to be bullied to get on planes for tournaments. Once he was old enough not to live full time at the Finca, he found a home with a family of fellow Holguineros to look after him. 'Julia' became his landlady and his surrogate mother. Her son Pepo became his best friend and surrogate big brother. They lived in central Havana in a place called San José and Espinosa had to get from the centre to the Finca regularly for training at six a.m. There was no public transport and Espinosa usually cycled the ten or so miles to the farm. Sometimes, if the bike wasn't working properly, he ran it. His landlady's son used to wake him up at four and pull him out of bed or off the floor to get out to the Finca in time.

'I went to the world youth championships even though I

had never really trained with the youth team at all. I went to a youth tournament in Romania and got silver and when I got back I was selected for a tournament in Mexico, which never actually happened. At this point I was a 63kg fighter. When I went to the junior world championships in the Dominican Republic I won the gold medal and the prize for best boxer. In 1984 I was entered in the Cuban national championships as a light welterweight, which I won. In the semi I remember I had to fight Carlos Garcia, from Camaguey, who was the senior world champion at the time. I mean I was the junior champion, but he was much more experienced and a lot of people came to see the bout, which I won by knockout.

'When we got back from that I was put in an awkward spot. Alcides took me aside and said, "Look, Espinosa. We have a problem at light middleweight [71 kg] and we think you are the man who can solve it. We believe in you, Espinosa, we think you can switch up in weight, but it all depends on you, whether you are happy doing it or not." It was flattering but a little confusing. The guy who was the Cuban team's light middleweight, Orestes Solano, was the Pan-American champion so I didn't really see the problem. "Look," said Alcides, "Garcia is a world champion and you beat him. You can step up."

'I had to train twice as hard and eat twice as much to make the weight. My first fight at that level was against Armandito Martinez, who had been the Olympic champion of 1980 at light middleweight, and he beat me. And the next trip was West Germany. It was a pretty sharp step-up in weights, but when I got to Germany I won the gold medal and the prize for best young fighter. When I got back it was the Cordoba Cardin, where I got a bronze.

'But the really big thing was the Olympics of 1984 in Los Angeles. While we were training for that in the Isla de la Juventud they told me I was in the team for sure. When they told me that we weren't going to the Games because of the boycott it was probably not as sad for me as for other people. I was still a kid and for me the Goodwill Games, which replaced the Olympics in Cuba that year, were a big deal too. In the Goodwill Games I had a few problems, I picked up a bad cut boxing against a Russian and had to carry on competing against a German in the next round. I can't remember the guy's name now, but it was a really hard fight and I had to be given a standing count at one point and he knocked me down once as well. I knocked him down too. All that was in the first round. In the second I got to grips with him, controlled the rest of the fight and won.

'I don't remember much about 1985, but I won everything I touched in 1986. I got gold in Czechoslovakia, in Halle at the Copa Quimica. I think I beat Enrique Richter in the final. They asked me to fight at middleweight in a team competition in Cuba and my weight went up again. I was having real problems with my weight and when I arrived back at training camp I weighed 87kg, which is a heavyweight. They got me down to 72kg, but I looked really thin, so they decided that from then on I was a middleweight. It was an important time because we were preparing for the Pan-American Games in Indianapolis. I beat Dari Allen there in what everyone said was the best fight of the tournament. He was the middleweight world champion and I was the light middleweight and a lot of people had been looking forward to it. It was a good fight.'

It certainly was a good fight, probably Espinosa's finest in the ring. He was tireless, restless, impatient, in front of Allen. He stood relentlessly in the middle distance, right on top of his opponent but quick enough and slippery enough somehow to be just out of reach. He bobbed up and down on the tips of his toes throughout the fight, darting in and landing hard blows before darting back. He took a few shots too for his trouble, but barely blinked. He bobbed and bobbed, up and down, up and down, slam, slam, slam, and caught Allen flush with a right hook. Allen's legs just gave up on him and he sank to the floor and lay on his side motionless. Espinosa retreated to his corner, still bobbing up and down, expressionless, locked in a world of his own, bobbing up and down, up and down. While Allen was helped back, dazed, to his corner after a minute of lying on his side surrounded by doctors, Espinosa went over to the corner, still dancing, and checked he was all right. He hadn't put his dressing gown on, he had just tied it around his shoulder like a Superman cape. Even after Sagarra left the ringside Espinosa was there enjoying his moment, full of energy, up and down, up and down. Espinosa won the prize as best boxer of the games.

'We had some problems at those games with Miami-Cubans. We call those exiles *gusanos* [maggots] because they are the rubbish of our country. They tried everything they could to distract us, first of all offering to buy us beer and when we declined they decided to insult us. Anyway, a huge fight broke out in the hotel and we got into a lot of trouble. I grabbed one of the flags that they had brought with them and kept it.'

'Angel was always getting himself in trouble,' said Corinna. 'He always had this incredible respect for authority and at the same time this teenage kick against it, this urge inside to rebellion. He constantly acted like a fourteen-year-old just learning that they've got a bit of independence. He was like that in everything he did. On one side he would take authority and on the other he would just think he knew better. He never seemed to get past that teenage approach. It happened all the way through his life. It was always extremes, one thing or the other, one day total silence and obedience, then another day he wouldn't believe a word anyone said. The only one who could get through to him was Sarvelio Fuentes, his trainer. More than Alcides, who was very distant and strict, Sarvelio was like a father to him, knew how to coax him through his moods. And it was always me and Sarvelio who had to get him out of trouble whenever and wherever it happened. In that sense I was like his mother and Sarvelio his dad.'

'I won in Yugoslavia in the World Team Cup in the final against Henry Maske. I won the best pound-for-pound boxer's trophy.' Espinoza paused. 'Hang on a second.' He stood up and disappeared into the bedroom. He shouted to his mum, who shuffled through from the kitchen to join him. By the sounds of rustling and banging, Espinosa was looking for something. He came back with a small cutting from a German magazine, a profile of Henry Maske, who was Olympic champion in Seoul in 1988, and who became a professional world champion. I didn't understand much of it, except one paragraph that Espinosa had marked with a pen. Deducing what I could from the few German words that looked vaguely English, Maske was asked who his most difficult opponent had been. And he had told the magazine that it was Espinosa. Angel folded the cutting up, like a certificate, and tucked it into the photo album before carrying on.

'I beat Maske three times around '87 and '88, in Halle, in Yugoslavia and a few months before the Seoul Olympics, which we didn't go to. It still hurts to think that I didn't get to go to the Seoul Olympics because I know I would have won. We spent the whole of 1988 training for it and then in the end they told us we weren't going. I felt really hurt by that and things started to go wrong for me.

'In fact, 1989 was the worst time of my life. I had problems with my wife, with my mother, things happened that shouldn't have happened and I didn't have anyone to help me out. I'd got married in 1988 and I was really in love. We were living in my mum's house. Her family didn't like me and my friends all said that she was going to be a big problem for me, but I didn't listen because when you're in love you don't. All this was going on and I stopped training properly.'

What was actually happening to him was much more complicated. At this time he had started drinking heavily, possibly because he was starting to taste life outside the Finca for the first time, and his new wife, Xiomara, a doctor, was drinking heavily with him. She was the niece of Julia, the woman who had taken him in as a lodger in Havana. She wanted him to give up boxing and live with her in Holguin. She would ring him and tell him she needed him with her, so he would pack his things and catch a plane back.

The team had no idea how to handle him. They sent Teofilo Stevenson to visit him in Corinna Chute's flat in the Focsa building, an ugly high-rise block close to the centre of Havana by the sea with fantastic views, largely occupied by foreign workers. 'Teofilo came to see him when I had just moved there and there was no furniture. They just sort of grunted at each other like boxers do and I left them to it for a couple of hours, the pair of them sitting there on cardboard boxes hardly saying anything. When I got back Teofilo just said that Angel had decided to pack it in, but he was making a terrible mistake and he would never be able to get back in the team. That was how they were, always forcing him to choose, making things black and white, threatening him, never trying to find some room for manoeuvre. Angel knew that if he carried on boxing his marriage was on the rocks, but that if he gave in he might lose the team as a support. It was choose us or her.' For a while he tried to juggle both.

'Despite all that was going on in 1989,' said Espinosa, 'I still won the Playa Giron that year and the Copa Cardin and was in the team that went to Germany to prepare for the World Championships in Russia. I was really out of condition and everything, but I still got into the team. The first few fights there were easy, absolutely fucking simple, but then I got in the ring for the final against this Russian, Kurniavka, and there was nothing in the tank at all. I tried to impose myself and I just couldn't. And that is what it is like when you haven't trained. Alcides is right. The truth is that titles are won in the gym and I hadn't trained properly. I got home from Moscow and went straight to Holguin to see the family and once again things had got even worse while I was away. So at the end of 1989 I just decided to get out of boxing for a year and sort it all out.' He was twenty-two.

At about this time Espinosa was involved in an incident with the police, which is so mind-numbingly stupid it is hard to imagine what he thought he was doing. A few people came round to Corinna's house for the evening. One, a friend of hers, was a driver from the Ministry of Culture. Also present were Julio Gonzalez and Espinosa. The group had a pleasant evening, got heavily stuck into the rum and crashed out. When Corinna woke up the next morning, the official car in which the Ministry of Culture driver had arrived was not there. Neither were Espinosa or Gonzalez.

'They had just decided in a drunken state that they wanted to go to Cienfuegos because Julio wanted to see his girlfriend and they wanted to go right that minute. So, pissed out of their heads, they took the keys off the table where the driver had left them, got in the car and tried to drive. This was an official car with red number plates which everyone could recognise. I don't know how it happened, but they ended up in Matanzas, where they were picked up by the police. You can just imagine what it must have looked like. They hadn't put any shoes on and they were in their shorts, so there were these two black guys in shorts driving all over the road in an obviously official government car at four a.m. They could hardly have done much more to attract attention to themselves. They got nicked and put in the cells. When the police realised who they were, they phoned the Finca to sort it out and everything looked like it was going to be all right.'

Corinna meanwhile had gone to the beach with some friends, where Julia, Angel and a few others were supposed to join them. 'After a while I rang Julia,' she said, 'and asked her why she wasn't at the beach. She just told me that Angel had been detained and I had no idea what that meant at first. I thought it meant he was going to be late or something, but eventually it clicked that he had been arrested. I drove out and went to pick him up at Sarvelio Fuentes's house. Things had got much worse. Just as Angel was leaving the police station with everything sorted out, he asked for the keys to the car and they told him he couldn't have them. He didn't mean anything, I'm sure, just that he wanted to return the car because he knew the driver would be in trouble. But they told him that it was government property and it wasn't going anywhere. He went berserk and they all jumped on him to stop him. Anyway, about eight of them had a go, but they were just bouncing off him, bang. The only way they could control him was to hit him hard over the head with an iron bar. And that shut him up. When I went to get him from Sarvelio's house he had this huge gash on the back of his head and he was covered in marks.'

'After some time away I went to the Copa Cardin of 1991 and had a word with comrade Alcides Sagarra and comrade Cheo Barrientos [the Commissioner of Boxing] and told them I was ready to come back to the team and they got me back in training again. I had nine comeback fights, won them all, won the Playa Giron, went to Spain and won there, then to France and won there. In France there were a lot of people hanging around offering me money to defect, but I had no intention of deserting my country, which is, and always will be, Cuba.'

The temptations in France were large. One associate of

Espinosa's told me that he was offered three and a half million dollars to turn pro. It's a plausible figure. Elio Menendez, Cuba's most respected boxing writer, says that he rates Teofilo Stevenson and Angel Espinosa as the two greatest Cuban amateurs of all time. 'I will probably stir up a hornets' nest by saying it. There were and are better athletes who put more time in at the gym, but no one else, with the exception of Stevenson, possessed the range of punching that he had, nor his charisma, which are things that you can't teach a boxer or buy for him.'

In France Espinosa flirted with his suitors and in Paris accepted the loan of a Mercedes, which he drove around the streets recklessly before returning it. But Espinosa meant what he said about his country. He was considered one of the most trusted members of the team as regards defections. He believed strongly in the revolution and in Fidel. The team, however, were starting to lose faith in Angel. No one apart from Sarvelio knew how to keep him on the straight and narrow.

'When I got back to Cuba I won the Cardin again against Solano and was looking forward to competing in the Cuba versus United States match later that year, but they went and picked Solano, a decision I still don't understand to this day. It wasn't such a big deal, though, and I just got into training for the Pan-American Games, which I thought would give me a good chance of being selected for the 1992 Olympics. But one day I was out training and I suppose I didn't warm up properly and, bang, the ligament in my right leg just goes. They gave me injections for the leg and I carried on training as best I could, in a seat hitting the bags from a chair and doing anything I could that didn't involve putting weight on my leg. But with fourteen days to the Pan-Americans and unable to put any weight on my leg I didn't reckon I had a chance, so I went off to Holguin to see the family. I was there about three days, but when I got back they slapped a fine on me for indiscipline and wanted to punish me. That just made me mad – I wasn't fit, I couldn't train. What was the big deal about going home for a couple of days? And I quit boxing again.' The Olympics were only a year away.

'I spoke to Alcides before I left and he said that if I wanted to go he wouldn't stop me, but that if I wanted to return to boxing once again the only way he would let me back in was if I won the 1992 Playa Giron. I didn't think anything of it until a week before the tournament and then I thought I might as well give it a go and with a week's training I won the silver medal. I lost to Solano with a week's training. I had proved my point and I knew inside that Solano had only beaten me because of my lack of fitness and that there was no fucking way he was a better boxer than me. I kept going and went to the Copa Cardin, where once again I got beaten by Solano. He hit me hard and early and by the time I had recovered he had scored a lot of points and it was too late to get back in the fight.

'I thought that was that as far as any Olympic chances went. I had a couple of fights in Moa [a grim nickel-mining hell-hole about an hour from Holguin], but I reckoned that they would pick Solano for Barcelona in the light heavyweights because he had beaten me twice. But they had a tournament to make the final selection for the Olympic team and I was invited. Solano's first bout was against Yosvani Vega and he lost, so suddenly it was all open again. I beat my first opponent, Guerra from Pinar del Rio, and then beat Vega in the final and I was right back in the frame for the Olympic team.'

Espinosa, as usual, is not quite telling the full story. In fact he received two counts of protection against Vega and was docked two points for breach of the rules. Espinosa got to the final round needing a knockout to win, with the youngster Vega knowing that all he had to do was keep his distance. He didn't. Bang, bang, Espinosa caught him massively to the head, concussed him, and the referee had to stop the contest and declare Espinosa the winner.

'We really trained hard for those Olympics. But Alcides took me aside and said he thought I looked slow at the weight – 81kg – and that he wanted me to get down to 76 or 76.5 kg. But I was training so hard in Spain with the team that my weight actually dropped to 75kg, which is a whole division below the one I was entering in Barcelona. When it came to it, if I was fighting someone in the afternoon and they weighed in at 81kg in the morning they probably weighed 83 or 84kg by the time we got to fight in the evening, whereas I was 76kg maximum the whole time I was there. In my first fight I realised that even though I was catching my opponent flush on the face I couldn't actually knock him down. Although I had gained some speed by losing the weight, I didn't have the strength in my punch. I was never noted for fast punching anyhow, I boxed more like a spider, tricky, unpredictable, all over you, so I wasn't getting any advantage out of this speed. I guess I was just losing the things that I had taken for granted as a kid, I wasn't as hard as I had been and the weight difference was really counting against me. I lost the quarter final in the Olympics against a guy who, to be honest, ought to have been easy meat for me. I was losing it as a boxer. And that, my friend, is my career pretty much over.'

Espinosa failed to mention the blame that the team themselves had to take for this debacle. When his coach Sarvelio Fuentes arrived at the airport to fly to Spain he was told, on the steps of the plane, that there was no room for him on the aircraft and that he wasn't going. Angel had to sit on the plane and fly off to the Olympics without the one man he knew would look after him and see him through. Why the team dropped Sarvelio, one of the founders of the Cuban amateur set-up, at the last moment on the way to Barcelona is not a matter of record. But several people have suggested that he and Alcides were involved in a battle for power in the camp, that Sarvelio might have been planning to defect with some of the boxers, that there was a debate about professionalism going on and Sarvelio was on the losing side. I have no idea which of these is true, but they are all plausible reasons for an extraordinary decision. Espinosa was given a new trainer whom he considered to be worse than useless and felt he had been betrayed by the team. He remains too loyal, however, to tell his story himself.

'After Barcelona the team went back to Cuba and we had a few days in Varadero by the beach. In my head then I thought I couldn't keep going, I couldn't make myself do it any more. But I steeled myself for one last go and went back to Havana with the team and trained at the Finca for fifteen days. It was really hard work, but I was determined to do it and not let anyone point the finger at me for lack of training. I never arrived late because I didn't want anyone to have an excuse to kick me out of the team for disciplinary reasons.

'Anyway, one morning at four a.m. I left the flat I had in the Focsa complex in town on my bike to train in the Ciudad Deportiva and as I'm going up the hill it just falls apart. What am I supposed to do? I had to arrive on time for training, but now I was sure to be late. There was nothing for it but to wait for a bus, which eventually came and got me to training by seven a.m. When I got there everyone was all kitted up and ready to go. Anyway, before training Alcides always gives a speech about how things are going and he said something, that I took to refer to me, about indiscipline and arriving on time and I thought about quitting the team. Honorato Espinosa came over to me and told me to get changed, but I was angry and I told him I wouldn't because I didn't feel like it. I stormed off and had a lie-down in the rest area for a couple of hours to try and get myself together again.

'I carried on training for two or three days more after that until one day I was there hitting the bags and I just thought, "What the fuck am I doing here?" and just as I'm thinking it the trainer comes over and yells, "Get stuck into it, Espinosa," and I turned round and told him that was that, that I wasn't going to box any more, that I was finished with it all. Imagine it. This is a sport that I have had in my blood for years, the only thing that I really know how to do well, and suddenly along comes this day when I just don't want to do it any more. Think of it from your own view. What you once used to do easily isn't there any more. Try and imagine what sort of a moment that is. It's like if you as a writer go through your life writing until one day you wake up and don't see the point of it any more and just stop. That's how it was for me. I was only twenty-five or twenty-six years old at this time and I had spent fifteen years in boxing and now I just didn't want to do it any more.'

This time he meant it. After a time he found his way back into boxing as a trainer with the regional team in Holguin. His marriage ended and he moved back with his mum. He had never been given a house in Havana by the team because he had always refused to accept it on the grounds that he was from Holguin and having a house meant that he would live the rest of his life in Havana. He was in Havana in 1998 for the Copa Cardin to receive an award, but because of some bungle, someone not turning up, he never received it. He was never given the car that all the top sportsmen expect when they win major tournaments. In February 1998 he wrote a letter to INDER, the overall governing body of sport in Cuba, and the boxing authorities, asking that they give him the car he had been promised when he was active. It's a sad letter, one paragraph, followed by a randomly ordered long list of his medals and tournament wins. The list takes up a full page of

A4. His signature is a tiny, shy scribble barely bigger than the typing of his name.

As I look at the letter, James, his and Corinna's son, now aged ten, comes bounding in, up and down, restless, energetic, with Espinosa's cheeks and lips and the boxer's spindly legs. James is a happy kid. He wants to play Nintendo. He runs out into the yard to play football with the Asian kids next door. He doesn't seem frightened by anyone or anything and his mother loves him very much. It hurts a little to see a son so like his father physically and yet so different from the lonely, hurt thirty-three-year-old boy who gave everything for Cuban boxing but whom Cuban boxing seems to have given very little in return. But the good in Angel lives in James's cheeky young face. And there was a lot of good in Angel.

'I look back and it makes me sad now,' says Angel, as he shows me out of the gate of his mother's house. 'Once you are out of this sport you are ignored and forgotten and kicked around. And you find out that things weren't quite how you thought they were. But you just have to keep on going. I don't see any point in being happy or sad about who I was or who I am because for me it's destiny that decides these things. I know that in other countries they say that there are diamonds lost in rubbish bins and that is what I think I am. I had the chance to leave this country, but I always came back. And who am I now?'

11 *Running with the Hack Pack*

My first meeting with Felix Savon was not as auspicious as I had expected. I had hooked up with Cuba's boxing press, a bunch of universal journalist types amongst whom it was impossible to feel uncomfortable. Hacks work in packs, as a team, and the Cubans were no different from any of the other groups I had ever worked with. The usual camaraderie and teamwork, mixed with a splash of suspicion and ego, were made more relaxing among the Cubans by there being no question of competition for stories. In fact there wasn't even any question of looking for stories at all: just straight results and the odd smattering of mildly expressed opinion, which could be quite forceful if it was the official line. The job of the journalist, even in sport, was to transmit to the people what the official organisms of the state wanted the people to know. It wasn't to get stories. These guys were in Holguin to get away from their families, enjoy a bit of time outside Havana, eat and drink as much as they could at the expense of their employers, then turn up to the sporting event and report it in pretty much the same manner as all their colleagues but with a couple of personal spins according to mood or style.

There was one guy from the Party's national daily (i.e. the only national daily) *Granma*. His name was Miguel Hernandez, he was about forty-five, a bright, softly spoken, greying man who looked at his most comfortable in faded red tracksuit bottoms. He was a good journalist, always mixing and mingling, always finding out what was going on, but with barely any space in which to publish anything.

Granma comes out Tuesday to Saturday. It is a terrible newspaper with eight tabloid-size pages, an embarrassingly charmless and dull outpouring of Communist Party propaganda, deeply, fundamentally unreadable. But it was the only paper in Cuba – and the only paper that printed the TV schedules – so it sold out everywhere by about eight each morning. People queued or sent their old folks to queue for them, as much out of habit as a desire to read the paper. It was rubbish, but it was all there was. And there were so few things that you could actually buy with local currency that it would have been reckless to waste this chance.

I had occasionally joined the queue at the kiosk near my flat in Miramar if there was boxing abroad or some interesting baseball to catch up on. I would sit with about fifteen old guys in string vests and worn-out brown pants and wait. And wait. Occasionally the paper wouldn't come at all and I would have to give up after an hour or so. Or occasionally the voices of some of the blokes in the queue would grate too much and I would have to get away. Or the sound of the fifteen-piece band wailing in the windowless room next to the kiosk would get too repetitive. The worst queuer was a man in a loud shirt. He had the sort of fog-horn voice that alone would have guaranteed him a place in the top 10 per cent of the world's most irritating men, but he combined it with a tone that was deep and hoarse and grating. He had an opinion on everything and swore blind he knew everything about everything. If the paper was late – and given that the delivery depended on a man on a bicycle doing a round of the whole of this part of Havana, that happened quite often – we would all have to listen to him spouting off for maybe an hour. It was exactly the same as it would have been in England: everyone silent and annoyed, hating the man in the loud shirt who wouldn't shut up, while we were all trapped, waiting in the increasingly hot sun. But everyone was too polite to say anything. His only audience was a small, thin, sunbeaten man with one tobacco-stained front tooth that might have discouraged him from smiling but didn't, who seemed to think that this kind of exchange could pass for conversation. He made his money directing people into parking spots on a nearby road. He had a piece of paper in a laminate with a faded piece of newsprint which gave him the minimum air of authority. And I suppose occasionally people paid him a few pesos.

When *Granma* didn't come out, on Sundays there was *Juventud Rebelde* (literally 'Rebel Youth'), Cuba's only Sunday newspaper. It was exactly the same as *Gramna* except it had more arts and television. The correspondent who had come to Holguin to cover the national championships for *Juventud Rebelde* was Elio Menendez, a well-respected boxing writer and author, who had last seen his own *juventud* about forty years before. He was a greying, thin man who never looked hurried. He had the distinguished air of a minor golf club treasurer, a senior citizen, proper, someone who knew he'd earned his right to be old. He was also respected enough to have written Cuba's only mainstream boxing biography, about Kid Chocolate.

On Mondays the only paper to come out was called *Trabajadores* (Workers) and its correspondent wasn't immediately obvious. I think Miguel Hernandez filed to them too, but we never saw a copy in Holguin.

It was Miguel who gave me my first introduction to Savon. I was strolling across the hotel lobby with him the day before the tournament started. We were about to undergo the by now daily ritual of grabbing a cheese toastie in the bar – the only bar food available – before sitting on the third-floor landing and watching a film on the TV that was in a corridor next to the lifts. And just as we were getting to the door of the bar, into the hotel ambled – as far as anyone of his height and stature can amble – Felix Savon. This was a strange moment. Savon was the reason I was here, but I had never seen the guy close up. The photos didn't do him justice. In them he always had his head protector on and a mouthguard in and, to be frank, he just looked like a big ugly lummox with a huge body. But up close, in the official red and blue tracksuit of the Cuban national team, he looked powerful and at ease. He wasn't clumsy or awkward in the way that a lot of really big men are, certainly not in the way that Frank Bruno almost seemed to apologise in public for being so huge, with his scared eyes and a stooped, hunted, sorry look. Bruno looked liberated from his embarrassment by being in a ring, where everything was on his scale at last. Savon, by contrast, looked just as comfortable in a hotel lobby in a tracksuit.

Savon is taller than the average heavyweight, about 6ft 4in, and actually quite thin around the waist. His legs are like sticks. He spoke with a chuckle, always looked you in the eye, was quite tactile, and while he was no Einstein he made up for it with a warmth that came through in every sentence. He chatted a while with Miguel, who he thought might be able to help him get a new house. At that time, from what I could make out, he lived in a modest flat in Nuevo Vedado. His wife had just given birth to twins and he needed something bigger. As Miguel was with the Party newspaper he wanted him to have a word with someone. Miguel chatted and agreed to try.

'This is a *companero*, Yon Dooncan from England,' said Miguel.

'Aaah. *Que vola?* [How's it hanging?]' he said.

'Er, fine, thanks. How are you?' I said clumsily in Spanish.

'Good, good. See you around.' He smiled and was gone.

So that was the man. The good part was that my theory of it being relatively easy to speak to the right people in Cuba was obviously spot on. The journalist cover was working beautifully and I was getting access to whoever I wanted. The problem was that taking it all a stage further was difficult.

'Is it true, that story of Don King turning up in Mexico and offering Savon $10 million to turn professional, to fight Tyson?' I said.

'Yeah, I think so. Why?' said Miguel.

'Because I can't understand why anyone would turn it down. If I was offered that sort of money I would take it, even if I thought I would get myself battered and bruised for it. Wouldn't you?'

'It's not as simple as that, Yon. This is his country. His wife, his children, his family, are here. He has a good life and everyone likes him. He knows well enough that if he goes to the United States and turns professional he will lose all of that. And it's not as if he was given the money in a suitcase. What happens if he gives everything up and then the money doesn't turn up? He'll have given up everything he has for nothing. Over there he'll become a piece of meat, being bought and sold by promoters and gangsters. Here he is a star, he has a nice house and everyone loves him. He believes in the revolution, so why would he leave? What people from outside Cuba don't understand is that there are more important things than money.'

I suppose he was including me in that generalisation, but I was starting to understand what he meant. What I saw the evening of 31 January helped me to understand it even more.

The journalists were transported from the Hotel Pernik to the arena every night by bus, a creaking, uncomfortable, no-trimmings vehicle that would normally be used for agricultural workers. It left on time every evening whether it was full or not. This was an unusual occurrence for anything Cuban and it caught me out the first night, when I turned up to catch it five minutes late because I assumed that, like everything else, it wouldn't be leaving when it said it would. The journey to the arena, which was a giant hayshed attached to a concrete swimming pool with a corrugated iron roof, was on the outskirts of the city and getting there meant taking a short cut through the centre of Holguin. The city was designed on a grid system, with narrow streets criss-crossing right the way across town. It was hard enough in daytime knowing whose right of way it was, but at night, with little or no streetlighting, it was impossible. The bus relied on its size and the noise of its groaning diesel engine to bully its way through the traffic. The driver seemed to have impossible faith in people getting out of the way and liked to measure the distance between him and other traffic, not to mention walls, in millimetres rather than inches. All of which he would do while chatting to his wife, who he picked up on the way. Well, I assume it was his wife.

This particular evening we rounded a corner and squeezed past another bus on the narrow street. We slowed down to edge past it and our man parked up to talk to the other driver. Around the coach was a collection of young men in tracksuits and even in the pitch dark you could make out that they were boxers. Their bus had broken down. After a lot of shouting and laughter the boxers, of whom there must have been thirty or so, got on to ours. The trouble was it wouldn't start. So about twenty of the boxers got off and started pushing it to get the engine going again and as I looked down through the back window at the huge men who were push-starting a bus on a flat street I was sure I saw Savon, laughing. Only in Cuba, as Don King never said.

When we got to the arena we went through the familiar ritual. Get in, sit down, wait for it to start, watch, make notes.

No one was allowed to sit at ringside apart from press, boxers, trainers and police. The crowds sat in a raised stand which went down each side of the arena, with a concrete wall and a decent drop between them and the floor. They didn't have seats, just stone steps to park their bums on. They got there early to claim a bit of concrete and sat on it until gradually there was no room to move. The crowd was mainly men, but there was a smattering of women and kids too – it was only a peso to get in and there wasn't much else to do.

We arrived and the radio boys chattered away. Television wasn't covering the night's events – it was considered too early in the tournament to provide any real competition for the top boxers, but it looked like a good programme with seven Olympic finalists boxing. The commentators came anyway and teased the radio boys. And there was Savon sitting on a plastic seat at ringside in the VIP area to the left of the press's wooden ringside table, marked off from the rest of the officials and VIPs by a limp dirty rope. He looked so happy and relaxed, deep in his own thoughts, occasionally turning round and smiling as people in the crowd tried to chat to him. No entourage, no press, no hassle, patting a balloon back to a small kid, joking with a few of his friends and signing the odd autograph, laughing at himself when someone in the crowd tried to take the piss out of him. He looked like one of them and they loved him for it. It was the sort of freedom that the free world doesn't offer its stars and celebrities. He just looked content to be there, doing what he did well, among people who liked watching it.

The programme started. Angel Comendador against Guillermo Valenciano in the light flyweight. Comendador was a technician, Valenciano a scrapper, and it was a great contest. I scored it a win for Valenciano, 17–12. The judges, primed to favour technique above the aggressiveness which marks good professionals, made it 20–11 for Comendador.

Then Maikro Romero, the Atlanta Olympic flyweight champion, fought out a surprisingly difficult bout with Juan Carlos Palma, a local from Holguin who ought to have had no chance. Palma unsettled Romero and attacked him and for once Maikro, whose reputation was as a defensive boxer, got caught out. Romero had gone to Atlanta as one of the Cuban team's least-lauded fighters and, having cantered to the final, overturned a two-point deficit in the last round against a tough Kazakh to win 12–11 on points. This time he edged the local boy 13–8, shook his head when he heard the result and apologised to his opposite number with a shrug. He left the ring to the roars of the crowd chanting 'Fix!' and left the arena. They were just doing what any home crowd would have done and the judges were probably doing what any judges would have done – you don't beat a champion that easily. The fourth bout pitted Neslan Machado against Exer Rodriguez, a world under-nineteen champion. It was another non-stop slugging match, which was scoring about even when the referee stopped the contest after fifty-five seconds of the fourth just as Rodriguez took a squelching left. We had only just finished with the flyweights and this was the best night of boxing I had ever seen.

The lightweight Olympic silver medallist Arnaldo Mesa breezed past an opponent who just covered his face and stood there. The light-welter contest between Diogenes Luna and Victor Romero was the dullest of the night, though enlivened by a small fight in the crowd. A small dose of police brutality and it was over in an instant. Juan Hernandez Sierra, Olympic silver medallist, dished out a first-round thrashing to a boxer from his home town of Pinar del Rio, whose corner very sensibly threw in the towel. Alfredo Duvergel, who had been leading comfortably in Atlanta when he was dropped by David Reid of the United States to give the hosts their only boxing medal in Atlanta, was leading 15–2 on my card when his opponent retired in the fourth. Ariel Hernandez, another Olympic champion, faced Mario Dovirne, a game boxer, in his next bout in plain red trunks and a dirty vest which contrasted with Ariel's red and black striped Adidas-sponsored shorts with his name written on the hip. Ariel whipped him, but couldn't knock the kid down or stop him and despite a 26–0 win for Hernandez it was a crushing moral victory for Dovirne. And a great spectacle.

My notes on the fights got increasingly excited as it started to hit me how deep the quality of boxing in Cuba goes. In the midst of a series of scribbles punctuated by exclamation marks I wrote in small capital letters WORLD SERIES OF BOXING with a scribble of arrows and bullet points written in tiny letters so the guy from the Party newspaper sitting next to me couldn't see what I was doing, a slightly paranoid precaution given that he didn't speak English and even I could barely read what I was writing in all the excitement.

I was thinking of a world series fight-off between amateur and professional boxing in a series of carefully selected weights, specifically constructed so there would be contests between Americans, Cubans and Brits. They would fight on one card in the United States over eight rounds of professional rules, then in Cuba under amateur rules. A points system would be devised over the two legs of the fight which would allow winners to be determined. I got so excited I decided to take a risk and pulled out my *Ring* boxing almanac (which felt like whipping out the Koran in the middle of an audience with the Pope) and played fantasy boxing and came up with the card. Heavyweight (Savon versus Tyson), welterweight (Juan Hernandez versus Pernell Whitaker), lightweight (Neslan Machado – who in the end was voted the most aggressive boxer at the championships – against Naseem Hamed) and flyweight (Maikro Romero against Danny Romero). The only pity would be the lack of real, name fighters for the light-middle and middleweights Duvergel and Ariel Hernandez. But that was being picky.

The problems were minor, I decided. Though amateur boxing and professional deliberately isolated themselves from each other to such an extent that training in the same gym as a professional could theoretically get you kicked out of the amateur ranks, the people who ran the amateurs were coming to realise that some accommodation had to be made with the pros, who were robbing them of their best boxers at an increasingly early age. It would be good publicity for the amateur code to have fighters people had actually heard of coming back to fight under their rules. It might even encourage boxers to stay in the ranks for big fights against boxers of world quality they would need years to get a sniff at if they turned professional as a teenager. And if it brought in cash to a code which had lost a lot of its kudos and finance with the collapse of the Eastern Bloc then I didn't see how they could resist. For the Cubans it would bring hard currency and a breach in the US trade embargo – the two things that dominated Cuban politics. For the pros and their promoters it would be a few bob in the bank and an interesting diversion to fight with big television deals but no existing world title on the line. How could it fail?

The last two contests of the evening were the heavier weights, with two men on view who could claim to have beaten Savon. One was Freddy Rojas, who had moved down to light-heavyweight because his chances were so limited by Savon's dominance at 91kg. Rojas had beaten Savon in Cienfuegos in 1994 in the Cordoba Cardin, the annual tournament attended by Cubans and boxers from around the world – Canada, Latin America and the odd Angolan or Mongolian. That victory had been on points and Savon had always claimed that he was robbed. Rojas's desertion to a lower weight meant there were few chances to settle the argument.

The other man who had beaten Savon would be facing him again that night. There was no argument about whether Juan-Causse Delis had deserved his victory over Savon. Delis was a strong-jawed but temperamental heavyweight who packed in the boxing game for a few years because he stopped enjoying it. He had knocked out Savon in 1986 in a Torneo de Equipos, a boxing team cup, when they were both nineteen. The last time Savon had been beaten by a foreigner was when a Korean, whose name no one in Cuba could remember, knocked him out in Bulgaria in 1989. The guy he was fighting had been given two protection counts and Savon went after him recklessly to get the third count of protection, which means an automatic win. He got careless, got caught and was floored. He had only been beaten four times in ten years and had at one stage in his career scored ninety-six consecutive victories. He had twelve consecutive national titles from the annual Playa Giron under his belt. Even if you took his career right back to when he was a beginner he had over 340 wins and ten defeats. It was remarkable that there were two men in the same room who could say that they had beaten him, but to see two of them in a ring one after the other was extraordinary.

Rojas was on first. He lost a contest he probably should have won to the local boxer, in front of a screaming crowd whose baying and yelling, mingled with the curdling screams of the growing number of women at ringside, practically forced the judges to press their buttons every time the local guy Gerardo Deroncelo made any sort of connection. Rojas, in truth, didn't look that good. How had he ever beaten Savon?

Then it was time for Savon against Delis. Delis came in sweating hard, punching air, his head down, doing his best not to appear terrified by what was about to happen, but failing abysmally. Or maybe it just looked that way because it was impossible to avoid putting yourself in his shoes. He couldn't look up beyond the two feet of air in front of his chest and his hands kept moving. He looked miles away in a world, hopefully, where what was about to happen to him wouldn't hurt. Muhammad Ali used to talk about going behind a door in his fights, somewhere where you didn't think or feel, you just fought. But you were supposed to wait until the bell went before you shut it behind you. Delis looked as if he had already slammed it shut, locked it solid and pushed a wardrobe up against it.

And there was Savon. This was the first time I had seen him in his working clothes. He looked a different man from the guy in the lobby of the hotel. All the geniality was gone, he looked brutal, mechanical, leaping in the air and twisting his neck from side to side like a lion on a leash. He stared straight ahead, looking hard in his own mind at the brutal task ahead. Savon looked like he did this for some grim amusement; Delis just looked cornered.

Savon's gown, white and short with a bright red lining and almost certainly 100 per cent polyester, bore his name and his title as champion in red letters on the back. Delis was big, but there was an intake of breath in the crowd when Savon took off his gown and revealed himself. Boxers don't have muscles everywhere, the requirement not to exceed a certain weight means that anything that's not useful isn't there. Savon's lower leg is almost a straight line, a gentle long muscled curve at the calf, but little else. His thighs are taut but don't bulge. His upper body, though, is immense, accentuated by the tight dark-blue vest he is wearing. As he stretches upwards to flex his arms he has so much bulk around his shoulders and back that it looks as if he has a giant armpit ringed by muscle, like a volcanic crater. The proportions of his body are somehow wrong. His arms are long, but his wrists are not massive, his forearm too is long rather than muscled and his head, even with his strong jaw, jutting forehead and bone-hard cheeks, looks dwarfed by the shoulders and biceps amid which it sits.

The fight starts, three piercing distorted electronic beeps and then an electronic foghorn. Savon prods Delis, prods him, thwacks him; prods him, prods him, thwacks him; prods him, prods him, thwacks him. Through every other fight it was possible to observe and enjoy the art involved, the movement forward and backward, darting in and out, the ballet of boxing. In this one you could only feel the pain. Prod, prod, thwack. Whoosh, whoosh, oomph. Savon was just picking up points – there were bigger battles down the line than against this guy – and Delis was just hanging on in there. As they sat down for the bell at the end of the third round of five, my notes have Savon ahead by nine to two. They got up for the fourth and Savon was noticeably standing off Delis, going through the motions, and Delis was tempted a little out of his shell. Then put back in it by a couple of thwacks. The fight was only going one way.

After one minute and thirty-five seconds of the fourth round, the world stopped for a second. Savon ducked to his left and stooped to avoid a jab and put his head where Delis was swinging through with a right-hand uppercut, it wasn't planned by Delis, it just happened that Savon put his head there. There was a thud and Savon collapsed. No staggering, no arms-out stumble, not even a pause, Savon just deflated, unconscious, there on the spot and lay still on his front, his face on the canvas, one arm crumpled awkwardly underneath his giant frame.

Silence. Disbelief. Confusion. All in less than a second.

Then a massive roar, a maniacal hysterical moment of release and excitement. Screaming and screaming and waving. Delis jumped on the ropes in a neutral corner and raised both fists to the crowd, his teeth clenched and his head raised to the ceiling. No one was near him, four rounds of pent-up terror just bursting out in a flood of jubilation. A doctor rushed to Savon, still lying face down on the canvas where he had fallen. Completely motionless. In the midst of it all, Alfredo Toledo, one of Cuba's leading referees, a friendly, grey man, gestured Delis to his corner and counted Savon out urgently. The mouthguard came out, the team doctor cradled his head and turned him on to his side and still Savon didn't move. It was three whole minutes before Savon even regained consciousness. I know because I counted. I counted because I thought Savon might die. A minute later he was helped to his feet and another cheer went up. Delis left the ring, high-fiving and smiling, and the crowd started to file away from the stadium just talking and chattering, but filling the hall with noise. Others stayed there watching the empty space where Savon had fallen. Just stood as if they didn't want to let go of the moment. Among them was Ariel Hernandez, the Cuban middleweight who occasionally sparred with Savon, which given the difference in weight between the two and Savon's refusal ever to tread lightly had left him with more than a few scars.

'I just can't talk,' he said. 'I don't really believe what I saw there.'

And also standing in the shadow of the ring was Teofilo Stevenson, the greatest amateur boxer of all time, sanguine and knowing as ex-boxers always seem to be when everyone else is overcome by the drama and violence of the sport.

'He was careless,' said Stevenson. 'He let his guard down. But Delis worked hard for his win. He deserved it.'

The press room afterwards, where we went after each evening to drink soya milk from a dirty glass and eat a stale ham sandwich before catching the bus back to the hotel, was remarkably calm. I could imagine what it would have been like in England, a frenetic dash to meet deadline after looming deadline and to squeeze the last comment and opinion out of anyone who was anyone in order to fill up the inevitable front pages of every newspaper in the country and a few around the world. Here, though, the press room was barely stirred from its torpor. Only Miguel Hernandez of *Granma* had a newspaper that was publishing the next day and he had missed his deadline. Worse than that, he had had to scurry to phone the desk to change the story he had filed of Savon's victory to defeat. He had been so sure of the result that he had filed his copy before the fight.

The talk then was of who would get sacked at Holguin Regional Television for not sending a camera. It was possibly the biggest sports story in Cuba for a decade and the local TV head had said he couldn't spare any cameras. So there were no images of the fight, nothing to be broadcast, analysed, replayed again and again. It made the knockout all the more certain to enter into Cuban fight mythology. The TV had, it turned out, been covering a local Communist Party event somewhere nearby, so nothing was said. By the time the bus came ten minutes later the only man left was the guy from Cuba's Prensa Latina news agency, tapping into one of the giant ancient telex machines lining one side of the room.

As we got on the bus everyone was elated, as you are when you have seen something for yourself that people will talk about for weeks. But my doubts were multiplying. That evening I had not only seen a Felix Savon who appeared quite content with the life he had in Cuba, but a Savon who wasn't as invulnerable as everyone thought. There were even mumblings about his age in the bus, the undertone being that he was actually older than he had been declared for official purposes, thirty instead of twenty-eight. Maybe I was already too late.

The following morning I wandered down to the tiny room marked Public Relations, which was only just big enough for the desk, two chairs and telex machine that had been squeezed in there. Salmeron, Miguel Hernandez and Elio Menendez were sitting around talking. Too fast for me to know what they were saying. I asked them if there would be a press conference after what had happened. They didn't think so. Were they going to get some quotes from Savon or Sagarra? There were a few shrugs. Sagarra wouldn't say anything, they said. I told them I had to file a story to London. Nothing. Until eventually Elio got bored with my questions, took pity on me and stood up. 'I'll take the kid down to the hotel. See what's going on.'

We walked out of the Pernik and turned left down the hill, tramping along an overgrown roadside with boxers jogging past us up the hill towards the baseball stadium where the more junior fighters were based. The national squad were only 200 yards away in the Hotel Bosque (the Forest Hotel). Where the Pernik hid the fundamental fact that it was a grotty tenement block behind a sharp Soviet-style modernist lobby, the Bosque hid the same flaw behind a barrage of plastic fruit, raffia baskets and wicker chairs. The reception was adorned with fake strips of brown cane. If the cleaners had worn hula-hula skirts it couldn't have been more tacky. But it was smaller and friendler than the Pernik.

I'd assumed that Menendez would come down with me, chat to whoever dealt with the press, ask permission for an interview, get turned down and we could walk back to our hotel feeling that at least we had tried. Instead he asked the woman on the desk for Savon's room number. She gave it to him.

'Could you ring him for me, *mi niña* [luv]?' he said. Here we were less than twenty-four hours after Cuba's biggest sporting hero had been publicly and spectacularly humiliated and we were on the phone asking him if he wanted to come down for a chat. 'Hi, Savon. It's Elio Menendez here. I've got a colleague of ours from the *Gwardianne* in London and he wonders if he could talk to you . . . Yes . . . Yes . . . No, that's fine . . . Well, if he's there, bring him down too.' He turned to me. 'John, would you like to speak to Delis as well? They're both up with the doctor and they can come down in fifteen minutes if you can wait.' I nodded like an idiot.

I sat with Elio in the lobby in a cane and wicker chair the size of a double sofa. It seemed pretty flimsy, but there were two chairs either side which I assumed would be taken by the two boxers. That plan was ruined when Elio sat in one of them and the team doctor, Raul Foyaca, sat in the other. Which left 6ft 4in Felix Savon and 6ft 1in Juan Causse Delis to sit next to 6ft 2in hack from the *Guardian* on a chair that would have creaked dangerously with just me on it. 'Just ten minutes, John; they both have to get some rest and I don't want Felix getting too tired,' said Foyaca. I fumbled with my tape-recorder microphone and switched into Brit hack overdrive. I could hear my voice getting guttural and sports reporterish. I was turning effortlessly into Gary Newbon.

'So, Felix, what happened last night?' (Stupid question. I was there, I saw what happened: you got knocked out stone cold by the big guy on my left.)

'Well,' said Felix, 'it's no big deal, it's part of what happens in boxing. You get beaten sometimes. He's a good boxer and he caught me. I don't actually remember the punch at all really, but, well, you don't like to lose but it happens. Juan is a good friend of mine and we're good mates, I've boxed with him a lot and I've beaten him plenty of times before. But there you are.' (Ask a Gary Newbon question, get a Gary Newbon answer.)

'He's knocked you out twice now, Felix. What has he got, do you think, that makes him so difficult for you?' (Apart from a fucking big punch in his right hand which if you stand still and let him hit you with makes you unconscious. Stupid question.)

'Well, remember that I've fought him a lot of times before this and I think in the last ten years he hasn't beaten me. That was all a long time ago. I don't want to say that he didn't deserve to win, but I wasn't at my best yesterday and I should have done better, you know. I'll get him next time.'

'And you, Juan-Causse, how does it feel to have beaten a boxer as great as Felix?' (Stupid, stupid, stupid question. It feels fucking great, you idiot. He must be gloating like mad on the inside and you ask him a question like that when the guy he knocked down is sitting a yard away from him?)

'Felix is a truly great champion and it's an honour to have beaten him twice now. But remember he has won twelve titles in a row and I have not won anything, so I am not pretending that all of a sudden I am better than him. But I beat him and as a boxer when you get in the ring that is what you are aiming to do. So I am happy. I have worked hard. I gave up all this boxing because it did not seem worth it, I was tired of it, but, well, I'm back at a decent level now.'

We chatted a little more about his career, probably a relief for both of us. Cuban boxers switch into automatic when you do that; they're much more comfortable producing a list of results and dates which they pronounce with a little flourish. 'Mil noveciento ochenta y seis.' 1986. It sounds better in Spanish. I asked Savon when he would be boxing next, how his family were, when he was going back to Havana, and he answered every question patiently and politely until the doctor leaned across and suggested that he should get some rest. I could hardly object. I went to shake his huge right hand and he clenched his fist and put it next to my hand. I assumed it must be hurt, this big fist with a massive deformed lump on the back of his hand, so I wrapped my hand gently around it. He smiled warmly. He did the same to Elio, who made a fist of his own and gently tapped Savon's, knuckle to knuckle. I'd even managed to screw up saying goodbye to him. I had a lot to learn.

I went back to the hotel and scribbled some notes. Savon was a different man in and out of the ring. He wasn't a violent type, he wasn't mixed-up, though some of the punters I had spoken to in Havana thought he was a bit thick. They thought all boxers were thick, but Savon especially, not for his lack of culture but because he hadn't taken Don King's money and run. He was no rocket scientist, but neither was he the sort of jail-bait, fucked-up lump of tortured black flesh that the professional heavyweight division was throwing up. Look at them. Oliver McCall, a crack cocaine user on the permanent edge of a nervous breakdown or violence against anyone, who ended up washed out in a small-fry jail in small-town America. Mike Tyson, bullied and abused turned bully and abuser, a convicted rapist. What would have happened to Felix Savon if he had taken the money and left?

12 *Joel Casamayor*

I first came across Joel Casamayor running down the seemingly endless, relentlessly straight, crocodile-infested road to the Miccosukee Gaming Hotel on the Everglade fringes of Miami in August 1999. He was running, head down, mechanical, in the way that boxers do, preparing for what was supposed to be a big fight the next day against Adam Vargas, but he was having problems making the weight. That went some way to explaining why he was jogging at midday in 90 degree heat and 100 per cent humidity in a heavy orange tracksuit that looked as if it was made of towelling.

Casamayor was the first person I had seen in Miami on foot who wasn't walking to or from their car. Beyond the tree-lined tourist honey-pots and art deco-dence of South Beach or the imposing self-confidence of the skyscrapers of downtown Miami, the city is a giant, soulless monument to the car, a criss-cross grid of roads and huge four-, five- and six-lane motorways with a permanent flow of trucks and traffic. Alongside each road and highway are shops and warehouses dedicated not to what is good in life but what is cheapest. The dollar stores, as they are called, have been superceded by the

99 cent store and I even spotted a 98 cent store. There was one sad-looking concrete monstrosity with tired-looking rags stuck to the wall with brown tape whose name was Coño que Barato, which I can only translate as 'Fuck Me, That's Cheap'. Even coming from a busy city like London I found the relentless, nagging, lowest-common-denominator sales pitch of Miami exhausting. Buy cars, buy cheaper food and make sure you drive. In Miami it sometimes seems as if human beings live in the slender gaps between the roads, the sprawl of malls and adverts, knitted together by a veneer of fake politeness that only half-heartedly covers the obvious fact that ordinary Americans are the dullest, most conformist people on earth, wedded to regulations and red tape and lacking in any kind of imaginative approach to anything.

Miami has a massive Cuban community, measured in millions, most of whom live in a part of the city called Hialeah, a twenty-minute drive from the glistening brochure image of Miami which tempts so many Cuban, Colombian, Venezuelan and Dominican immigrants to say bye-bye to families and businesses and lives and buy, buy, buy into the American dream.

The same magnets which draw every Cuban to Miami – freedom, a fridge and a late model Ford – draw Cuban boxers more than most. While the highest possibility for a car mechanic or a bus driver who has managed to get into Miami is that he can earn enough to keep his family and hope against hope for a better future for them, if not for him, Cuba's top-quality amateur boxers look across to the United States and see lesser men than themselves earning millions of dollars for doing what they still do for free. It must be torture.

It was to Miami that most Cuban boxers at first migrated after the revolution banned professional boxing on 23 February 1961. This was not a moral decision simply against the cruelty of professional boxing but against professional sport as a whole. Sport from then on was considered a right of the people and was to be about participation rather than earning money.

The last professional fight in Cuba was in December 1961. Just before that INDER gathered together the boxers from wherever they had been working. They were told that they could leave Cuba for any country they wanted if they felt they had to pursue their career. Those who stayed would be guaranteed a job of some sort. The majority decided to leave, though Sarvelio Fuentes and Luis Toca decided to stay.

I met Toca a couple of times. He was a quiet, undemonstrative fitness fanatic who was now a sports photographer but who had been with the North Vietnamese, among others, in the various wars in which Cuba was involved during the Seventies and Eighties. He used to find a space in his hotel room when we were at tournaments to lift himself on to every morning, up and down, up and down. He had told me he was a former boxer and that he had fought on the bill that last night of pro boxing in Cuba. They gave him a job as a gardener at the sports arena when he decided to stay – he hadn't really liked boxing much anyway – and from there he had taught himself photography. Things hadn't turned out too badly for him. But the decision to ban professional sports robbed Cuba of four soon-to-be world champions who were active at the time, three of whom were at the meeting.

The first Cuban after 1961 to win a world title was Benny Paret. Paret was an illiterate from Santa Clara who had a reasonable record as a pro in Havana, though he had lost twice to another Cuban great of the time, Luis Manuel Rodriguez. Paret's last fight in Cuba was in 1958 just before the revolution and he decided to pursue his career in the United States. How Paret, who was never an exceptional fighter, got a crack at a world title so quickly is anybody's guess. He started off fighting at light heavyweight, but was beaten three times.

He moved to middleweight, but found himself similarly outclassed. So it was down to welter, where those who ran the show at Madison Square Garden were looking for a successor to Don Jordan. Paret got his first fight with the champion on 27 May 1960 in Las Vegas, a fight he won after fifteen rounds by unanimous and justified decision. Jordan was left penniless and managerless after the fight, having agreed to pay off his managers with the whole purse from the fight.

Soon after, the first of a series of fights was set up with Emile Griffith, the most credible contender for the title, in which an even fight turned into a knockout win for Griffith in the thirteenth. The rematch six months later was a similarly even war of attrition with Paret working hard to the body. Most observers said that Griffith had won, but the judges disagreed and gave the fight to Paret. A mere two months after that gruelling battle, Paret stepped up to middleweight to take on Gene Fullmer and took a ferocious beating which ended with a knockdown in the tenth. Fullmer couldn't believe that Paret had lasted that long. 'I never hit a man so hard,' he said.

Paret's next fight was to be his last. Despite advice that he would need time to recover from the brutal lesson he had learned against Fullmer barely three months before, he signed to fight Griffith again at Madison Square Garden in March. Worse, Paret made the fight personal by crudely insulting Griffith at the weigh-in. In the twelfth Paret found himself backed up into a corner and beaten helplessly around the head while the referee did nothing. Half an hour later and Paret was on his way to hospital unconscious. He died ten days after the fight. He was twenty-five years old. Only months after the ban on professional boxing in Cuba, the authorities had their first and biggest martyr.

Luis Manuel Rodriguez was also at the INDER meeting. He had fought as a professional from 1956, but is probably the least well known of Cuba's world champions, largely because he held the title for a mere forty-seven days from 21 March to 8 June 1963. He won the welterweight crown from Emile Griffith a year and three days after Paret had died at Griffith's hands. Rodriguez deserves to be better known. Griffith, himself one of the greats, said that he was the hardest man he ever had to face. They fought four times in all and while Griffith won three times, the only unanimous verdict was the March 1963 title fight. 'He moved a lot. He was always busy and he threw a lot of combinations. He was more a boxer than a puncher, hit and move. He drove me crazy. Each time we met was a war and I had to make adjustments always changing my style. Was he an all-time-great fighter? I would say so.'

Griffith took the title back off Rodriguez the following June in New York. Neither could decisively peg down the other and the decision was split again. One year down the line and it was more of the same. It was an ugly contest, low blows and cheap shots after the bell, but Griffith edged it.

The fight which should have confirmed Rodriguez as a true champion came in Rome in 1969 five years after his previous welterweight world title shot. This time he came in at middleweight and was about to pull off a famous victory in Rome against Nino Benvenuti. Rodriguez was well on top, when out of the blue he was caught by a perfect left and went spark out. Rodriguez never did have much luck.

Another Cuban who was there the day pro boxing was banned was the young featherweight Urtiminio Ramos, born in Matanzas in 1941. The Americans drew on their limited lexicon of ring nicknames to christen him Sugar. As a sixteen-year-old pro in 1958 Ramos had killed José 'El Tigre' Blanco in the ring after knocking him out in the eighth round. Ramos had wanted to give up boxing, but was convinced by Blanco's mother that her son's death was not his fault and that he would be wasting a second life if he stopped.

On the 21 March card which featured Luis Manuel

Rodriguez beating Griffith at Dodger Stadium, Ramos found himself up against Davey Moore. From the fifth round onwards Ramos pummelled Moore, who fell finally in the tenth, with a sickening twist against the bottom rope that snapped his limp head forward. His manager threw in the towel at the end of the round. Moore was lucid enough to make the kneejerk calls for a rematch in the dressing room after the fight, but hours later he fell into a coma. Four days after the fight he was dead.

Ramos successfully defended his title twice, before a bizarre fight in Accra in Ghana, when the local boxing board ruled out a split-decision win for Ramos against local hero Floyd Robertson, who had hurt the champion in the fight. That may have accounted for why he gave in so limply to the Mexican Vicente Saldivar in his next fight, a foolishly short four months later. It took until 1966 for him to get another crack at the title and it speaks volumes for boxing's short memory that a man so closely associated with the deadly peril of the sport should have been part of what happened that night. Ramos, by now living in Mexico, took on Carlos Ortiz and knocked him down in the third round. But Ortiz plugged away at his face and opened a serious gash. Three times at the end of rounds the referee called on the Mexican doctor to look at Ramos's wound. Three times the doctor ignored the request. The referee stopped the fight of his own accord in the fifth. Ortiz and his manager were punched and kicked on their way back to the dressing room, only to be told that the Mexican board had overruled the referee and that Ortiz had to go back out. He stayed put and eventually kept the title. Ramos retired in 1972.

Though Ramos never got another chance, the featherweight title was in Cuban hands in July 1968 when the Kid Tunero-trained, Spanish-based Cuban, José Legra beat the Welshman Howard Winstone in Porthcawl on a cut-eye technical knockout. Legra tortured Winstone once the cut had opened for a couple of rounds, dancing around him until the referee decided he had seen enough and stopped it in the fifth. Legra was from Baracoa, where they make a chocolate they are very proud of locally, but which is sickly sweet to the point of being inedible. I met his brother there, who said that José still occasionally sneaks into the country for a visit from time to time. Legra lost the title to Johnny Famechon in January 1969, his first defence, but won it back in December 1972 against Clemente Sanchez by a knockout. He only hung on to it for a year this time, losing it in May 1973 to Eder Jofre in Brasilia, a fight for which he only spent twelve days preparing. He retired after he was knocked out in one round by Alexis Arquello, who went on to become one of the great champions of the weight.

Legra's reputation was as a thoroughly undisciplined fighter who never trained as he should but had enough natural talent to get past most people. 'Why should I give up the good life', he said, 'when the only reason I box is so that I can enjoy the good life? I don't make that much money. People don't realise that when you've paid for trainers and training camps there is scarcely anything left. But what I have I spend.' His career record was 133 wins, 12 losses and 4 draws with 48 knockouts. He fought too much at times. Three eight-rounders in eleven days in 1963 was his worst spell, but he fought four times in a month in October 1966 and four times in June 1967 alone.

Mantequilla Napoles was arguably the best of the lot, but once he left Cuba he adopted Mexico and many people regard him as a Mexican champion. Napoles took the welterweight title in 1969, beating Curtis Cokes in what was his forty-first knockout win in sixty-one professional fights. He won the rematch before losing the title to the doggedly ordinary Billy Backus in December 1970 when Backus opened up a gash in Napoles's eye and forced the fight to be stopped in his favour.

The rematch in Los Angeles the following June was stopped because Backus's face was so swollen that the doctor refused to allow him to continue. Napoles's attempts to step up to middleweight were given short shrift by Carlos Monzon, who knocked him out in a title fight at that weight in the seventh round in 1974. Then finally John Stracey took the belt off a tiring and slowing Napoles in Mexico City with Mexican judges, no mean feat against an adopted Mexican whatever Napoles's diminished capacities. Stracey went down in the first, but battled back and overwhelmed him in the sixth to nick the title. The last anyone heard, Napoles had retired to a farm in Mexico.

The stark fact is that since those pre-revolutionary professional fighters there has been nothing. There have been a few defectors, but no one outstanding. But with the special period and its accompanying poverty, the pull of Miami for Cuban sports people is stronger than it has ever been.

Since 1997 the lure has become even stronger, not because of boxing but because of baseball and the extraordinary stories surrounding the defection first of Livian Hernandez, a Cuban pitcher who joined the Florida Marlins after getting on a raft to the West Indies and a year later pitching the Marlins to the World Series. A year after that came his half-brother Orlando 'El Duque' Hernandez, who escaped from being the trainer of a psychiatric hospital team, where he had been banished from top level baseball in Cuba for thinking about defecting, to win the World Series with the Yankees.

Cuban boxing had taken a few hits with defections, but had not suffered from the sort of million-dollar success stories which fed the desires of its baseball stars to go abroad. In fact, quite the opposite: the refusal of Stevenson and Savon to countenance professional careers in the most lucrative divisions of all gave Cuban boxing an image of moral purity. No Cuban who defected after 1961 has become a world champion or even made the smallest impact on the world of boxing. Every single world champion of Cuban extraction since 1959 was a professional before the revolution. After forty years, however, Joel Casamayor looks as if he might change that.

Casamayor came from pretty much nowhere to win a gold medal in the Barcelona Olympics and then disappeared from a training camp in Mexico in 1996 with the heavyweight Ramon Garbey just before the Atlanta Games. There were tales and rumours everywhere.

On the same day I saw the orange-clad Casamayor jogging along the road, they held the weigh-in for his fight at the Miccosukee Gaming Complex. What a revolting place. A giant hotel and gloomy casino, suffused with constant electronic noise and the smell of cheap food. It was packed with lines of electronic gaming machines, their jackpots flashing above them, and sad-looking people staring wistfully at screens which every second or so teased another dollar from them and then bleeped for more. Armed guards strolled around the floor, not doing much but positioned, I assumed, to protect anyone whose machine spewed out cash. Next door was a brightly lit bingo room with rows and rows of tables all facing a giant scoreboard. The venue for the fight was a white plastic dome at the far end of the hotel carpark, kitted out to hold a couple of thousand punters, with the ring at the far end surrounded by ringside seats in three corners and the main crowd area all down one side. Tickets, at thirty dollars, were not cheap and the woman at the kiosk where they were being sold had them stacked beside the till. The telephone credit-card booking service wasn't working and the sales people seemed barely concerned that this meant a forty-minute drive out to the reservation to pick up tickets in person. They were ever so polite, but had no idea how the problem might be solved. They just did what they were told.

The weigh-in was in a suite on the hotel's second floor, a

clean, featureless room with a table at one end that looked set up for a press conference and another table to one side for accreditations. The room was half full of the usual lurkers wondering who everyone else was. The security people, mainly young black men, muscled but not boxers, were being signed up and quizzed as to whether they had any felony charges against them, which seemed to be the only disqualification for the job. They crouched over the tables and filled in their forms. Around them the boxers, with their entourages and trainers, stood together in groups. Most of the attention centred on Miguel Angel Gonzalez, the world champion from Mexico, who was top of the bill. He wasn't milling around, but was accorded the honour, along with his opponent Kostya Tszyu (a Russian amateur who defected to Australia and turned pro after the world championships in Sydney in 1991), of making an entrance of sorts. Cameras flashed and the undercard boxers milled around and carried on talking. The hanging around went on and on and on until at last the scales, which had been sitting in front of the main table, were surrounded by officials. José Suleiman, who runs the WBC, of which Gonzalez was world champion, scrutinised the weighing of the two men in their pristine underwear. Both stuck their index fingers up in the air after making the weight to indicate they felt they were Number One, but neither did it with much gusto. This was just the routine of the fight game trundling through the necessaries before the event itself. A PR man from HBO, the major player in America's cable sports market, pointed Casamayor out to me, so I sat down with him and launched into my spiel about the book and an interview, but he was constantly interrupted. A sixty-year-old skinny Australian came over to ask if Casamayor would sign his boxing gloves. Casamayor said yes, at which point the man produced a giant kitbag of the things. Casamayor didn't bat an eyelid. He was too eager to please in this still new world to make a fuss.

Then two kids came over and wanted their picture taken. He posed with one on either side, their right fists clenched alongside his in the middle, while the man with the camera struggled to make it work. They chatted to him in English and he nodded in all the right places, though he plainly didn't understand a word they were saying. Casamayor stood there fixed in his pose and didn't move until it was obvious the camera was broken. At which point he smiled, shrugged and shook their hands as they walked away chattering. On to the next person who could provide them with a few moments of entertainment at no cost. A young white Latino was looking after Casamayor, taking him through the bureaucratic rituals of the afternoon. He had a goatie beard and a fashionably bright green T-shirt. Casamayor trusted him.

'Look, why don't we talk after the fight tomorrow,' I said to Casamayor. 'We can't get any peace here.'

'Yeah. This is my number at home, my sister's house. And this is my bleeper. Call me on Monday.' We could have been in Cuba, it was that easy.

I arrived late for the fight on the night. I had assumed that because of all the publicity for the Casamayor fight, which implied that he was up against a serious contender (a misprint in the flyer made it seem that he was fighting the WBC Number One bantamweight Adam Vargas), and also because it was the second most important fight of the night, that it would, as is traditional, take place just before the main event. Instead Casamayor, his record 18 wins, no defeats and 11 knockouts, was the first man on, boxing against a Mexican I'd never heard of called Enrique Valenzuela. I found out later that Valenzuela had 18 wins and 20 defeats, the sort of record that defines a journeyman, paid to get beaten up for the benefit of massaging the records of fighters who might be contenders. As I walked in, Casamayor, in red and gold trunks, was on top. I had barely sat down when he delivered, in the second round, a crushing right that sent the Mexican tumbling. There was a muted cheer and then silence. Even though we were in Miami, the majority of folks in the Miccosukee were there to see the Mexican Miguel Angel Gonzalez and there wasn't much of a Cuban atmosphere.

Casamayor climbed out of the ring barely sweating. His dressing gown glimmered with its gold fringes and before he went to the dressing room he went to give some early copy to the hacks who leaned across their ringside seats to hear him. That, I presume, was why he was on first, to give the local Cuban press something for that night's edition because the Gonzalez fight wasn't happening till midnight for the benefit of HBO. Written on the back of the gown was his nickname, El Cepillo, which means The Hairbrush (or just Brush), perhaps not in the fearsome tradition of the Razors, Princes and TNTs, or Iron Mikes of boxing tradition, but it was a name that definitely was his alone.

Within thirty minutes of the fight, in a tight black T-shirt and pristine black jeans, with a thick gold chain around his neck, he was back in the arena wandering around shaking hands and mixing with his friends, for all the world just another Cuban wide boy in Miami.

Gonzalez was beaten by Tszyu. For round after round Tszyu hunted him down, jabbing and poking, but Gonzalez just would not submit. He hadn't scored a point in the whole contest and under amateur rules the fight wouldn't have gone much past the second round. Instead I could feel a thrill that the amateur stuff had never really given me, something inside that was awestruck at what I was being permitted to see close up, someone really hurting someone else and it not being stopped, both edgy and desperate, aware that their financial welfare depended on it. This fight really counted and that was its thrill. It wasn't so much that someone was going to win but that someone was going to lose when neither could afford to.

It wasn't about jabs and technique for the people watching, it was about hurt and pain of the best kind – someone else's. I loved it.

I rang Casamayor on Monday, as promised, at ten a.m. His sister said he was still in bed. He was still there at eleven when I rang again. But at midday he answered and gave me his address. My driver squinted when I told him where to go. It wasn't a good part of town, an area that they just called Norwest (NW). I had already been there looking for a place called the Wilfredo Vasquez gym, where there might be other Cubans, but when I got there it was a concrete, graffiti-covered hut. It had been closed for a while. Norwest was a poor corner of town, with scruffy, single-storey houses and half-mended cars cluttering up crumbling drives. Casamayor's house was in a block where a lot of Dominicans lived. In front was a broken-down Seventies American car. I walked to the right house past a row of monotonous square concrete buildings, one step up from shanty-town dwellings, and there he was walking towards me, immaculate again in blue jeans and a loud flower-patterned shirt.

'Hi. How are you?' he said warmly. 'Come in here.' We went into one of the square buildings, which were single-storey one-bedroom flats. It was clean, there were plastic flowers in ever corner and the red sofas were new. The furniture was cheap, but looked barely out of the wrapper. As I sat down, the reason why this part of Norwest was not sought after became clear. A plane flew over from the nearby airport and I had to lipread for a few moments, which was made harder by the fact that Casamayor stammers slightly and talks so fast you just have to pick up the general sense of what he is saying. He sat down, leaned forward on his chair, fidgeted nervously with the tape recorder, and looked at me as if to say it was my turn to talk.

'You were born in Guantanamo, weren't you? What was it like there?'

'I was brought up in a fairly poor neighbourhood. I was a street kid around there, always fighting, but there weren't any drugs or anything. Well, I suppose there are drugs everywhere, but honestly I never saw any in my neighbourhood in those days. It's not like here, where people talk about drugs every three minutes. I never heard a word about it. It was a pretty tight community, quite calm, to the point that if I started fighting with some kid the neighbours would run in and tell my mum straight away. The boxing gym was right in front of my house. I used to sneak away from my mum, jumping over the fence in the backyard and I was in the gym in an instant. But every day my mum would give me a thrashing for it. She used to try and beat me into understanding that boxing was pointless, that there was no logic in hitting people until they fell over for the entertainment of other people, but I used to tell her that it was the only sport that interested me.

'My mum stopped hitting me once she realised that it wasn't doing any good. So out of the blue one day she just said, "OK, if that's what you want you go ahead and do it." So I started training officially in a gym that belonged to Hugo Fernandez, who is dead now. He was my first trainer when I was seven years old and he trained me until I was fifteen. It was a difficult time because we didn't have much food or clothes or anything really. But Hugo told me that I was his favourite and he was going to look after me and he bought me things. There was a group of us, but he always said that it was me who had the brightest future and that I would be famous one day. At thirteen or fourteen he made sure I got into the local EIDE (the first rung on the ladder of the national Cuban sports network) in Guantanamo, where I spent four or five years and he kept on working with me. After that I just kept moving up the scale little by little. It was at this school they gave me my nickname El Cepillo.'

'Why did they choose Cepillo? The Brush is . . . [don't say stupid, remember he's a boxer] an unusual nickname for a boxer.'

'They chose El Cepillo because my mother's husband worked in the school as the headmaster's chauffeur and gofer and his nickname was Cepillo, so the other kids called me Little Cepillo and it stuck with me even as I got older. At sixteen I went to the national ESPA (the next rung on the ladder) and took part in some schoolboy championships for the first time. In 1987 I was in the national youth team, trained by Pedro Roque, and in 1989 I was called up into the senior squad.'

He was rattling through this at a frightening pace. Time to slow him down a little. 'Havana must have been very different from what you were used to, coming from a small city like Guantanamo.'

'It wasn't a difficult change for me really to leave Guantanamo and move to Havana because almost all of the youth team were from the east like me – Hector Vinent, Ariel Hernandez, Garbey, we were all together – so it wasn't so much of a shock. Once I left the east I couldn't really ever go back except for New Year's or Mothers' Day and very quickly Havana was just where I lived, was where my life was. I really loved that time of my life.'

Like most of Cuba's really outstanding boxers Casamayor's talent was both obvious and rapidly exploited. 'Alcides Sagarra wanted to call me up into the national team from the youth team, but Pedro Roque told him that I wasn't ready and that he should wait. So they agreed to wait until after the world youth championships. When I was preparing for them in Puerto Rico they let me take some bouts with seniors and I was beating people from the national team like Orlando Reyes.

They didn't let me out much, but they could see that I had enough quality to be in the senior team. I won gold in Puerto Rico and moved up a grade, where I always had good results and was among the best three or four boxers there. I had seven years in the team until 1996.'

Two questions and he's already rushed full pelt to the year he defected. It was as if he didn't really want to linger, that this was a time he had not thought about at any length for a while. Time to drag him back.

'What was it like being with the national team at the Finca when you were just a kid?'

'When you get to the Finca you are aware that this place is full of the heroes of Cuban boxing and you approach it a little scared. I was nervous as hell. I had never stood in the same room as so many champions. I mean, I'd seen them all on the television before, but I never really thought that in such a short time I would be standing next to them. The senior boxers were great, though, people like Adolfo Horta. They told me they would show me the ropes. But the basic fact that hits you when you get there is that these are great boxers and you are nobody. They just laughed at me and said that they had had their day and now it was my turn.'

This process of institutionalising that every Cuban boxer has to go through, channelled from EIDE to ESPA to the Finca, controlled, monitored, disciplined, a system designed to filter out those with the talent but not the self will, can be hard on a kid from the east.

'There were times when the fear overwhelmed me. I remember once I just packed my bags and went back to where the youth team all lived. The next day they came looking for me, shouting and screaming, and eventually convinced me to go back to the Finca. After that I was fine. Life in the team is very hard, though, very sad in some ways, because you train every day and you never have a break. If you don't do exactly what the coaches say, they chuck you out of the team. The diet there is designed around the weight and is very strict. It reflects Alcides, I suppose, who is an iron disciplinarian. You have to give it to him, though, he's a great trainer, and he is the reason that Cuban boxing is the best in the world. And the truth is that overall I enjoyed my time in the Finca.'

One of the things Cuba does to avoid losing young, impressionable boxers to Western promoters is carefully restrict who is permitted to go to international tournaments. If there is a hint of doubt over the political dedication of a boxer or if he gets caught even thinking out loud about the world beyond Cuba, he is liable to find his opportunities to travel limited. And, in the absence of cash, the opportunity to travel, and the opportunity to make a few dollars on the side, is what keeps some of the boxers going. The younger boxers are watched especially carefully because it is they who have the most chance to make a career in the pros. By the time a boxer reaches his mid-twenties his chances are limited by the amount of time needed to build a reputation and a decent enough record, maybe three or four years. Thus the younger fighters rarely go to major tournaments.

'In 1992 I wasn't supposed to go to the Olympics. I was only eighteen and they had said to me that I would be in the team for the 1996 Games, but that I wasn't ready yet. That seemed fair enough to me and when the team went off to Germany to prepare for Barcelona I went home to Guantanamo and I was pretty pleased with myself. One day, though, the president of INDER, the president of the province and the regional head coach came into my neighbourhood frantically asking everyone where I was. Eventually they found me sitting on a wall with some friends eating an egg sandwich. I was on holiday, after all, and for the first time in months I didn't need to worry about my weight. They came up to me and said that Carrion [Cuba's No. 1 in Casamayor's weight class] had broken his arm in Germany and that they needed to call me into the team at the last minute. I thought they were kidding. "This is not my idea of a joke," I screamed at them and told them to fuck off. But they told me to shut up and that I just had time to pack my bags and set off for Havana to catch a flight to Europe. I barely had time to say goodbye to my mum, who was very pleased. I just left with the clothes I was wearing. This was two weeks before the Barcelona Olympics were due to start.

'I had nothing to lose, nothing was really expected of me. I'm a pretty positive person, but I told myself that I had no chance of a medal and that my job was to get as many points as I could for the team, to stay in the tournament as long as I could. I looked at the opponents and I knew how hard it was going to be. There was the Irish guy [Wayne] McCullough and a Russian whose name I forget now. I had five hard fights, but I suddenly found myself boxing for a guaranteed bronze medal. And it dawned on me as I was getting in the ring that I was only two fights away from gold. I knew I had to up my game to have any chance of that and I found an extra gear from somewhere. I beat McCullough 17 to 7 in the final.'

The seeds of Casamayor's defection were sown by his victory in Barcelona and what happened next. 'Well, you know what it's like when you win an Olympic gold medal for your country.' (I don't, actually, but what could I say? I nodded.) 'Everyone loves you, they put tributes to you on the telly, they give you a week's holiday in Varadero. They also gave me a house, but to be honest it was a pretty lousy house and not a very nice area.' His present house wasn't exactly Beverly Hills, but he was going too fast to interrupt. 'It wasn't in great nick either, this house they gave me. But I'm the sort of bloke who keeps his thoughts to himself. I knew they could have found me something better and it really pissed me off that I had won a gold medal and they couldn't do better than that. They didn't even give me a car either. There are only three Olympic gold medallists from my province, Savon, me and Rogelio Marcelo,' light-flyweight gold medallist in Barcelona, 'and they couldn't even rustle up a measly car as a thank-you.'

Just in case this seems a bit odd, let me put it in context. These are the only perks you can get as an amateur sportsman. You don't compete for yourself and you can't be paid, but a house and a car of your own, difficult things to obtain legally for a young Cuban, are the biggest status symbols you can have and the only things the state, for whom you are effectively competing, can give you. If you get a gold medal in the Olympic Games and then the car doesn't materialise and the house is rubbish it would be natural to feel cheated. These are the only perks you can aspire to and having fulfilled your part of the bargain not getting the reward is bound to leave you feeling pretty short-changed.

'Things went around in my head at the time and I felt depressed at how things had gone. And I thought, "Fuck it. I'm a good enough boxer to fight as a professional and they would have to pay me good money in the pros." But it was just a sort of vague idea. I never seriously thought of defecting from the country. It was my country after all, it was where I lived, where my family were. And right from a young age you get told about how terrible professional boxing is. Sagarra, in particular, was very good at making everyone afraid of professional boxing. He said that you got killed in the pros, that it was very dangerous, that boxers were exploited and ripped off. Well, now I know what a load of crap that is, but I didn't then.'

'Are there a lot of boxers who would like to leave?'

'Yes, I think there are a lot of boxers who would like to get out. But they are afraid.'

He didn't elaborate and for the first time in the conversation fell silent. I didn't push him. Perhaps Casamayor's plans were a little more advanced than he likes to admit. When he returned to Havana he appears to have waited and waited for the right moment and never given a hint to anyone of how much he wanted to get out. Many of Cuba's boxers have found their frustration transformed into indiscipline and drifted away. I never heard anything of Rogelio Marcelo or Juan Lemus, both medal winners in 1992, when I was in Cuba. But Casamayor kept training and bided his time. 'I didn't say anything to anyone and I was more disciplined in training than ever. I hid my feelings completely. Buried them. It didn't matter how much they shouted at me or whether they put me on the toughest diet in the world, I did it without a murmur of complaint. Inside I was thinking, "Come on, do your worst, treat me as badly as you like, because I'm not going to be around for ever." I knew I would be picked for the 1996 Olympics in Atlanta if I stuck at it and, sure enough, I was. We went to train in Mexico in Guadalajara before the tournament began and I knew that the moment had come.'

'You didn't have firm plans or contacts or anything before you got to Mexico?'

'No, none at all. In my own mind when I left for Mexico I was going to go on with the team and win a gold medal and come back to my five-year-old daughter and my mother. But when we were in Mexico things happened that made my mind up for me. In fact it was the trainers and security police with us on the trip that decided me. Everywhere you go they are there, one step behind you, telling you that you can't do this or that. I got to the point where I couldn't face going back to Cuba and having all that secret service shit the rest of my career. I figured that all I wanted to do was earn some money and help my family and I couldn't do it in Cuba. All of this sort of thing was knocking around my head and in Mexico I got to feeling that it was now or never.'

The mechanics of defecting are not easy, however. First,

getting away from the training camp without being noticed when there were guards with the team to stop precisely that is not simple. Second, even if you get away from the team what are you supposed to do next? You're in a foreign country, you have no money, and you are effectively an illegal immigrant. The only place you can be sure you won't get sent back from and where you might find some kind of support network is the United States. But how do you get across the border?

'I had a friend over there in Mexico, a Cuban guy. He and his wife used to come back to Cuba from time to time and I knew him because I sold him Cohiba cigars. Every trip the boxers went on we used to take a few boxes of good cigars to sell and have a bit of money to spend. Quite a few of the boxers used to sell cigars to him because he seemed to be well-enough connected to shift them. He also used to know people at the border who helped him smuggle the cigars into the United States. One day I went to his house and told him straight out that I didn't want to go back to Cuba any more. He sat there dumbstruck when I told him. He said, "You know what you are saying?" and I told him I had never been surer of anything in my whole life. He told me to give him three days to find a place where we could hide out. He told me he didn't want my cash, he just wanted to help me along my way.

'I left at night. We were in a summer school complex in Guadalajara and basically I had to sneak out of the dorm and jump over a fence to get away without anyone seeing me. I went and woke up Garbey and he came with me. I tried to wake up Vinent, but he said it was too dangerous and stayed. Look at him now. I heard he attacked a policeman and was going to jail for ten years. It just makes me even more certain that when you get a chance you have to take it.

'There was a security guard with a gun, but he was always asleep. So one night we climbed the fence and there was this guy waiting in his car to drive us away from the city, where no one could find us. He got us across the border in the boot of his car and we drove up to California. He wasn't that clever about it, though, because he took us to a luxury hotel in Los Angeles and we weren't exactly hard to spot, these two black guys with no money and no clothes in a five-star hotel. The plan had been to go to Las Vegas and sign a contract to box there, but in the end we didn't do it. We were in Vegas for a while, but I hated it. While I was there I met Luis de Cubas, who people said was a good manager. So we met and talked and I said that if he wanted to call me he could. After a while I signed up with De Cubas and came with him to Miami to join his Team Freedom [a gym of thirteen Cuban defectors].'

If you glance at the stories of the boxers who make up Team Freedom, Casamayor had a pretty easy time of it. Eliecer Castillo, a half-decent but unspectacular Cuban light heavyweight, whose highest achievement was a bronze medal at the 1990 Playa Giron, sailed out of Cuba on an inner tube in 1994 only to be picked up by the US coastguard and taken to the Guantanamo naval base. He spent a year there before being allowed into the country in November 1995 and making his professional debut three months later. It wasn't until May 1998 that he lost his first bout. The same happened to Ramon Ledon, who got on a raft with ten friends in 1994 and spent eight months in Guantanamo before being let in. Ledon was hailed by De Cubas as 'the best-kept secret in boxing' and compiled the same impressive record as almost all his stablemates. The trouble is that whenever any of them get a real title shot they somehow manage to blow it.

Diobelys Hurtado always looked like the best Cuban to defect in the Nineties. Hurtado had run away from the team as they caught a connecting flight on the way back from a tournament in Connecticut, making a dash for it at Miami International Airport and charging out of the terminal on foot. This was October 1994 and by December he was fighting as a pro. He was, as are all Team Freedom boxers, nursed to a decent record, protected and projected until the time was right and then given a world title shot. Hurtado got his chance against Pernell Whitaker, a legendarily classy boxer and WBC world welterweight champion, when the pair met in Atlantic City in January 1997. Hurtado dominated Whitaker in a way that shocked those who had followed Sweet Pea's lengthy and successful career. The fight was eleven rounds old, Whitaker had been knocked down twice and there could be little doubt that the WBC championship was about to go to the Cuban. Then Whitaker found a couple of swinging lefts and floored Hurtado. He didn't get up. Hurtado was nursed back to credibility, recognised for what he had nearly achieved against Whitaker and when the super-lightweight world title fight between Miguel Angel Gonzalez and Kostya Tszyu was postponed because of injury, Hurtado took his second world title shot (interim world title, they called it, whatever that means) at two weeks' notice against Tszyu. There were five knockdowns in the fight, but the one that counted left Hurtado on the floor in the fifth. He had come so close yet again. Bearing in mind how Tszyu had dismantled Gonzalez on the night I saw Casamayor going through the motions against Velanzuela, Hurtado must have been pretty damn good.

What the bald numbers and statistics don't reveal is the personal cost of leaving your family and going to another country, from where you can never return. 'I spent a whole year crying,' said Casamayor, 'wondering what on earth I was going to do now. I was here in the USA on my own, I didn't know anyone, I didn't have a car. Eventually I got to know a few Cubans who helped me out and they all told me that it was normal, that they had all felt the same when they got here, but that the sadness passed after a while. Anyway, bit by bit I got used to the idea and they took me out and showed me the city, we went out for a few beers, a bit of dancing, and I felt better. But it's not easy here because you have to have work or you die.'

Nagging away too was the price his family were paying back home for his defection. The state machinery moved in to punish them for the embarrassment Casamayor's defection had caused.

'When you leave you know what will happen to your family. In fact, a good example is my mother. I can't really telephone her and she can't be seen to telephone me. She doesn't have a phone so she would have to use someone else's and they daren't take the risk of being seen to help her. If I call I have to telephone someone else's house because the secret police are always checking up on her and trying to find out if she has had any contact with me. When I left, my mother lost her job and I can't be sure if she is eating or not because the situation in Cuba is really hard. The other day my sister's boyfriend rang me from outside Cuba. Halfway through the conversation he told me to brace myself, he had news about my mother. I immediately said, "What? What? What's happened to my mum?" And he told me that since I left she has had two heart attacks. She's all right now, but was pretty bad. He said I ought to call her because she really misses me. And I felt this real pain inside because I know that in part what has happened is my fault, because I left and I can't come back.

'But on the other hand I also know that in the long run I can help her and the family better from over here. I don't earn a vast amount now, but that will change and I hope that in two years I can have my mother here with me. In fact, I'm sure of it. But as I said I know that for a couple of years I'm not going to be able to help her. I gave a boxer friend in Cuba the telephone number of the house so she can call me and I arranged for him to have some money to take back for her. But I have two dreams that I have to achieve. One is to be a world champion, which I have already done, and the other is to have my mum here with me. And I'm telling you today, 23 August 1999, that when she turns up I'll introduce you to her. I know it's going to turn out all right. I know it, God willing.'

It is said often by people associated with the pros, but by quite a few amateur experts as well, that the transition from amateur to pro is a lot more difficult than you might think. The rounds are longer and there are more of them to get through. The process of adapting, of working your way up from four-, six- and seven-round pro fights to get comfortable with the twelve-round marathons that bring world titles and big bucks, is potentially a very long one. 'The first thing I had to do was get hold of a trainer who could change my style from the classic amateur style to a more professional one and the key to that is the trainer. But the difference between the two isn't as big as people make out. My trainer is a Latino and he says it's basically the same. You keep your head lower' – in amateur boxing the head must not bend below an opponent's chest – 'and other bits and bobs, but I can't say it seems that different to me. I always learned things pretty quickly anyway and I've watched a lot of the pros here and I have learned to copy them. I'm not a brawler by any stretch of the imagination, but I know how to fight in close better than I did, I keep my head down and I work harder to move around the ring and I'm getting better all the time.'

Casamayor's professional career started remarkably quickly after his defection on 20 September 1996, only a couple of months on from Guadalajara, when he pulverised David Chamendis and knocked him out in the first round, an emphatic victory which he repeated three times in the next two years. In fact he developed such a reputation as a power boxer that the line was put around that the nickname Cepillo was a reference to his uppercut. Casamayor adapted quickly to the rigours of the pro game and it seems that his style and temperament helped him, although none of the opponents they put in front of him had ever been heard of before or since.

Mariano Leyva, a Cuban coach attached to the Mexican team, who defected during the Atlanta Games shortly after Casamayor and Garbey and who now helps Casamayor, is certain that Casamayor will make it. 'American fighters always move forward. Very often they are off-balance and they lunge at their opponent. Because Casamayor has great movement and because he knows how to work on his opponent, he'll be able to counter-punch that aggressive style.'

On 12 July 1997 in Lake Tahoe Casamayor punished the aggressive Salvador Montes, knocking him down twice and forcing a stoppage in the second round. Six months later, on 23 January 1998, he outpunched and overwhelmed Javier Diaz to capture a unanimous decision in a four-round contest.

On 21 July 1998 he got a four-round stoppage over Gary Triano, and a month later a stoppage in the second against Miguel Figueroa, his ninth victory by knockout. On 26 September 1998, a year before I saw him in Miami, Casamayor outpointed Eugene Johnson for a unanimous decision in a six-rounder, despite an early cut from an accidental headbutt. The irony was that he was fighting less and taking less punishment than he would have done if he was back home in Cuba fighting as an amateur, a mere thirty-one rounds in two years to September 1998. So much for cruel professionalism.

'One of the problems is that you come straight from Cuba and from a system where everything is very controlled and the discipline is very tight to here, where no one can force you to do anything. But it comes down to whether you love boxing or not. Look at me. No one tells me what to do now, but if you want to be good you have to impose a discipline on yourself. I could smoke and drink if I wanted to, but I always think about what is really in my best interests because if I don't I'll just die in poverty. The difference between Cuba and here is that here if you don't have money you are nobody, which I just had no idea about. In all honesty, I didn't know what I was getting myself into. I thought that when I got here they would give me a house straight away. I didn't even know about paying rent or anything because it doesn't really exist in Cuba. Here you have to pay for everything and that's why you have to work and work and work. If they had told me what it was going to be like I wouldn't have believed them. In Cuba you train and they give you your salary because you train. Here you have to pay for the right to train, to pay trainers and gyms and all that. And you get your money when you win fights. But the biggest shock was that there is nothing free here, there is no such thing as a gift. Even your best friend charges you for the tiniest thing.

'So you have to be clever about it. I don't want to be one of those boxers who gets ripped off. I have an accountant and I make sure I can understand where my money is going and in that sense I'm not as stupid as a few boxers. I'm well aware that to make money in this business you have to lose a bit along the way, but the purses I earn are pretty good. Of all the Cuban boxers here I'm the best paid and a few of them envy my position. I have to be careful about the people around me more than ever now because I'm just getting to a higher level, where you can genuinely earn some money. Now I'm close to my first world title shot. My trainer is pretty cool. He won't let me take fights where I am getting ripped off because if I don't earn good money he doesn't earn anything either. And he told me that in four or five years we are both going to be millionaires. And I believe him. Next up I'm going to fight this Mongolian' – Lavka Sim, the WBA champion – 'who is avoiding me because he knows I can beat him. If he turns me down I'll get another shot at someone in the top ten rankings.

Then I reckon I will be in the frame for a fight against Tom Manuel for half a million bucks or something like that. But whoever it is I'm getting to the level now where I can earn serious money. Which is what I came here for. I have to make it. I have to get to the top. Otherwise all the sadness and pain will have been a waste of time. I have to make it. I just have to.'

13 *Introducing Señor Yon Doooncan*

The morning in Holguin was bright and sunny. Much like the one before that and the one before that, except that this morning was the regular fixture at Cuba's national boxing championships when the referees and judges take on the press at softball. The match always takes place on the middle Sunday of the Playa Giron and the venue this year was a small softball field next to a tumbledown corrugated-iron hut which housed a children's boxing gym. The field was remarkably well kept, with a proper fence and a roughly constructed concrete stand to the right of home plate which held about fifty people. I had been invited to make up the numbers for the press team on the basis of a few confused conversations about cricket and a series of bare-faced lies about my own skills in the hand–eye co-ordination department. Well, it's just rounders played by blokes, isn't it?

The match was organised by Modesto Aguerro, who had brought his bat and gloves with him from Havana and had imported a few ex-boxers from the heavier weights to our cause. My role was to stand on the field in the position where there was least likelihood of the ball ever coming, which would have been mid-on in cricket. There were only enough gloves for one team, so each time there was an out the team fielding took off their gloves and threw them down for the team replacing them. I picked up the gloves where they lay and stood there out in left field, with the crowd laughing at this skinny white guy in a vest that was too big for him who obviously didn't have a clue what he was supposed to be doing. They were especially amused by my batting style, which drew heavily on a cricket stance, none of this bat-held-back-coiled-and-ready-to-explode nonsense, my bat was straight in front of me, horizontal but at ninety degrees to my body. The ball was thrown underarm to me and I left the first couple just because the batter in front of me had done the same thing. Then one came along which just begged to be hit. I had a swing and it went about ten yards straight across the ground behind the pitcher. I threw the bat down and charged for first base, I touched my foot on the plate as the ball came over, slightly fumbled and poorly thrown from second base. 'In,' declared the referee. A furious row broke out. I had definitely done something wrong. I think you are supposed to stand on the plate rather than touch it and run past. This was really serious. They were shouting and screaming and a friendly game had turned into a ruck. Except that I quickly realised that half the fun of this game, of any game, for Cubans is to shout and scream and complain and sulk. The next time at bat I did the same. Again a pathetic short hit. Again it was fumbled. Again I made it to first. The crowd, the first of any kind I had ever played any sport in front of, went mental. I was run out at second.

In the early stages of the game I had been switched from left to right field depending on whether the batter was left- or right-handed, i.e. I wasn't left in a spot where the ball might come to. But eventually they forgot. Up to the mound came a giant of a man, black, an obvious ex-boxer, left-handed like me. He swung madly at the first pitch, swished air and staggered. Then he connected with the second pitch and this ball, which I had only managed to propel a meagre twenty yards at most, went sailing high into the sky. In my direction. I stood underneath it and felt my heart pounding. I could hear the crowd yell. Even when I played football I only ever heard the muffled groans of team-mates if I fluffed an easy chance to score. Oh dear. The ball started to plummet to the ground and I moved to get myself underneath it. That part was easy, it was just the same as cricket. Except that I had this big leather glove on. And the ball was bigger and softer. The bad thing was that the glove was a hindrance to catching the ball in a cricket style, hands out cupped in front of the chest. The ball was supposed to be caught one-handed, the gloved hand held high in front of your face and snapped shut when the ball arrived. No, John, I thought. Nothing fancy. Do what you know best. I stood my ground, the gloved and ungloved hand in front of me, the ball dropped into the gloved hand and stopped dead. The crowd burst into a mixture of hysterical laughter and cheering. I bowed. The runner on second stole a base. 'Throw the fucking ball,' shouted Modesto. 'Throw the ball, Yon,' shouted the pitcher. I threw it to Modesto wildly and the guy on second scored. But it was the sweetest of Pyrrhic victories. The batter turned around and went back to his team-mates scowling. What I had done was just not cricket, I suppose. It was considered showboating, showing off how easy the catch was. And he had been caught out by the geek from England.

There were no reporters in any press box, just thirty or forty blokes with nothing better to do that day, but in a country where there is little official news of human interest I found myself plugged into the most effective news network in Cuba – word of mouth. From then on I was famous in Holguin. I couldn't walk anywhere without blokes pointing at me and gesturing as if they had a softball bat in their hand and smiling.

One guy on a building site stopped what he was doing and shouted, 'Hey, John. Softbol. Hey.' And he made a cup-handed catching gesture. He even knew my name, for God's sake.

It turned out to be the smartest catch I had ever made. In any situation as an outsider coming in, people take time to accept you. In Cuba it seemed as if everyone wanted to know you, but those who took most interest in you usually wanted something. The boxing people, beyond the journalists who recognised a member of an international brotherhood, were more stand-offish. Now, though, when I went to the arena for the evening's boxing, the referees greeted me like an eccentric but welcome friend. And while I was chatting to them they introduced me to some of the boxers who came by. And the more that people saw me in the company of officialdom the more they assumed I must be OK and were happy to talk to me. I was even introduced to the commissioner of the Cuban Boxing Association, José Barrientos, a smartly dressed brown-skinned young bureaucrat who rarely smiled and never seemed excited by anything, one of those guys who looks as if they are permanently burdened with some awful secret. One of the referees convinced him to let me go back to Havana in the official bus instead of paying for a flight. I felt the door to the world of Cuban boxing opening slightly.

Emboldened, I started to think about the man who stood in the way of everything: Alcides Sagarra. Sagarra was to be found every day at the national championships, sitting in the middle chair of three behind a plain wooden table to the right of the press benches. He sat in splendid, visible isolation in his tracksuit, with a clipboard and a file for company, reading and making notes. For Savon and one or two of the other fighters he would disappear discreetly minutes before they were due to come on and lead them into the arena, strolling and not making eye contact with anyone while they bobbed and shadow-boxed behind him. But most of the time he sat there looking impassively at each contest, expressionless, neutral. Occasionally a greying member of the national training set-up would wander over and whisper in his ear while he would look at the ground blankly, maybe nodding slightly but nothing more. I only ever saw one boxer approach the table to talk to him and that was Savon, who looked at him in awe and admiration as the pair talked. Savon sat on the chair beside him, his long legs stretching out before him, his huge arms resting with his elbows on his knees and a child's desperate-to-listen-and-please face. I spent one lunchtime talking to the Cuban journalists about Sagarra, what he was like, what he thought. They confirmed what was obvious if you had been watching him for a couple of days, as I had: that he was suspicious, reserved, wary of foreigners, protective of his boxers, fearsome if you were on the wrong side of him and ruthless in protecting the discipline of the Cuban boxing team. One of his gold medallists from Atlanta, Hector Vinent, had failed to make the right weight at Holguin and had moved up a weight in consequence. Two days into the tournament it was announced to the press that Vinent had therefore been kicked out of the national squad for a year. Sagarra allowed no deviation from the will of the coaching staff and if it meant losing a boxer who was a certainty for a gold at that year's world championships then so be it. He had been elected to the central committee of the Communist Party. He was pivotal to the success of my plan and I had to speak to him. The chaps helped me translate a few questions into Spanish so that he wouldn't lose patience with me when I tried to speak to him, and I got on the bus shaking, knowing that I was going to talk to him for the first time. It was like the journey to meet Warren only worse, a terror of being exposed, laughed at, treated like a fool.

Maybe it wouldn't be so bad, I kept telling myself. I'd

watched him being interviewed by a camera crew from Holland the day before and you wouldn't have recognised him. Once the camera came on his face lit up and he smiled and answered the usual questions, about Savon, why Cubans were so good, whether Savon would beat Tyson (the same list I had, really). The minute it was over he shook hands, still smiling, strolled off and was back to his expressionless best at his throne in the corner of the arena.

The camera crew from Holland, however, had paid for the privilege and done everything by the book. In Cuba public relations for all sportsmen is done centrally through the commercial arm of the Ministry of Sport, Cubadeportes. They employed a series of fixers to guide foreigners around town and introduce them to whoever they wanted and they charged them an arm and a leg for the privilege. For a TV crew over from Holland it was no big deal, but I hadn't paid anything. He didn't have to talk to me if he didn't want to. When our bus arrived at the stadium, Sagarra, unusually, wasn't there. I sat down and felt the confidence drain out of me. I was getting involved in serious stuff now. I had come to Cuba to convince them to change the laws of their country to accommodate professional boxing. Who did I think I was? What had I been thinking? Just as I was starting to wonder if it was too late to get out of all this, to forget about spying and hustling and get back to being an unremarkable journalist in my unremarkable country, Sagarra ambled in.

Miguel Hernandez pointed him out to me. 'Come on, I'll introduce you.'

'Not yet, Miguel. I need more time to think about my questions.'

The boxing started. The semi-finals. I made not a single note. I sat in shivering lonely silence with Sagarra fixed in the corner of my eye. I didn't notice anything until one of the chaps from Radio Rebelde (Radio Rebel) gestured me to his seat. I went over and he made me put on some headphones. I assumed he wanted me to hear something funny that was going on. Roberto Pacheco, Cuba's leading sports broadcaster, was chatting away and his co-commentator Robertico was handing me his microphone.

'And we are lucky to have with us Mr Yon Dooncan from *El Guardian* newspaper in London, the only foreign journalist here at the Playa Giron. Welcome, Yon.'

Well, it was better than going over to talk to Sagarra.

'Hello, Pacheco; hello, everyone in Cuba.'

'So, John, what do you think of the boxing?'

There are only two rules of radio, I had been told by friends back home who worked in it. Keep talking and don't say 'fuck'. Off I went.

'Well, last night was pretty spectacular with the defeat of Savon. But I have been amazed at the quality of boxer you have here. Almost everyone I have seen would do well in England.'

'Do you listen to Radio Rebelde in London, Yon?'

What on earth was he on about? But rule number three of radio: always play ball with the host. 'Absolutely, Pacheco, we all tune in to listen to Deportivamente [the name of the programme I was on].'

'The Queen? She listens in Buckingham Palace?'

'Yes, the Queen. And Paul McCartney.' Give me a break, he was the first Englishman after the Queen that came into my head. Pacheco loved it. 'And in Liverpool the Beatles, they all listen?' Well, they all lived in the United States, but it was too late to be getting all serious now. 'All the Beatles, except John Lennon, of course. They all love you.'

'Thank you, Yon Dooooncan . . .'

And with that I accidentally made myself even more famous. What in England would have been an interview that no one heard, broadcast to people who had more to worry about than some foreign hack talking rubbish on the radio, became another appearance for this funny English bloke who liked boxing and who was now, by popular acclaim, friends with the Beatles and the Queen. Six months later people in Havana were coming up to me and asking me whether it was true that I was a personal friend of Elizabeth II. The adrenalin rush of live broadcasting was in fact just what I needed. And I reckoned Sagarra must have seen me talking on the radio, so if I was good enough to be on state radio I was good enough to have a conversation with him.

'Good evening, Señor Sagarra. My name is Yon Dooncan' – well, there wasn't much point in pronouncing it properly any more – 'and I'm a journalist from England. Have you got a couple of minutes to talk to me about Cuban boxing?'

'Do you have any identification?'

'Errm. Yes. Here.' I showed him my three-month temporary hack's card. I was shaking. What a miserable unhelpful git. This was much more the sort of attitude I was used to back home. He examined it for a good ten seconds and looked on the back of it. He had plainly never seen one before in his life and was not about to take it at face value. He made me suffer. Then he looked down his spectacles at me. 'Speak.'

'Erm.' I scrambled for the list of questions, my dignity and cool crumpled on the floor at the spot where he had just stamped on them. And he proceeded to give me a brief interview which, looking at it when I got back to the hotel and transcribed it, was a masterclass in saying absolutely nothing of any real interest and ignoring the subtext of the question, the sense of it, in fact everything to do with the question in favour of wittering on. I thought he should have been a politician and then I remembered that of course he was.

'What do you think of the state of Cuban boxing now compared to the past?'

'Well, Cuban boxing continues to make progress. Here at

the national championship we had 275 boxers who particip-
ated to a high standard over ten days of competition. In each
division we had fifteen to twenty boxers taking part, which
pretty much demonstrates that Cuban boxing is on the way
up.'

'The rules have changed much,' my Spanish was starting to
fail me, 'the five rounds and two minutes . . .'

He finished my sentence for me: 'Well, the world changes
and in every walk of life there is change and sport is just one of
them. This isn't new, it was always in the rules but it just
wasn't ever used. Some countries are against it still, but the
Amateur International Boxing Association [AIBA] says it must
happen so it happens. After the next congress of AIBA they'll
decide. We ourselves are looking into it quite deeply and we'll
give our own opinions on it when that's complete because it's
still too soon to say how the boxers are responding and how
they behave in this sort of combat.'

'What would you do if you were made coach of the British
team, which isn't at the moment all that strong?'

'Well, that's a complicated question because I know the
British, I've had dealings with them but I don't really know
how the people are so it is a bit difficult. The first thing that I
would have to do is find out how to get inside the people in
order to know their personalities and I would also start to do
some work from the bottom upwards in British boxing in
terms of getting more participation because the British also at
some time have had good fighters. We would have to see what
is the matter once we were inside the problem.'

'What do you think makes Cubans such good boxers?'

'Cubans are a naturally rebellious, aggressive people. It's our
history and culture. And we are a mix of a variety of cultures,
black African and Hispanic, dance cultures. You don't need to
educate a Cuban how to move in the ring because they already
know how to come forward and backward in a co-ordinated

way because of dance. Boxing is ballet with aggression and Cubans are well equipped for it.'

'What idiosyncrasy is it that makes Cuban boxers so great not just now but since the triumph of the revolution?' I was crawling now, trying to impress him, make him like me: Cubans talking to officials always called it the triumph of the revolution, never just the revolution.

'The Cuban situation. Well, it has exceptional character-istics for sports and also in our country boxing is one of the national sports. We have a large pool of talent and that gives us the chance with all the coaches and the experience we have had over the years to progress.'

'Finally, in the squad you've chosen today, who do you think are the stars of the future?'

'At this time we have an enlarged squad of about 120 boxers, more or less, and they are all of different ages, so they will reach 2008 in the condition we hoped for. We are planning for 2008 not just 2000. It's the long game that will pay off for us in the end.'

'What inspired you to be a coach in the past?'

'I have loved boxing since I was a boy and I was brought up beside a gym, but I had bad breathing and so I didn't even think about actually becoming a boxer until someone told me it would be good for my asthma. They said the lungs had to develop greatly and boxing was a tough sport and you needed to have a strong will. So that was it.'

'One last question. What do you think, compared to 1961, of professional boxing? Is your objection to professional boxing moral still, do you think it is as immoral as it used to be or a bit better than before?'

'Well, we had professional boxing in Cuba until 1961 and we also had amateur boxing. I believe at this time that, as with everything in life, it has advanced. Boxing is on the up, it's shown on TV, it's popular and all those things, but I don't know anything about pro boxing because I don't work in that branch of the sport.'

'Do you think that Felix Savon is a better heavyweight than Mike Tyson?'

'I don't know anything about professional boxing. I don't follow it and I'm not interested in it, so it is impossible for me to say.'

And with that he switched off the friendly face and asked me if that was it. It was. I now knew that Alcides Sagarra was in no way inclined to be friendly or explore any of the avenues I had thoughtfully plotted out for the transformation of Cuban boxing. My fantasy train had just hit a very real brick wall.

'Don't worry about it,' said Miguel Hernandez as we got on the bus for the twenty-four-hour ride back to Havana. 'He is like that with every foreigner. He's a very serious man.' I sat down at the back of the bus as we prepared to leave. I positioned myself in the emergency exit seat at the back of the bus, where the extra leg room was quickly filled by a huge pile of kitbags full of boxing equipment. The man on the seat next to me introduced himself as Pedro. He was a boxing coach in Havana. I told him who I was and that I was writing a book on Cuban boxers. 'Well, if you like, you should come down to the meeting we're having next month of the Association of Former Cuban Boxers. It's at a place called the Arena Trejo. All the great Cubans who were world champions used to fight there and train there. Bring a bottle of rum and you'd be welcome.' He wrote his name on a piece of card and a telephone number. I rang it a week later, bought a bottle of rum and two cases of beer and got in a taxi. I had no idea why I was bothering. It was only supposed to be a cover story after all.

14 *El Gallego Alvarez*

You find the Arena Trejo down by the port, fifty yards from the main road which whisks lorries and buses through the docks, in the maze of narrow side streets. The meeting of the Association of Former Cuban Boxers, run by Pedro and his friends, was supposed to take place on the first Sunday of every month. 'But we can switch it to the second Sunday if that's more convenient,' he told me over the phone. The reason for the flexibility may have been that I was the first person to be paying admission at the Arena Trejo since the banning of professional boxing in 1961.

The pitch was this. If I turned up with two cases of beer (about $14 each) and maybe a bottle of rum (about $4), I could sit in on one of their meetings, which would always start with a former boxer, usually one of the old pros from before the revolution, running through the details of his career.

'The beer is for us to sell so that we can raise some money towards restoring the old stadium,' said Pedro. Which seemed fair enough, although when I arrived with a friend on the first Sunday in October we drank all the admission fee in a very pleasant couple of hours.

It was hard to imagine that this stadium had once been a major venue. The entrance was tiny, maybe three bodies wide, and when you went in the skeleton of a rusting ring sat in the middle of an open piece of derelict land. There was no roof and you could see the walls of the buildings on either side and piles of rubble in three corners. There was a little shack and store cupboard, and but for the ring and the fact that I had checked the address in what record books there were, this was just another dying Havana building. The major figures of Cuban boxing had all fought here at some stage – Kid Chocolate was mentioned a lot – and Sugar Ray Robinson had trained here once when he was preparing for a fight or an exhibition, no one was quite sure which. The only major figure who hadn't was Kid Gavilan, who, they said, was too snobbish.

'Welcome,' said the chairman. 'This is a meeting of boxing veterans, as you know, and we have with us today El Gallego Alvarez, who had a great career as a boxer. He also wrestled occasionally before the revolution. He was tortured by the Batista tyranny and was a figure recognised all over Cuba. He was a boxer and a referee for many years. Most of us remember El Gallego for his physical strength. The Cuban boxer with probably the biggest punch, Orlando Cepeda, was never able to beat El Gallego. Many foreign boxers came here to Cuba to take him on and not one ever managed to knock him out. He was tough and a real fighter. Comrades . . . El Gallego Alvarez.'

We were sitting in what would have been the entrance to the arena when it was a working building. The corridor between the street and the arena itself was the only part that could be described as a building, about six foot wide and twelve foot long, with chairs placed along the sides and a small noticeboard on the wall. We were sitting only a few yards from the road, which meant that the conversation was punctuated by shouts and car horns and the musak and mayhem of Havana street life.

'The problem is that it seems that I was born to box. I was born in Havana, in Compostela between Teniente Reyes and Muralla, on 21 July 1926. I am now seventy-one years old. My parents bought a place, a small farm, in Mantilla, which was where we worked. I was twelve years old before I wore shoes for the first time and went to school. On the way to school I always walked past the house of Castor Fernandez, a Spanish boxer who was living over here. He was a friend of my dad, who was a cook and worked near Fernandez's place, which was called La Panera, right here in Habana Vieja [old Havana]. I had to walk past the gym every day and I really got excited when I saw what was going on inside. My parents were dead against it though, so I wasn't allowed to go in. Anyway I was hanging around outside one day when I decided to go in. And when I was in there the trainer was saying, "OK, who wants to glove up and have a go at Piton?"

'Well, everyone knew Piton because he was hard as nails, but I stuck my hand up anyway. Piton and me fought like wildcats and effectively beat each other up. So when I got home that night I was covered in bruises and my mum went spare. But after that Castor Fernandez suggested I take boxing up as a sport and promised he would have a word with my dad. There was no convincing my mother, mind you, but there you go. I went down to training with a mate, Miguel Penas Santiago, who had already had a few fights, and a kid he knew from Lawton [a rough Havana suburb] called Ignacio Jardines. When Miguel introduced me and we shook hands you should have felt the size of his hands and I thought I would never be as strong as that. They put me in the ring with a guy called Casanova, who had already had a few fights as well. He gave me an almighty fucking pounding, knocked six shades of shit out of me, and even knocked one of my back teeth out.'

El Gallego smiled at the thought of it, an old man's smile, wistful and gentle. His face was very much like the Arena Trejo itself. There was a lot of history, but a present that was nothing to shout about.

'The gym opened at five p.m. and at four the next day I was outside waiting. They put me in the ring with Casanova again. He was a tough boxer and not bad, but he was quite thin and I had a right go at him in the stomach and put him on the canvas. He went down making a sort of cow noise and he soiled himself. Think about it. I had beaten the hardest kid in the gym on my second time out. I had a few fights in Regla [another hard Havana suburb] and then I moved up to the Arena Cristal. I won almost all my amateur fights.

'In the qualifiers for the Golden Gloves title in '42 I beat Rogelio Cespedes, but I lost against Chano in the next round. No one thought I was going beat Cespedes and no one thought I could possibly lose to Chano and I missed out on a final against a kid from Route 28 [I'd never heard of this place, but El Gallego was in full flow and I wasn't about to stop him and ask].

'I wanted to turn pro after that and I went to a new gym to do it. My debut as a pro was against Panchito Castaneda and I lost, which shook up the trainers, who thought maybe I shouldn't carry on. I lost to him twice again in rapid succession after that, but it was what I wanted and they gave in and organised fights for me. They put me up against Angel E, who was quite a stylish boxer, and I won on a technical knockout in the second round.

'At about this time a manager called Pepino Prieto wanted me to sign for him and told me that if he was running me I would be the featherweight champion of Cuba within a year. But he wanted a five-year deal and I only wanted two and after going round in circles I didn't sign the contract. Then a guy called Alejandro, I think, was sniffing around me, but he was offering only five years as well so that fell through too. I fought lightweight and featherweight, but I lost against Lino Garcia, then Povei, then Patterson Carale. I beat Joe, er, I don't remember his second name, and another guy. Funny, I never forget the names of the guys who beat me. I won eighty-nine fights, drew twelve and lost twenty-two.'

El Gallego reeled off a whole list of names at this point, counting them on his fingers as he did so. This was a speech he had rehearsed and given many times before. It was fascinating. He was no champion and had plainly messed up his career pretty badly. I had no idea who he was, had never heard of him or read about him. But he talked in colour of an era that I could only see in black and white. He took a sip from the glass of rum that was on the floor beside his seat, an armchair with torn covers, and carried on.

'You know, I never complained about a decision. They robbed me sometimes and I robbed them sometimes. Though I probably got robbed more than I did the robbing because I had no one hustling for me. I never signed a contract with anyone.

'I suffered for that. When I fought Miro, for example, his manager also happened to be the commissioner of boxing, who wanted to do a bit of managing on the side. He wanted a fight with me because I was supposed to be a proper test for good fighters. It was hard to knock me down. His manager's idea was that he would knock me out, get great publicity and move on to better things. To help Miro they cut the fight to eight rounds and then to six. Well, my strength was that I never tired, so that took away my best weapon. I was really fit for those days, I could go ten rounds as easily as drinking a glass of water. We started the fight really going at each other, but he couldn't put me down because more than anything I could take a punch. It was an even fight, but I thought I just about edged it. He got the decision.

'So anyway they set up the rematch for a few weeks later, but the promoter came to me the Tuesday before the fight and told me it was off because Miro had gonorrhoea. I was a young bloke so I went out on the town and stopped training for a few days until they came and found me in a bar on the Friday, the night before the fight, and told me there had been a mistake. Miro was fine and the fight was on. I was furious. I remember throwing an inkwell at the promoter and getting myself covered in ink. But the fight happened and it was just like the first one, very even, and yet again they gave the fight to Miro. These two fights were the saddest and most hurtful moments of my career because I knew I could beat him.

'I fought seventeen times abroad, in Miami and Tampa. I fought twice in Venezuela, three times in Jamaica. I won all seventeen in Miami because in those days if you lost a fight there you didn't get another one. I fought one guy who was a middleweight champion three times and they were great fights. Over there I was with Charolito, with El Cheo Olivera, against Layalo and Williams. In Miami I remember fighting Tommy Borsano and Xavier Chu.' He was back to the names again, a roll-call, a summoning of journeymen ghosts who had long since died in the public imagination, but who lived on in the memory of their journeyman comrade in a derelict venue in Havana. 'I never got paid all that much in Cuba because none of my fights were really big deals, but in Venezuela I cleared $1,000 for a fight and $750 for another. In the US too I was earning $500 or $600 a fight, but here in Havana I never made more than $200. There wasn't actually that much real corruption here in Cuba, it was much worse in the US. I remember being offered money to throw a fight in Jamaica and when I refused they threatened to kill me. Because of the threats they had to put police all around the ring when I was fighting to protect me. But that was the only time.'

Alvarez quit and came back to Havana. 'I lost most of my

cash trying to start a gym back in my home town with a local baker. It only lasted a year. It was a financial disaster though we did train a 112lb champion called Herrera. But he decided to become a pianist and packed in boxing, so that was that.'

El Gallego got a job in a factory and trained to be a referee. But his trade union activities quickly brought him to the attention of the state. 'I was about five months into a six-month course under the supervision of Johnny Cruz when they came and arrested me and put me in prison. The special police took me in to the station and tortured me, beat me up, gave me a right knocking about and then sent me to prison, the Principe prison, which became a model prison after the triumph of the revolution. After the fall of Batista I got out and tried to get back into boxing but they told me that I couldn't because I hadn't finished the referee's course. Eventually I passed and became an amateur referee, but I was never allowed to take part in international competition because they told me it wasn't allowed because I had fought as a pro. I don't know if that's true or not, but anyway I was a referee here in Cuba for years. The biggest honour was when I got to referee Teofilo Stevenson against a kid called Benito Diaz. It was an honour just to be allowed in the ring with Stevenson. He was awesome.

'I'd like to still be working but my knees have gone and I can't get around a ring like I used to.' He stopped and looked towards the chairman of the meeting. This was it. He didn't want to talk any more. He didn't like this part. Like the Arena Trejo he was never going to recapture what he once had. He was a journeyman and his journey had ended.

15 *Go Away and Don't Come Back*

A couple of weeks after the meeting in the Arena Trejo I decided to go home. Well, it was decided for me because my visa ran out. I went with Martha Gonzalez to the International Press Centre to meet the moustachioed bureaucrat who was in charge of journalists from England. He was distinctly unhelpful this time around and it was obvious he did not enjoy the same rapport with Martha as he had with Susanna, my old landlady. 'We only give out these visas for three months and your three months are finished now. We cannot issue another one from here in Havana, you will have to go back to England and apply to the embassy in London for entry as a journalist and come back.'

'But all that the embassy there will do is ring you up and ask for authorisation and if you accept they will accept. What is the point?'

'Those are the rules and there is nothing I can do about them. But don't worry, when the embassy call us I am sure everything will be OK.'

I was less frustrated by this than otherwise I might have been because in truth I wanted a break from Cuba. Living abroad in a country where the opportunities to talk without having to think of every word or find a simplistic way round grammatical problems is exhausting. The requirements of speaking in a different language make you a different person. You don't understand how much of your own personality is defined by the words you use and your ability to play with words until that ability is taken from you.

There were good things. I had adapted to Cuban Spanish by becoming more flamboyant in gestures and speech, I made faces of confusion, or disappointment, or annoyance, that I didn't need to make in England because I had words to convey them for me. I had become more melodramatic than was my custom because that was how people spoke and much of learning a language is about mimicking, copying gestures and accents and faces. The words, I had found, were not enough. But not only was I a different person, I didn't have anyone to whom I could unburden myself about what I was actually doing there, no one to bounce ideas off. Having to lock away a part of yourself at the same time as becoming a different person in a different language is psychologically gut-busting.

And I needed to see Frank Warren to ask him what he wanted to do next, whether the defeat of Savon affected his view of the project, whether he even knew about it, whether he wanted me to set up some official meetings so he could take the project to the next stage. I also needed some money. The first payment of £10,000 had arrived after some prompting and cajoling in early January. The second was due in March and I wanted to make sure that it was going to be paid.

There was a slight logistical problem in that the airline on which I had come to Cuba, Viasa, the Venezualan national airline, had gone bankrupt in the three months after I arrived. I discovered this in February when I went to change the date of my return flight and found a typewritten notice in the window of their offices in the Havana Libre Hotel.

Iberia, the Spanish airline, which had caused the collapse by pulling all their money out of Viasa under pressure from the European Union, were offering alternative flights to those stranded by the collapse, but the flights before my visa ran out were fully booked and all they could do was put me on a waiting list. Enter Martha Gonzalez. She took me down to the Aeroflot offices. She had a neighbour in Aeroflot bookings, who had a friend who worked in Iberia next door. She explained that I was on the waiting list, but that I had to get out before my visa ran out. He listened, took the waiting-list number and disappeared. We sat and waited, with my private visions of being banned from the country for overstaying my visa festering and itching. And waited. Until Martha's neighbour came back.

'Take this piece of paper, go next door and ask for Carlos.'

We went next door to the Iberia office, which was an exact replica of the Aeroflot office apart from a series of posters showing the history of the Iberia livery on its planes, from the Thirties to the modern day. We waited for Carlos while the usual gaggle of people came in trying to change flights or get refunds, only to be told that what they wanted was impossible or cost money. Carlos finally appeared and I handed him the piece of paper. He looked around quite casually and started tapping into the computer. He said nothing. We said nothing. He stopped when a supervisor walked past. He started again when the supervisor was gone. At that moment I loved this man. Then a wailing dot-matrix printer burst into life on the table and he handed us the Viasa ticket with a faintly printed slip of paper and a confirmed flight out of Havana on the very night that my visa ran out.

I arrived at the airport three hours before departure in the habitual but entirely hopeless expectation of getting one of the emergency exit seats. After failing, I checked in and sat in the café outside the immigration desks to read *Our Man in*

Havana, a book I hadn't picked up since I was at school. Now seemed as good a time as any to give it another crack. It made me laugh out loud. It was hard to believe that any city could have changed so little in the forty years since Graham Greene had captured it so perfectly. It wasn't surprising to find familiar streets and locations dotted throughout the book. Though the Wonder Bar and the Havana Club didn't exist and the Seville Biltmore was just the plain Sevilla and the Havana Hilton was the Havana Libre, it didn't take much imagination to see that the geography and architecture of the city were the same. Even more striking was that the atmosphere of the city, which should have been so different, forty years and a whole new social system later, wasn't. There it all was in Greene's book. The corrupt death rattle of the last days of a dictator, the heavy fog of misinformation, suspicion, veiled intimidation, the overpowering sense of a larger invisible power being used both brutally and comically, bureaucracy and chaos and a shoulder-shrugging approach to what was the law and what was acceptable behaviour, the difference between the untorturable foreigner class and the seeming worthlessness of the local and the instinct for survival that was the foundation of a thriving black market. It wasn't exactly the same. People weren't as afraid. They didn't disappear. They wanted things to work out. They didn't want a new revolution. There was pride in much of what the revolution had achieved, where there were only resignation and disgust at Batista and his American cronies whom Greene had portrayed so well. But only an idiot wouldn't have noticed that Greene's Havana and Castro's didn't feel as distant from each other as they should have done.

There were two hours to go to the flight, via Madrid, so I headed for immigration, a row of booths with narrow entrances that led to a wooden door with no handle. You couldn't see who was inside the booth until it was your turn.

There was no indicator to tell you even whether there was an official in the booth or if there was anyone having their documents checked inside it. You would wait in line for thirty minutes at least, listening to the sounds of the airport, the announcements of flights being punctuated by the thud, thud, thud, buzz, which meant that some sunburnt tourist had in fact got the right documents, everything was in order and after five minutes of furious scribbling and studious noting they were to have the honour of being allowed to leave the country.

It was my turn. I handed over the passport and my temporary journalist's visa. It was to be expected that this would throw a system which took ten minutes to process a normal passport with a tourist visa. I had come in as a tourist, had changed my status to journalist (stamp in passport to confirm the fact, journalist's ID card to reconfirm it) and was now leaving the day before my visa expired. I reckoned maybe twenty minutes. After only three minutes, though, he called the top man over, army uniform, green, neat and pressed. He ummed and aahed and pointed at the passport, flicking over the pages violently and looking puzzled. 'Could you step aside, please? We are going to have to make some security checks. Please confirm the address at which you have been resident.' Neither I nor they realised what a wonderful moment they had just handed me. Well, not a moment but an hour actually. As the Cuban secret services checked out my identity and my cover story and my documents, not knowing that I was in fact a total fraud, I finished off *Our Man in Havana* – sleazy, scary Captain Segura, lists of secret agents, vacuum cleaners and constructions in Oriente, poisoned whisky, the torturable classes – leaning against the window of their control post. The darkness at the end of the book which follows the comedy was powerful and moving. A good man dies in *Our Man in Havana* because of Wormold's fantasies and inventions. I wondered whether I too should be taking what I had got myself into a little more seriously.

Finally the immigration official called me back to his booth and actually smiled. He made polite conversation – utterly unheard of and I'm sure totally against the regulations. It spooked me badly. Why was he being so nice? Did they know? Did they reckon I was a friendly spy just doing my job, one of them maybe, a harmless foreign agent whom they had covered and who was now going home with nothing useful? Did they know that from whoever had been watching me? Was it Martha Gonzalez? Had they deliberately made space for me on this plane so they could be sure I had left the country? Aeroflot. Russia. It all made sense. Who had they been talking to in that hour? This sort of paranoia was the reason why I was going home for a few weeks.

It was the strangest sensation to be driving back into central London after three months away. Of course I'd been out of town before for a month at the Olympics, but the whole of the profession had decamped there as well and it wasn't that different from life at home. But on a sharp sunny February morning after three months in a run-down, fume-filled capital where everyone stares at you and everyone wears the same sort of clothes and the faces on the street come from a fairly narrow selection of colours and styles and races, London seemed a great city.

I stared at the people crossing the road outside Euston as I headed in a black cab for the office to drop off some film from Holguin for the *Observer*, which was publishing a small piece about the championships. Asians, Chinese, Latinos, Africans, Afro-Caribbeans, white English, blond, red-headed, brown-headed, dyed hair, curly, straight, men in suits and in tracksuits, women in smart clothes dashing through their lunch hour. Tall buildings, old buildings, new buildings that weren't falling down, new architecture with glass and metal, old architecture with sandstone and statues. I fell in love with London again as willingly and helplessly as I had fallen in love with Havana twelve months before. I felt calm and at home for the first time in three months. I went into work and talked to everyone I had left behind. It was the same bunch of people in the same desks, but I just wanted to grab them and tell them how much I loved them. I felt like a sentimental old hippy.

I had arranged to stay with some friends, Mike Ellison from the *Guardian* and Lucy Cavendish of the *Sunday Telegraph* magazine, in their sparish room. It was only for a couple of weeks anyway, so I figured they wouldn't mind too much. I'd brought them a framed Cuban film poster back as a thank-you. I ended up on their floor for close to two months.

The problem was the Cubans. The guy in the media centre in Havana had lied to me. After five weeks of phone calls about when they were going to renew my journalists' visa the embassy rang me up to say that it had been refused. The press centre in Havana felt that I had had three months and that ought to have been enough. I didn't buy a ticket back to Havana. To keep myself busy I went into the *Guardian* office each day and did odd bits of work. I even got dragged in to helping design a new Saturday sports section with the deputy sports editor. Next to my notes on Holguin I have notes for a couple of matches at Leeds and Crystal Palace which I covered. I wrote a column on Joe Royle, the Everton manager, which may have contributed in some small way to his demise as manager not long after. I kept in touch with Cuba intermittently, once ringing Martha to ask her what had been the favourite television soaps in Cuba during the past few years for a short *Guardian* feature. I still owe her £30 for that. In short I was slipping willingly back into my old life.

Except that I couldn't, could I? I'd put the phone call off for two weeks, but eventually I had to pick it up and dial Frank Warren.

'Hello. Sports Network.'

'Hello, Jean. It's John.'

'Hello, John. How are you?'

I think she remembered me from when I was trying to set up meetings with Frank before. Or maybe she was faking it because the one time I tried to call Frank from Cuba reverse charges, as you had to do if you didn't have a special international phone line in your house, she refused to accept the charges. Maybe it was company policy.

'Can I speak to Frank's secretary?' I said.

'Putting you through,' she sang back. Click answering machine.

I left a message this time and another a few days later and then another until I was practically best friends with Jean. She was always charming and it didn't really worry me that no one seemed to be replying to me. Eventually I got a call. A meeting was scheduled for a Thursday in March. Phone in the morning to confirm. As I expected, the meeting was cancelled. I forgot about the rescheduled meeting and was in the bath when I got a call saying that it had been cancelled as well. I did my best to sound disappointed and not splash around too much. The next possible reschedule was in two weeks, by which time I had decided I would be back in Havana. I never did get to see Frank. And I never saw any more money from him. It felt as if he had moved on and had other fish to fry. In a way it was a relief because now the decision on what to do next was mine. There was no question of doing it just because Frank expected it because it seemed as if Frank had forgotten who I was.

I was tempted not to go back to Cuba at all. Warren didn't seem bothered about the money he had already spent, and I still had a few bob of it left. But then I didn't have anywhere to live any more – my sister was in my flat and although I was house-sitting for a friend who had moved to Scotland that wouldn't last more than another month because the flat was being sold. Neither did I have a permanent job – the sports correspondent position had been given to someone else on a twelve-month contract. Worst of all, though, not going back would have been a terrible admission of defeat, a desperate and cowardly veering away from what the year had always been supposed to be about – not being a journalist, having an adventure, changing the person that I was. I had to go back or know in my heart that I was a failure however much I could justify it to myself. I also knew that I had already got closer to the Cubans than anyone before me. So when I booked my ticket back to Havana it was less out of fear this time than personal pride.

But I needed to know I could stay longer than a thirty-day tourist card would allow me to. Martha Gonzalez, with a predictable instinct for protecting her dollar income, came up with the answer. Around the corner from where I lived in Cuba was the former training institute of the Foreign Ministry. Before the Russians upped and left it was a thriving Marxist institute in which students and post-graduates studied Marxist foreign policy and theorised about the Cold War, but latterly it had had neither the teachers nor the resources to offer more than one or two courses for workers in the Ministry or up-and-coming functionaries. Martha had found out that, in order to survive, they taught Spanish to wealthy foreigners and diplomats, whom they charged $1,000 for the privilege. However, because she knew the people there, they had agreed to charge me $500 for a year and they would organise the visa when I got there. Given that their Ministry issued the visas, it was pretty much guaranteed that I would get one. I would have to study for three hours each weekday morning, which didn't seem too bad given that I needed to improve my Spanish anyway. It was perfect, if a little expensive. I said goodbye to England with a six-month return ticket in my pocket, from Cubana this time, after stocking up on CDs, books and magazines and buying vitamins, paracetamol and Tampax for friends back in Havana. As usual I failed to get the emergency exit seat and as usual there was a group of musicians at the back, smoking and drinking and chatting. As usual my bags came off last. As usual I promised myself that I would get luggage insurance next time.

While I had been away, however, a great deal had changed. A string of fast-food restaurants had sprung up all over town practically overnight, a state-owned chain of dollar burger bars called El Rapido (The Quick One), knocked together on street corners and city-centre sites that might attract tourists and the Cubans with dollars who lived off them. They were passable imitations of franchised low-rent burger bars like McDonald's, with a kitchen out back where the food, mainly chicken and chips and fresh-from-a-tin hot dogs, was lined up. The staff wore clean uniforms: stripy shirts, red skirts or trousers, and baseball caps with a cute company logo. There were even colour photos and comforting modern plastic furnishings, which stood out in Havana because they were neither crumbling nor obviously Soviet influenced. The one Cuban element in the operation was that no El Rapido I went in had burgers because, though they were advertised and looked great in the photos, they didn't seem to be supplied with them.

But there was something else too; more fear and less hope than there had been before. There was a sense that the government wanted to claw back what it had given out during the special period. There was talk of swingeing new taxes against those involved in legal private enterprises such as taxis and renting rooms to foreigners. There were plans for a change in the identity card system which would enable the police to identify anyone who did not have official permission to be in Havana. There were yet more police in the city. There were loud rumours of mass deportations by train of those who fell foul of the new regulations, though in true

Cuban style none of the stories of the brutality of these random expulsions was ever substantiated, although this didn't stop people believing them. The atmosphere was different, altogether more menacing. For the first time what I was doing didn't feel jolly and quixotic. It felt dangerous.

16 *Felix Savon*

If the atmosphere around Havana was tense, the atmosphere around the boxers as individuals remained friendly. I met Felix Savon Fabre, around whom all my plans supposedly revolved on a number of occasions. Two months after my return we talked in the cafeteria above the Arena Ramon Fonst, a multi-purpose indoor stadium which looks like an oversized Soviet-designed chicken shed and is named after Cuba's greatest fencer. I had come to see Savon box and found him sitting tracksuited by the window with an ice cream, chatting to an Italian tourist, polite and friendly but disengaged, one eye on the boxing but pausing to smile at the Italian who had two young black women with him. I went over to say hello, to ask if he remembered me from Holguin, and he smiled in recognition. 'Yes, Eeenglish,' he said with a wry smile, and tapped my outstretched hand with his fist. And then he was gone: he was fighting in thirty minutes against another Cuban international who represented little more than a routine work-out for him. He won at half pace on points. But there was something lacking: the defeat in Holguin seemed to have damaged his desire.

Then, a month later, I met him again at the National Sports Museum, a sad place next to the Arena Fonst which housed a bowling alley on the ground floor and the museum above. The bowling alley was apparently in pristine condition, but none of the machinery worked so it wasn't in use. It had been built by the Eastern Bloc, but there were no spare parts to be had, so it just sat there, polished, gleaming, utterly useless in a city where there was nothing to do. What a waste. Above the bowling alley was the Sports Museum, which with a little imagination could have been turned into a tourist attraction but was a limp collection of old shirts, shoes and photographs in glass cases, with bad and sometimes incorrect handwritten labels. It was permanently deserted. I went there one day and the roof had leaked in a storm, so part of it was cordoned off to the imaginary public. Felix Savon and Juan Hernandez Sierra, two of the biggest stars of Cuban boxing, were coming to give a talk to schoolchildren. Only one group of about twenty turned up.

Savon gave a brief chat and asked for questions. All he got was open-mouthed, awestruck silence.

'Who wants to be a boxer?' he asked. Silence as every boy in the room stared at him transfixed.

'What about you?' he said, pointing at a terrified-looking girl of about ten. She shook her head rapidly.

And then he chatted about how he hadn't wanted to be a boxer either, about how important it was to be good to your parents and do what they say and eat everything if you wanted to grow up to be big and strong like him. They warmed to him and he played with them. He lunged unexpectedly at one kid on the front row, who practically fell off his chair in terror. Then Savon ruffled his hair and the kid had a story that would keep him in playground credibility for the rest of the year. With kids he looked at home, normal, happy.

'One of the things that I had always missed in life was not

having kids because we thought my wife couldn't have them,' he said when I asked him if he had enjoyed the day. 'But it used to depress me because I love kids and there are always kids around me asking me questions and all my friends had kids. It was my ambition for a long time to have kids. We got some treatment for my wife in Havana eventually and we had twins and I feel my life is complete.'

A little while after the museum talk I told him I wanted to have a chat about his career. He said politely that he didn't really have time, but if I bought him a couple of bucks worth of petrol he would give me a lift home. So we got into a car he had borrowed, a red open-topped Cadillac, battered and worn but a cool enough car none the less. It didn't have a starter motor, so he dragooned three passing youths into giving us a push. Smoke billowed from the exhaust and we were off.

Savon talks awkwardly, slurring every word in the way that eastern Cubans do. His speech impediment had been much worse until he came to Havana and had it corrected by specialists brought in by the team. They thought about surgery, but instead gave him speech therapy that involved reading more and repeating difficult words again and again. We talked a little on the way home, but I couldn't really understand what he was saying. We stopped at a petrol station and put in a couple of dollars of fuel. Some soldiers in the back of a lorry watched with the same gaping wonder that the children had done earlier. This reaction was obviously a constant of Savon's life. But no one bothered him and no one did anything more than look. No one wanted to take him on or abuse him from a distance. Tyson could never have got away with this in New York.

We met a few times more over the following months until I knew Savon well enough not to have to introduce myself and he would chat happily. One day I asked him for his telephone number and suggested I buy him lunch. He accepted.

Getting to Savon's house, close to the airport and away from the easily comprehended grid system of the centre of the city, is no easy matter. He lives in a neat residential area of single-storey houses with small gardens. Every road looks much the same as another, and although they still have a grid there are few hints as to which street is which. The taxi driver's strategy for finding the house was to get as close as he could and then just ask where Felix Savon lived, in the certain knowledge that everyone would know. His confidence was not misplaced and we arrived after only a few brief interrogations and mistakes. Savon's house stands on a corner at the edge of the development, with fields and trees beyond the front door. The house is fenced in, less to protect the contents from burglars than to contain the goats that Savon still keeps (you can take the man out of the countryside but you can't take the countryside out of the man). The goats, having mown the strip of lawn around Savon's house down to the soil, make occasional dashes for the lush grass on the verges and unfenced gardens surrounding the house if the gate is left open and the neighbours regularly complain when their shrubs and bushes are ripped up. I suspect they do it from a distance.

Savon is in the garage with the bonnet of his car up. The taxi driver shows me to the garage and then immediately starts talking with Savon about the engine and pointing. Savon nods and sucks some petrol from the carburettor with a piece of plastic tubing. The job done, Savon ushers me into the house and waves goodbye to the taxi driver. Inside the house is neat and tidy with a large sitting room and a huge sofa that faces a cabinet which contains a television. The television is on and loud and there are three other people there, Savon's friends and relations. Just off the living room is a dark room where Savon keeps his boxing stuff. It's full of boxes and old furniture, but he manages to pull out a few less than gleaming trophies and pennants with Cyrillic writing from tournaments in Eastern Europe. The rest, as I have come to expect by now, are kept for him by the team. His wife is watching television too. She takes the bottle of rum I have brought into the kitchen and returns with a full glass and an ashtray. Before we can talk one of Savon's friends is discussing with him how they can get into the bedroom where his twins are sleeping. The bedroom has a Chubb lock on it. The key to the door has accidentally been left inside with the children, who are too young to know how to open it. The choice being discussed is breaking the window above the door or trying to break the door down. Eventually a small boy is summoned to climb through the window and open it. Finally we sit down.

Felix Savon Fabre comes from the province of Guantanamo, the site of the US naval base, which is a wonderful symbol of the childish relationship between the two countries. The base was leased in perpetuity to the United States by the pre-revolutionary government for what now seems a peppercorn annual rent. Castro receives the cheque each year and refuses to cash it. In bad times the Cubans try to cut off the water to the base or try some administrative ruse to make life difficult. But things go on pretty much as normal despite it all.

Havana Cubans regard the east of the country much as southern English regard northerners, northern Italians regard southerners and New Yorkers regard Texans. It's a rural area dominated by coffee and sugar production but it's where the revolution was born, in the mountains of the Sierra Maestra, where Castro, Che and Camilo Cienfuegos fought the world's first guerrilla war against the Batista government and won. Those from the east think Habaneros are unfriendly and money-grabbing. Habaneros think that those from Oriente are barely more intelligent than the pigs they are all believed to keep in their front rooms. While Havana has lost faith in the purity of the revolution's ideals, the eastern provinces, where the plantation owners and their semi-feudal system of working was most hard felt and loathed and where the benefits of the revolution were strongest, have kept the faith alive.

Savon was born on 22 September 1967 in San Vicente, which is a tiny farming community a couple of kilometres from the town of Jamaica. He rarely went to the provincial capital, the town of Guantanamo, and spent the whole of his early life going between San Vicente and Jamaica, for school, for play, out of boredom and to help his family.

'I used to have to fetch water from the tank outside San Vicente. Now they have a water tank right in the middle of the village, but in those days they didn't. The trouble was that the village was getting bigger and bigger all the time and the nearest well, which was about a kilometre from my house, was always running dry. So most of the time I would go to the river which was three kilometres away with a big bucket, which I used to put on my head. If I needed to fetch more water I used to get a towel and wind it up tight and tie the buckets together and balance them across my shoulder. As a kid I made that journey two or three times a day.'

Savon's family lived in a former slave dormitory, crammed in with several other families until eventually they got a place of their own. 'My parents divorced when I was only a few years old and I was the man of the house very early in my life. I didn't have an older brother and I was brought up among women with my mother and my four sisters. I had to do all the heavy work like fetching water because of that and because my mum had a job in the fields. Outside the harvest season she used to work in the sugar fields and during it she worked in a canteen for the farmers. When I was seven years old, I think, I started school in San Vicente and it was in the fourth year there that I started to do athletics practice. To be honest, though, there wasn't a lot of time for playing for me in those days because whenever I got home from school my mum was washing or getting water and so I just put my stuff down and helped her. My sisters would always have a row with her if she asked them to help. They'd start saying; "Oh, Mum, why don't you ask one of the others?" and there would be a row. It was easier for me to just get on with it and help her myself. I hated to see my mother slaving away on her own. I've always been more close to my mother than my father, while my sisters were just the opposite.'

Savon was not a naturally aggressive child and laughs as he says his sisters had to stick up for him when he was young. It was following his sisters' example that drew him into organised sport.

'When I was about nine or ten I was actually a bit of a coward and my stepfather used to have to force me to stick up for myself if someone did something bad to me. I didn't really know anything about sport, I was just a little peasant boy. I used to play a little baseball with the other kids and I liked it. My father played baseball. But I used to drive the other kids mad because I was very quick and I was constantly robbing bases and starting rows and the kids were always laughing at me. They used to call me the Mad Machine [*Carro Loco*]. When there was a semi-official game I was always picked because I was pretty good and distracted the opposition. But I wasn't there a lot of the time because I took my housework seriously. The neighbours knew I would always help them out and they would send me to Jamaica on errands for rum or cigarettes and I used to make the journey four or five times a day. But I was happy. I liked walking and being out in the open. Even now I can't sit around in the house for long.'

Savon's size drew him into fighting. Despite his nature he was, from an early age, tall and thin and muscled. That meant, as he got older and the kids organised themselves into gangs, it was Savon who was always put up to fight kids from other gangs. 'In those days there were some rivalries among the villages around there that got quite nasty – the police have clamped down on it now. Well, San Vicente's rivals were San Emilio. The kid who always ended up having to fight for the honour of San Vicente was me. When I was ten I came up against this kid called Moreto, who was much bigger than me. He was eighteen years old and, me, I wasn't even in secondary school. He scared me. But I hit him with everything – headbutts, bites, knees to the groin, kicks, elbows – and all he managed to get me with was one bite. I beat him pretty good. Then I had to take on a little black kid called Libusnay, who was also older than me and who terrorised the neighbourhood. He was the leader of the kids' gangs there. He frightened me too. He used to try and wind me up, pushing me, patting me on the bum, trying to get a rise out of me, but I was too scared of him. Someone told my stepdad that I wasn't taking this guy on and he told me to just get on with it and fight this kid. I did and I won and from then on I was the unofficial head of the school, all the kids looked up to me.

'There was a boxer living in my town at that time called Armando Gomez. He was in the national team at the Finca in Havana. When Armando was on holiday back in San Vicente or at Christmas he would bring some gloves back with him and put them on the kids and mess around. The only one who actually did any boxing with him though, only playing of course, was me. I took quite a few punches. We used to have little exhibitions which the neighbours used to come and watch and even though I took a few shots from him it was a good training and I used to enjoy it a lot. That was, I suppose, my first introduction to boxing as such, but being a boxer couldn't have been further from my mind. I'd never seen a proper boxing bout because there wasn't any television or even electricity where I lived.'

With no driving ambition to be a sportsman, the main impulse behind Savon's entry into the Cuban sports system was still his family and his physical attributes, but these were qualities that could be exploited in any number of sports. Savon bent with the wind, helped his mum, did what others suggested and tried to stick as close to his sisters as he could.

'In about 1979 or 1980 my sister started in athletics at her school. When I joined her at secondary school in Jamaica they put me in the athletics team too. This was a tough time for us and getting into sport didn't help. I was growing very fast and my mother kept on having to sew my kit back together with a few extra bits tagged on to make them fit because I grew out of them so quickly and she couldn't afford to pay for new kit. We didn't have money.

'One day a sports coach came to the school looking for volunteers to try out in rowing. I loved the water and I could swim like a fish so I put my hand up. I did well at rowing and I attended EIDE, which is the first stage to entering top-flight sport in Cuba, the local elite teams. Initially I went there two or three times with the rowing team and the kids used to call me Teofilo because I was so big, though I had no idea what they meant. I didn't make it into the team. My friends told me it didn't matter, that I was big enough to do whatever sport I wanted, but by then it was too late, the other teams had already been picked and I was out of EIDE. I begged my sister, who was already there, to speak to the teachers and see if they could find something for me. After a while, about halfway through the year, just as people were dropping out with injuries or being kicked out for indiscipline, they sent a boxing trainer, Hugo Fernandez, to look for me. He turned up at my school, stood in front of the class and said, 'Which one is Felix Savon?' and then asked me if I fancied doing boxing at EIDE. Of course, all I wanted in the world was to go to EIDE with my sister, so I said yes straight away. The only thing they told me I had to do was take my ration card in and have my meat ration taken off it because they were going to feed me in EIDE now. They told me I had to get a grown-up to do it for me, but everyone there knew me and trusted me so I did it myself that same day and went home. When I told my mum what I had done she didn't like it one little bit. It was my dad who convinced her it was OK. He told her that if she loved me so much she should let me go because otherwise I could end up being drafted by the army to fight in Angola or Ethiopia or somewhere in Africa and that I could end up dead. He scared her pretty well and convinced her to let me try it out. My mum took me the first day but never came again. My father came after about a month and he had totally changed his tune. He was shouting at me and telling me if I didn't get out and forget about being a boxer he was going to kick my ass all the way back to San Vicente. He said I wasn't born to be a boxer I was born to be a dancer – I'd been to Havana as a kid and won a prize on a TV programme called *Para Bailar*. My dad went to see all the trainers and all the teachers at the school and told them that I was stopping. They asked him who I lived with and when I said that it was my mum, they said it was up to her to decide. I don't remember exactly why, but she let me stay.

'When I went to EIDE everyone wanted to have a go at me. When I walked in on the first day they were whispering, "Here comes fresh meat," because I had never been away from home before and I must have looked intimidated. They all tried to wind me up, but I didn't get into any fights because I thought it wiser to save myself for the ring. I beat everybody there so they sent me straight from the juniors to the national team. There used to be competitions between the various regional EIDEs to see who would move up to the national junior team level to the ESPA; and the boy who was supposed to win that year was called Lino Famide. In the final to decide who was going to Havana he was beating me, but I let this swinging right go and put him flat out on the floor. So I went to the national junior team and not him.'

In his first few months at ESPA, Savon's rise had been

impressive. His style was chaotic and unpredictable, but he was being noticed. At fifteen, with a seriously damaged hand, he lost the 1982 national youth championships. His hand was injured in the semi-final and the trainers kept it in ice until the moment before he got in the ring. He tried to ignore the pain, but couldn't and was knocked out. This only acted as a motor for further self-inflicted punishment when he tried to treat the hand with vinegar, ice, warm paraffin, anything that might make a difference. At the same time he hit walls – as he had heard Stevenson had done to strengthen his own fists – and got to work on the bag of sand with added gusto. He even sought help from santeria, the Afro-Catholic religion which combines the Catholic saints with African gods and superstitions. It was still popular in Cuba despite a theoretical ban on religion. The treatment he was given by the santero (priest) involved making cuts in his hand with a knife to sacrifice blood to Ogun, the god of war.

'People say to me now that they knew I would be a champion from the first day that I entered boxing. I honestly had never heard of Teofilo Stevenson until people egged me on, telling me to jump over the ropes like Teofilo did. I didn't like the idea much, but I did it for them. And then as time went by I tried to copy Teofilo in every way that I could.

'Alcides Sagarra came to the ESPA after a short time and moved me to the senior national team. I remember in those days I had a bag of sand above my bed so that if I woke up during the night I could hit it and practise combinations. Everyone else had one pumped up with air, but I wanted sand to harden up my hands. They brought me straight into the national set-up in 1985. I started that year by winning the national championships at the age of sixteen, beating Hermenegildo Baez, who was still the best in the division then.' He beat Baez again in the international tournament, the Copa Cardin, which was held a few months later. Savon knocked him out easily and then sent a Russian to the floor with a right hand that broke his nose.

'It ought to have made me feel excited, but to be honest I'm not a deep thinker. I've never thought much of the future nor of the past. I just trained and trained and I never really thought about why I was doing it and I'm still like that and I think that's why I'm successful.'

Savon, however, had problems with schooling. One condition of entry into the elite of Cuban athletics is a certain level of education and he did not have the pre-university requirement. It says a certain amount about Cuban socialism that it insists on educating sports people rather than chewing them up, ripping them up and spitting them out as had happened, undeniably, in pre-revolutionary boxing, whose myriad sad tales of boxers made good then bad fed the revolution's loathing for professional sports. To suggest either that this is a convenient way of giving their athletes a spurious career outside boxing which might maintain the amateur illusion (Savon is listed in competition directorates as still being a student at the age of thirty-two) or that it merely mimics the US college system, where even the greatest basketball stars have to achieve a certain level in exam results to keep the right to their scholarships and their keys to the professional world, would be to invite a big row.

Like the United States, the system could be stretched to include sports-related studies to smooth the intellectual progress of sports people, but it couldn't be broken entirely. So Savon, as a young boxer, was obliged to get up at six in the morning to train before heading off at six in the afternoon to study, returning at midnight on the deeply unreliable bus service to the Finca on the outskirts of the city. These studies continued into his university days, though at least those were a mere three days a week of long days training and studying.

Once he was brought into the Finca at the age of sixteen,

Savon entered a world of adults. It was a team of well-established stars who had little in common with him. Sagarra took him under his wing and made him realise that he was not yet a boxer. His advice to Savon was, 'Don't keep going forward when you throw a punch, don't let your guard down, don't get over-excited in the ring and forget where you are.'

In 1986 he was judged ready to represent Cuba at the world championships in Reno. 'That championship was Teofilo Stevenson's last major international tournament and my first. In fact I had to help prepare Teofilo for that competition. We really helped each other out in the build-up, sparring and talking a lot during the tournament. I was a cocky kid and while everyone, including me, respected Teofilo it was me who was responsible for getting in the ring and giving him a proper work-out and testing him. It was the moment when the handover took place between me, who was just starting, and Teofilo, who was about to retire.

'We were different weights, remember. He was superheavyweight and I was heavyweight, but a lot of people were already looking to me to fill his shoes – they used to call me Little Teofilo (Teofilito) and I didn't really like that because I wasn't Teofilo I was me. They used to tell me that I was his successor, the new Stevenson, and I hated that too because I wanted to be known for me, for who I was. I didn't want to be the new anyone.

'We fought in a sparring contest in Isla de la Juventud in the run-up to Reno. I was cheeky as hell, still am. In the sparring I was beating everyone up and they put me up against Teofilo and I was beating him up too and he was looking the worse for wear. So I let him rest a while and we started again. He caught me with a glancing blow that I barely felt and they stopped the session. No, no, worse than that they gave me a count of protection. I don't know whether it was me or his pride that they were actually protecting there. Then we carried on and I won the sparring easily.

'A while later we sparred again in Reno and this time Teofilo caught me with a combination that left my mouth cut and bleeding and I fell over on to the ropes. I remember Alcides stopped the session and came over to me. He whispered in my ear, "When the lion is asleep you can play with him, but when he is wide awake he'll bite your head off."

'The truth is that Teofilo was one of the main psychological influences on me. He made me really hungry to win the world championship. He was the best boxer of his generation and when we sparred he took me to places that I didn't think anyone could take me, I thought I was untouchable, but he showed me what real greatness was.'

Savon's career could have ended in shame right there in Reno. He was fighting the Ecuadorian Pavel Castillo when he caught his opponent hard in the stomach. Castillo turned away and, doubled in pain, claimed a low blow. A furious row developed in the ring. It was, according to observers at the time, largely because the Ecuadorian coach was so insulting when the ringside doctor tried to question whether Castillo was really hurt, that the Cuban team's appeal against the alleged low blow was allowed and the fight was judged a Savon win. A unanimous decision against the Dutchman Arnold Van der Lijde, the start of a long rivalry, ensured that Savon was a world champion at the age of eighteen.

'I felt a real responsibility after those world championships because Stevenson was gone and Adolfo Horta as well. After Reno I became the flagbearer for the Cuban team. It was an honour to be chosen because they don't give the flag of the country to just anyone. In 1986 they gave me the flag to carry in the Pan-American championships. That was the first time I actually met face to face with our commander-in-chief, Fidel Castro. He gave me the flag with his own hands. When I saw him coming towards me I felt my legs go to jelly because of who he is. It was the same feeling you get when you nearly get knocked out. I was so terrified that when he gave me the flag I had no idea what to do. I just stood there rooted to the spot when I was supposed to march forward and stop at a place which they had shown me beforehand. But I was completely transfixed, nothing was getting through. Eventually I got myself together and went to the appointed spot and as we lined up Fidel came down the line talking to the athletes and he stopped and talked to me. He asked me some questions and made some comparisons between me and Teofilo, but I just stood there, dumbstruck, not uttering a word, my mind was just blank. Eventually he realised what sort of a state I was in and he put his hand on my chest and said, "Keep this safe for Cuba".'

On another trip to the United States, for the Pan-American Games of 1987 in Indianapolis, he nearly found himself banned again. 'In the hotel where we were based there were a bunch of Cuban exiles who were determined to try and upset the concentration of the team. They were everywhere. One day I was in the bathroom at the hotel and I heard shouting and saw them trying to burn the Cuban flag and raise some flag of their own that they had made. I heard later that one of our lads had gone down, grabbed the flag off them and punched one guy's lights out right there and then. And that he had been followed down by another of the team, who had punched one of the others. When I heard this I ran down to the lobby myself and when I got there I could see people with bloody noses and someone from our own delegation, the smallest one there, bleeding from the head. They'd picked him up and thrown him against a wall when the fighting broke out.

'Of course, the story got to the papers and when the police got involved they came to the hotel to charge us with public order offences and made out that it was the biggest boxers who had picked on these guys, which was just not true. I hadn't been there at all, though I can't say I would have stood by and done nothing if I had been. They deserved it. They provoked trouble knowing that they would not be touched by the local authorities, who would be all too willing to blame us.'

The year 1988 is one that it is difficult to get Cuban sportsmen to talk enthusiastically about, if they'll talk about it at all. They look away from you, tell you that they agree with the decision not to go to the Seoul Olympics, in response to fraternal requests from the fellow Communist North Koreans. It was a bizarre boycott. The rest of the Communist world went. Only the North Koreans and Cubans felt strongly enough to stay at home. 'No, 1988 was not the best year of my life,' said Savon. 'We had prepared across the whole of the Olympic cycle for the games of 1988. I thought I had a chance at a first Olympic medal and I really wanted it badly, I kept dreaming about it. As a matter of principle I supported the decision not to go, and I haven't changed my mind. But I won't pretend I was happy about it.'

If 1988 was psychologically difficult for Savon, 1989 offered the first doubts over his ability as a boxer and a hint of his Achilles heel. Savon found himself humiliated on a trip to the Communist-organised Spartacist Games of the Friendly Armies (which would have won the gold medal for tautology in any grammatical Olympics) when he came up against Lee Dal Hen. An unknown North Korean, he was shorter than Savon and heavier, easily within Savon's capabilities. Having hit Lee so hard that the referee had given him two counts of protection Savon came forward mercilessly to finish the Korean off. 'I didn't think he had any energy left, but he caught me as I came forward and put me on the floor. The referee stopped the fight.' The defeat seriously damaged Savon's self-confidence and a series of tournaments was hastily arranged during the year to nurse him back. It was a success.

He won the world championship for a second time in Moscow in 1989, knocking out Van der Lijde in the first round of his first bout and winning the gold over a tough Soviet 18–12 on points, a remarkable decision in a competition in which the Cubans complained bitterly at corruption of the judges and in which the overall title was lost.

The rivalry between Van der Lijde and himself is the one boxing theme that really animates Savon. 'He has always been my hardest opponent because he's taller than me and he boxes more than me, in a technical sense. I've always had to dig deep against him, get in close and trade blows. I have to work a lot harder and box differently and he always makes me look a bit mad in the ring because I have to keep the punches coming to get points off him. I have to change my style completely and not try to outbox him. You have to grab the initiative off him, keep coming forward relentlessly, hitting and holding. That's how I've managed to beat him.'

His confidence back, Savon steamrollered on. The Olympics in 1992, the worlds in 1993 and 1995. The Olympics in 1996. All gold. It just never looked possible to beat him. He was too big and too powerful and the minute anyone became even half as good as him they turned professional. More than a few contenders for professional titles came a cropper against him. In one fight against Shannon Briggs, talked of recently as a possible heavyweight contender, you couldn't have fried an egg, let alone boiled one, in the time it took for Savon to knock him out. No one could live with him and everyone knew it, including the professional promoters.

In Seattle at the Goodwill Games, Savon was offered money to become professional. He never says how much money. He turned it down. In Mexico, as the team prepared for the Atlanta Games, Don King had tried to tempt him with a reported $10 million. He turned it down just as Teofilo Stevenson had done before. 'I did it because when you leave the island you lose everything, you don't think about anyone else and no one thinks about you. Here in Cuba I have the confidence of eleven million Cubans. But I could be a professional, I know that for sure because people I have fought and beaten have turned pro and become champions. I can't do it and won't do it because it is illegal and unpatriotic. But if the time comes when it isn't illegal then I would do it happily. The pros think they are better, but in fact the real boxing is in the amateurs, though no one pays any real attention to it because there is no money in it, I suppose. I'm physically strong enough to do it and I'm pretty confident I could beat any of them. Just imagine it. "Tyson comes close for the short stuff, but there's Savon jabbing and jabbing and keeping on top of him. There goes Savon's right. And Tyson is out.'"

It wasn't hard to imagine at all. It was a great deal harder to tell Savon that I had imagined it a great deal and that I was in a position to make it happen. I switched off the cassette recorder. I didn't know him well enough yet to tell him why I was there. I smiled and Savon, his wife and I got in his car and went out to lunch at a nearby *paladar*. And we didn't mention Mike Tyson again.

17 *Behind Enemy Lines*

Ed Hobart was as good a representative of the UK as the country could have asked for. He worked as the second secretary at the British embassy in Havana. He was charming to everyone, threw himself into Cuban life with gusto, worked hard, mixed well and enjoyed himself. I first met him at the university sports stadium, where I had wandered to look for a scratch game of football to get involved in. To my great surprise I discovered instead Cuba's one and only rugby club, a happy bunch of blokes charging into each other on a rock-hard surface cajoled and led by this tall white Englishman in an Oxford University top. That was Ed. The rugby club trained three afternoons a week and the team travelled for two hours or more to get to and from the stadium. There were international-class athletes who had competed for Cuba in the pack and backs: a shot-putter, a hammer thrower, a judo star who could run 100 metres in under eleven seconds, and a former 400 metres junior world champion.

Ed and I hit it off. We were unusual beasts in Cuba: two single men alone in Havana who were not disposed to sleep with as many Cuban women as possible. Ed didn't want to because he was a diplomat and had a girlfriend in England; my excuse was that I didn't want to get taken for a ride and the only way to be sure a relationship you had with a Cuban woman was genuine was not to have one at all. So we hung out together when Ed got tired of the diplo-circuit. Our favourite venue was the Rio Club, a disco which had been called Johnny's before the revolution, just by the tunnel that led under the bay from Miramar to Vedado. It had a curved art deco bar with stars inset and very few foreigners went there. It was packed with young Cubans who had money and was the one place where no Cuban women would make a serious effort to pick you up. They also played the Spice Girls. A lot. Which at the time seemed like a good thing. We had a rule when we went to the Rio that we never went in with anything that we weren't prepared to have stolen. On our first visit a Brit who worked for an investment company in Cuba had had his wallet with $200 in it stolen, and more impressively someone had snatched five bucks from my back pocket. But, despite all that, it was never threatening. It was closed down for two months during the summer after a raid by the army because it had become Havana's number one venue for buying cocaine, something of which I had been blissfully unaware. Luckily we weren't there at the time.

Ed wasn't typical of the diplomats in Havana. Many of them didn't seem to like Cuba at all and spent much of their time moaning about it and rigorously sticking together. It was a little puzzling why some had ever joined their countries' diplomatic corps if they hated it abroad so much. Through the British I got to know the Canadians and the Americans (they don't have an embassy as such, but they have what they call an Interests' Section in a massive building by the seafront which dwarfs every other diplomatic mission on the island). And through the Americans I discovered the US Marines. I didn't know before I went to Cuba that there are marines wherever there is a US embassy (sorry, guys, Interests' Section) abroad. The US Marines were based in a compound close to where I lived in Miramar and every few weeks they had a party to raise money for their annual ball. I used to go because they had Havana's only functioning pool table and just because it was weird that they were there at all. They raised a lot of money for the ball on beer sales and a few on a T-shirt they sold, which had a huge eagle with Cuba in its talons and the slogan US Marines Havana 1997: Behind Enemy Lines. You had to leave your sense of irony at the checkpoint for their house parties or you would have been beaten up within moments of entering. They were not allowed to leave the compound alone and I once went with a group of them to a disco in two people carriers (the ones made by Honda rather than those things with guns that traditionally ferry troops around, I'm happy to say).

The other advantage of mixing with diplomats was that they had equipment that just wasn't available elsewhere on the island. One of my American diplo-friends had satellite TV with pay-per-view access and we watched the NBA finals every night of one week at his house. His name was Artie and he was not very American at all, quite sarcastic, with eclectic tastes in music. He was a former Marine himself and so got on well with the lunks at the compound, but he was a million miles from being one of them. He always seemed more comfortable around the Brits. Artie's other big plus as a diplo-friend was that he had two fridges full of American food.

On the boxing side of things all I could do was keep turning up and seeing what happened. The next big boxing event was the Cordoba Cardin, an international tournament rotated around the country, at which Argentinians, Canadians, Angolans, Mongolians, Peruvians, Guatemalans, Mexicans and Hondurans spent a week getting beaten up by the best fighters in Cuba. It was named after a young lightweight boxer with six fights and a draw under his belt, who failed to turn up for a fight at Havana's Arena Trejo on the night of 25 July 1953. With a group of revolutionaries including Fidel Castro, he was preparing to attack the largest barracks in Santiago at the other end of the island the following night, a suicidal gesture in which he and many others were killed. With him that night was Pedro Marrero, after whom the national football stadium is named. The tournament was set up in 1968 and given Giraldo's name. His mother attended each year.

That year's Copa Cardin, as it was colloquially called, was held in Pinar del Rio in the west in the heart of Cuba's tobacco-growing country. Once again I booked myself into the same hotel as the journalists I knew, a cavernous Spanish colonial hovel that must have been quite grand when the town was built a hundred years ago. The shower in my room had a bucket and only a dribble of running water, a hygiene problem only solved because the designated press room had the hotel's only functioning hot shower. They were so shocked that a foreigner might stay there that they didn't know what to charge me and asked what I suggested. I offered five dollars a night and was given room which had no window and no furniture apart from the bed. It was such a terrible room that one night I woke up sweating with people banging on my door and lay there afraid I was about to be robbed. I couldn't believe the noise people were making at that time of night. When eventually I went out to find out who was causing such a racket I found that it was ten in the morning, broad daylight outside, and they were knocking to get me up for the day's excursion.

There being very little to do in Pinar, I went on more of the excursions this time. On the day of the quarter finals we were treated to a day out at the world's largest lobster-processing plant, on the coast near Pinar. We arrived on the usual bare blue bus, trooped out on to the docks, where Radio Rebelde was being played at full volume over loudspeakers, and walked past the usual dockside scenes of rusting boats and tackle surrounded by the swirling operatic cacophony of seagulls. They walked us through the whole process from where the lobsters came in, where they were boiled alive, to the benches where the women sat to select them for size and quality before ripping them apart with knives and to where they were frozen and stored before being shipped out. As our guide proudly told us, the majority of lobsters here were destined for Japan. Only through subterfuge and Cuban ingenuity would any of them end up on Cuban tables.

As for the boxing, it was pretty nondescript. Savon looked in bad shape in his first couple of bouts and appeared still not to have recovered from the knockdown by Delis that I had seen in Holguin. He patted his way past the Canadian Mark Simmons in his toughest challenge leading up to the final. But it looked bad.

Still, the first rule of promotion – I assume – is always to talk up your man. So when Cuban TV invited me on to their panel of experts to discuss live how the tournament had gone, I accepted. There were three other journalists, all of whom I had done lobster time with, Pacheco, Robertico and Miguel Hernandez. We were to sit beside the ring and as the night's action was about to begin the presenter Eddie Martin would come round and ask each of us in turn what we thought of the week. The Cubans were very downbeat. They (correctly) suggested that the low calibre of the foreign turnout had devalued the tournament, they (dubiously) suggested that Cuban boxing was in crisis, and they (tentatively) suggested that Savon had shown nothing to suggest he could return to being the unstoppable force of two or three years previously. And then he turned to me. I was terrified. The command of English and talent for keeping talking in the face of utter absence of any insight or knowledge which sustained me in such media situations back home wouldn't save me now. I hadn't even mastered the present subjunctive and here I was talking to millions of people on the Cuban version of *Sportsnight*.

'So, John, what do you think?'

'Well, to be honest I think my comrades' (good early use of *compañero*, establish yourself as someone who knows the rules of engagement) 'here are being a little, err,' (shit, how do I get round the fact that I don't know the word for downbeat?) 'err,' (use pessimistic, dummy, all those words are the same in Spanish. Just add an *a* to it and move on) '*pessimista*. As a foreigner,' (humble, good,) 'I have to say that I would never get the chance to see this calibre of boxing in one place.' (Flattery, even better.) 'You have five Olympic medallists fighting tonight.' (Was it five or was it six? Too late.) 'In England we would be happy to have just one. You Cubans don't know how lucky you are.'

Martin smiled. I got a smile in a foreign language live on TV. Nothing could stop me now.

'And, John, what do you think of Savon?'

Well, what was I supposed to say now? That from my own point of view he looked beat and that all my ideas of organising for him to fight for the professional heavyweight championship of the world looked as shot as his deformed right hand. Hell, no. 'Again, I think my friends', (damn, should have used *compañero* again,) 'are being too', (damn, damn, damn, I don't know the Spanish word for harsh,) 'err,' (how do I get round it? Think! Use hard,) '*duro*.' (Phew.) 'I've seen moments here of the old Savon, not as many as we would like to see, but I have this sense that someone is about to find out that Savon is not finished. I think the old Savon is back.'

'Gentlemen, thank you.'

Two hours later I looked like the greatest boxing analyst in Cuba when Savon came out fighting like a madman against Freddy Rojas, who had beaten him once when they were both youngsters. He was awesome, jabbing left, throwing rights, prodding, prodding, boom, boom. The old Savon was indeed back.

After the fight I was sitting with Pacheco, modestly rebuffing his compliments on my insight, when he pointed to a fat man sweating in a suit, his dark unkempt hair shining beneath the arena lights, sitting in the VIP area (a Formica table by ringside but a VIP area none the less). The man smiled and waved back at him. 'Yon. That's the Sports Minister, the head of INDER. You should talk to him about your book.' Pacheco pointed at me and stuck his thumb up so that the Sports Minister could see. 'Go and speak to him.' I went over and kneeled in front of the table. I ran through my story about writing a book on the history of Cuban boxing. He told me to call him in Havana and gave me his work and home telephone numbers. I suggested lunch. He smiled and nodded. I had made it to the very top. If the original plan to reach an agreement with the Cubans was to work, it would need political support of some kind within the government and I had found my door into the hierarchy.

It was a dash to Havana after the final night of the Copa Cardin because Artie had organised for us to watch the Tyson versus Holyfield rematch on pay-per-view at his house. Five of us had chipped in ten bucks each to pay for it, me, Artie, a guy from the British embassy and a couple of Marines. Having paid that much we were determined to squeeze the last drop of value out of it, setting ourselves up in front of the box a good two hours before the fight. The undercard from Las Vegas was decent enough, but no one in the room knew how important the big fight was to me. With Savon back to his best, a decent contact in the government and good access to the boxers themselves, if not to Sagarra, my situation looked better than it had done at any time. All I needed was Tyson back in play as world champion and Frank Warren would almost certainly reactivate his interest in the project. And Tyson was a big favourite despite his defeat in the first fight. Tyson had complained then that Holyfield had butted him in the clinches and fought dirty, but that he was ready for him this time and it wouldn't happen again. Most observers believed him.

The details of this rematch became something of a blur after what happened in the third round. There was barely any boxing of any real note. It was terrible stuff. The pair went head to head in clinches, there were elbows and heads everywhere. Tyson had a cut above his right eye after two ugly rounds which failed miserably to live up to the excitement that the fight had generated. A bleeding Tyson, unable to get away from Holyfield's stifling of the fight, might have known that his number was up. The referee Mills Lane had judged the butt that had caused his cut was accidental, but Tyson was having none of it.

Tyson came out for the third round without his gumshield, but was reminded by his corner to put it in. It wasn't in his mouth for long. After throwing a punch that fizzed pointlessly through the air, Tyson moved in to grab on to Holyfield, dropped the gumshield and attached his teeth to the top of Holyfield's right ear. And bit. The referee saw it and deducted a point as Holyfield, deranged with anger, jumped up and down and turned to go back to his corner. As he did so, he was shoved by Tyson in the back. The fight of the century had turned into a playground brawl. Two points lost for the first bite and the push, but Tyson was still mad as hell. When the fight restarted he went for the other ear and bit again. The referee looked at the damage and stopped the fight. Bottles and coins rained in, armed police were called, a brawl broke out among the hangers-on in the ring. Tyson had lost.

Worse than that, he was damaged goods yet again. He would make his excuses, claim he was provoked by Holyfield's dirty tricks, but the image of the bitten ear lying on the canvas, returned to Holyfield in a cellophane wrapper by an MGM employee later that night, was what stayed in the mind. Tyson was fined $3 million for his madness and his licence to box was revoked. He could apply again in twelve months with no guarantees. The Tyson part of my deal looked as lost and lifeless as that piece of ear.

Two days later I was with a friend from the embassy at their private swimming pool, which was attached to one of the diplomatic residences. I was drying off and settling down for a small beer when I picked up a copy of the *Daily Telegraph* one of the embassy staff had left behind. It was dated 20 June and was a fortnight out of date. I froze. This is what it said:

Frank Warren, the boxing promoter, was arrested yesterday by Customs officers investigating alleged VAT evasion. Warren, one of the most powerful figures in British boxing, was held with another man during a series of raids by Customs and Excise's National Investigation Service in Essex and Hertfordshire. They were taken to central London where they were questioned throughout yesterday.

Three premises in Herts and Essex were searched under the authority of search warrants and 'a quantity of documents' were seized. A Customs spokesman said that other premises around the South-East were also searched.

The promoter has made substantial wealth representing boxing stars such as Frank Bruno and Prince Naseem Hamed. He lives in a listed building in east Hertfordshire and currently represents more than 75 fighters, over 10 per cent of those active in Britain. He organises fights with Don King, the promoter of Mike Tyson.

A spokesman at Sports Network Europe, Mr Warren's company, said: 'We confirm that Customs and Excise investigation services attended our office today.

'They informed us that they had arrested Mr Warren and wanted to see documents at the office in relation to their inquiry. They told us that the inquiry related to VAT but they were unable to be specific.'

I had to face it. No Warren, no Tyson, no deal. The adventure was over.

18 *A Love Story with an Unhappy Ending: Kid Gavilan*

I was at the British embassy again later that week. One of the Cuban guards was chatting to me about English music – he liked Massive Attack, I'd never heard of them – so I changed the subject and asked him who he thought was the greatest ever Cuban boxer. It was a familiar game, half research, half social ploy: there were few Cubans who wouldn't make a passing attempt at offering an opinion or a morsel of information and it was the one topic on which I could feel by now that I knew as much as most Cubans. The language of the conversation was familiar – half of it was practically English (*nocaut, boxeador, el ring* were not the hardest translation tasks I faced in Cuba) – and you never knew when something extraordinary might come out of it. This was one of those days. 'The best Cuban boxer of all time was definitely Kid Gavilan,' he said. It was an unusual choice. Unsure people generally went for Stevenson, young people went for Savon, older people went for Chocolate and journalists suggested you buy them a beer so they could give it some proper thought.

Despite the fact that he was on the élite list of Cubans who had held world titles, few other Cubans had come up with Kid Gavilan.

Kid Gavilan was born Gerardo Gonzalez in Palo Seco, a small village outside Camaguey on 6 January 1926. His was the by-now familiar story of a kid who could fight but who knew nothing of fighting as an art. He took on all-comers by a cigarette kiosk, until gradually a group of men started to bet on his semi-organised scraps. They would egg him on, offering him a dollar if he could beat the next boy who came along and wanted to fight him. They even gave him his first nickname – Coni – which doesn't mean anything. In fact these fights became mildly notorious and more and more people gathered to watch as Coni, aged eight, weaved, ducked and attacked and pricked the pride of every kid in the area. Despite this minor celebrity, nobody told Gavilan's family for fear that if they did Gavilan would take his revenge on them. All his mother knew was that her little Gerardito would bring back a few dollars each week and give them to her. According to Gavilan, she thought it was money he had received for odd jobs.

Word finally reached his mother, Mariana, as she waited patiently for him to return and offer his little prize from the evening's entertainment at the kiosk. Gerardito had never at that stage even seen a boxing bout, but by the time his mother told him that evening he could never do it again it was already too late and, he says, he had got the bug. His mother beat him. And as he was sent crying to his room he looked back at her and said, 'Mum. These hands are for becoming a world champion, not for cutting sugarcane.'

The family moved to Camaguey in 1936 to find work and Gerardo, now ten, got work in a kitchen. He went to school regularly for the first time and without the money from the Palo Seco men had neither time nor incentive to pursue his previous employment. There wasn't even an official boxing gym in Camaguey. In fact, Gavilan's life looked set on a far more traditional course with his mother already preparing him for work on the Finca Luisa (Luisa Farm), which belonged to the Llanes family, who had taken them in in Camaguey.

Gavilan would never have taken up boxing again without the happy coincidence that, on the corner of the Avenida Martires where he was living with the Llanes family, they began to construct a boxing arena and gym. He was quickly hooked again. He went whenever he could and often when he shouldn't, neglecting his work in the kitchen and sneaking off to watch training, shadow-box and hit the sacks that hung from the wooden beams of the basement gymnasium. His interest and ability grew rapidly, but just as amateur boxing was starting to take off in the town, with the organisation of a Golden Gloves competition, the Llanes family, having spoken to his mother, decided to nip the boxing in the bud and sent him to the farm. After some time they let him return to Camaguey, believing he would have got over his desire to be a boxer, but twenty-four hours after moving back into town he was at the gym. There was no curing him. They tried to lock him in the house, but when they went looking for him he would be on the roof shadow-boxing and training, mimicking what he had seen in the gym. After a short time, according to Mr Llanes, he had bought himself a rope and used it to climb from the roof to the street and from there he was off to the gym.

The guard at the embassy invited me into his booth and I offered him a cigarette. It was air-conditioned to the point of being chilly, like the embassy itself, an escape, a safe place. We lit the cigarette. The guard had several issues of the Miami papers, *El Nuevo Herald*, the Spanish version of the *Miami Herald*, a dictionary and a clipboard. He was young, black and

236

fairly happy with life. This would have been a nothing job anywhere else in the world, but here, sitting in the air-conditioning with a decent lunch provided by the embassy, the chance of a few discreet scams to liberate a few discreet dollars and the opportunity to share, at the fringes, in the luxuries of being a foreigner in Cuba, it was pretty good.

'Why Gavilan?' I asked him.

'I don't know anything about boxing, my friend. The only boxer I know anything about is Gavilan because that woman over there was his wife and she has told me about him.'

'Which woman?'

He pointed at a frail black woman walking across the embassy courtyard. She was slightly stooped and moved slowly so you couldn't quite tell whether she was old and tired or just didn't see any point in hurrying. 'She is the seamstress at the embassy and she was married to him before he left the country. You should talk to her.'

Amateur boxing in Camaguey began officially in June 1938, with an appeal for anyone interested to come along to the gym in the Avenida Martires. The queue outside was 200 strong, many of them kids who were simply not heavy enough to be recognised in official weights. Gavilan was among them. This group was organised into a team called the *guasasas* (literally, the nuisances) and in October a tournament was organised to find out who among them could really box. Gavilan's first official bout was against Rafael Gonzalez. According to the local newspaper, Gavilan won easily on points. The wins kept coming, but his mother was unmoved.

'He would come back and tell me, "These hands are going to be the hands of a world champion, Mum, and when I win the world title I'm going to earn so much money that you will never have to work again," ' Mrs Gonzalez said years later. 'He always used to come back to the house with the couple of dollars he had won and give them to me. It didn't seem like much money for having to fight for a living, but he always said that one day he would earn a fortune and that I shouldn't worry. There wasn't much point by that time in trying to stop him. We used to lock him in the house in just his underpants to stop him sneaking out, but he would make himself a sort of loincloth and go to the gym. Or he would sneak out of school and go to the gym, which meant he had to go the whole day without eating.'

He kept on winning up to the point where no one in Camaguey wanted to fight him and they had to bring in opponents from other towns. He beat them too. But what looked like an unstoppable rise was halted abruptly when, due to bureaucracy and administrative infighting, the gym was taken over. With the founders gone, it rapidly deteriorated and months later it closed down. Many of the boxers gave up or were left only with occasional bouts in other towns. More and more drifted away. But not Gonzalez.

Nothing ever looked like happening. Gonzalez had fought in Havana with a Cuban team at the Arena Cristal, the brewery-funded boxing stadium which had seen most of Cuba's big fights up to that point. And he had won. But to make it as a pro he had to get out of the provinces. Eventually in 1943 the sports desk of the local paper, *El Camagueyano*, and a few friends got the money together to send him to Havana to try his luck there. They sent him with letters of recommendation to the two biggest promoters of the time – Pincho Gutierrez, who had developed Kid Chocolate and Black Bill, the greatest Cubans of the Twenties and Thirties, and Luis Parga. Both turned Gonzalez down, though Gutierrez, whose biggest dream was to repeat the world championship success he had had with Chocolate, claimed that Gonzalez never showed him the letter of recommendation and he had no idea who the kid was when he turned up at his offices.

Gavilan's Havana career eventually got off the ground when he found a trainer who was prepared to take a chance on him, Manolo Fernandez. It started in the traditional small way with his first fight in the capital, a decision victory against Baby Chango on 5 June 1943. He won $12. The problem for Fernandez was that he didn't have any money and he had to seek the help of a local café owner, Fernando Balido, to sponsor his pupil and keep him fed. Balido was pretty young himself, but harboured dreams of managing a world champion boxer right to the top. In photos from the time Balido always looks as if he can't quite believe his luck, beaming rather naively, while Gavilan's glow is more assured and composed. Gavilan looks as if he belongs in his world; Balido looks like a gatecrasher. I knew how Balido felt.

Balido tried to lodge Gavilan in his own house, but his family refused to let him. Balido battled on, found Gavilan lodgings and looked after him on the proceeds from the café. It was Balido who gave him the name Kid Gavilan. Gavilan in Spanish means 'hawk' and while it might well have suited Gonzalez – quick, elegant, difficult to get a grip on and with something of a bite to his punches – the title had nothing to do with the bird and more to do with Balido. His café, on the corner of Animas and Escobar in Havana, was called El Gavilan and Balido gave him the name to publicise the establishment. In marketing terms Balido was way ahead of his time.

'Excuse me. Olgita?'

'Yes.'

'Is it true that you were married to Kid Gavilan?'

'Yes,' she said, with the same face and tone she had used to confirm her name.

'What happened?'

'We're divorced now.' She looked sad. 'I got remarried and

I have a new husband. I still read stuff about him in the papers they get here at the embassy, but I had to get divorced in the end because I had to face up to the fact that it was twenty-nine years since he left for the United States after all.'

'But do you still keep in touch with him?'

'I can't. He's in Miami right now, being looked after by someone who says she is his daughter, but who I don't think is treating him very well. He's not well, you know. I saw an advert in the paper recently that gave a number of a woman to call if anyone wanted to help lift his spirits and I tried to call it, but when they answered they said they didn't accept calls. So I haven't spoken to him.'

She glanced around. She had work to do and it was hot out there in the carpark. There was obviously a long story to be told, but this wasn't the moment for it. We agreed to meet the next day in the embassy and she promised she would bring some of her mementoes with her to show me.

The pace of life for a fighter in Havana was as relentless in the Forties as it had been in the Twenties and Thirties, but the rewards were better. Cuba by now had a reasonably well-developed audience for professional boxing and it was supported by the breweries at venues where it was profitably promoted. Seven days after Gavilan's debut against Baby Chango he was in the ring again fighting Bartolo Molina. He received $15. He finished the year with a draw against Nanito Kid and a victory over Sergio Prieto. Four fights in six months. A mere $92 earned. The next year he really broke through and in 1945 he went on with nine successive wins and earnings in Cuba of nearly $7,000.

He travelled to Mexico and finally lost, after sixteen straight wins, to Carlos Malacara. He claimed that the decision was unfair. He beat Malacara with ease in Havana months later and with his biggest purse to date, $1,275.84. The names kept coming – Kid Bururu, Jose Zorrilla, Santiago Sosa – before he lost again on decision in Mexico to Tony Mar. Then back to Havana and with the money that he made Gavilan, and his manager, Balido, set off for New York. They didn't speak English, they didn't know anyone, they didn't have any idea who they needed to speak to. But they went anyway.

Olga turned up the next day with a plastic bag and we sat in an office at the embassy. She had said she would bring articles and papers that I could photocopy for my research, but when she arrived she seemed sad. She couldn't quite look me in the eye. I asked her what was wrong. 'I'm so sorry, John. My son didn't want me to come here. He says that you should pay money if you want to look at these papers because they belong to us. I don't want to ask you for money, but it's difficult because he looks after things. I had to bring them here without telling him.' She was upset. She wanted to talk and she didn't want money. But she felt obliged to ask. After we had talked for a while and she had told me her stories, she refused to accept any cash. 'I'll tell him you never turned up,' she said, and I took her for a pizza round the corner.

When we had sat down she told me her story. 'His first wife was called Leonor. Here, I've got a picture of her here leaving a hospital in New York after they had their first child.'

'How many kids has he got?'

'Three who live in New York, and three who live here in Havana. I don't know where they live, but I could find out. Look, here's a picture of him with Sugar Ray Robinson. And that's Sugar Ray's wife with Jake la Motta. Gavilan didn't say much, he was not a man who liked to talk, quite timid really, and when I was with him I looked after him. But then when he was on his own in the United States he got into trouble. He bought himself a cruiser and a gymnasium and I think he had the gym for a while, but eventually someone came along and talked it off him and left him with nothing.

'When we lived here we lived on a farm. It was a wonderful life with all sorts of fruit and vegetables and animals. The farm cost Gavilan $68,000 when he bought it, which was a lot of money in those days. He used to host massive parties there and everybody wanted to come to them. When he was resting from boxing he used to come and stay at the farm for two or three months at a time and all these artists and music hall people would turn up and start riding the horses around. I remember that there were three rooms in the farm that were off-limits. One was full of trophies, another was wall-to-wall with suits and the other was absolutely packed with shoes. He had about 500 or 600 pairs. He didn't use most of them or even know what they looked like, but these shoe firms used to send him free shoes all the time to wear as a promotion, I suppose. It wasn't a smart move because he was only with us a few months at a time and the rest of the time he spent training and he didn't have much time for them.'

Balido and Gavilan quickly found out that not knowing anyone in a city as large, unfriendly and fast as New York was not the same as not knowing anyone in a Cuban city. You couldn't simply start talking in a bar and find your way to the person you needed to see. But the pair had one stroke of fortune. In town at the time was Jess Losada, the greatest Cuban sports journalist of the time, who had worked on all the great society magazines, such as *Carteles* (a strange mix of the *New Yorker* and *Hello!*, which ran throughout the first half of the century in Cuba and whose covers, meticulous full-colour illustrations, reflected the art deco and art nouveau styles of its times) and specialist sports newspapers like *Nocaut* (a short-lived Cuban boxing magazine). If there was a need for sports writing on Cuba and the money was there to buy it, Jess Losada was hired.

The pair knew Losada and went to ask for his help. Being slightly more familiar with the New York scene than they he took them to the Stillman's Gym in Manhattan close to Madison Square Garden. Stillman's was one of the two centres of New York's boxing universe along with Gleason's in the Bronx. He introduced them to Nick Florio, one of the trainers who had worked with Kid Chocolate. When they got there, Florio looked them up and down and handed Gavilan gloves, shorts and a pair of shoes and told him to get in the ring. After a few seconds sparring with another fighter Florio told him to stop. He called Losada over and told him to tell Gavilan that he would have to change his style to survive in America. Gavilan boxed with a very untypical stance to American eyes of those days, not weaving and ducking but with his hand outstretched, at a distance from his opponent, ready to jab but keeping the other boxer away and dancing around the ring before darting in for scoring blows. Meanwhile Balido was introduced to Angel Lopez, who ran New York's Havana-Madrid cabaret and who had dabbled in boxing management helping the Puerto Rican Joe Basora. In the process he had picked up the sort of contacts and experience Gavilan would need to make it as a world champion. Many of those contacts were with the shady New York underworld, specifically Frankie Carbo, who took more than a passing interest in boxing.

It was November 1946 before Gavilan actually fought in the United States. He knocked out Johnny Ryan in five, decisioned Johnny Williams in eight a month later and won the rematch with Ryan over ten rounds two weeks after that. He and Balido returned to Cuba with the press ready to welcome them at the airport, Balido smirking as he came down the steps and Gavilan looking elegant in his cream overcoat and cap, holding a pair of black leather gloves. For a man who had only won three knock-'em-down beginners' fights he looked very much a world champion. Early 1947 offered little to stand in his way. Five fights, five wins, four decisions, one knockout. In April he was back in the States and in the next eighteen months fought twenty times, but was beaten himself in September 1947 by Douglas Radford. The roll-call of 1948 was a similar story. Gene Burton, Joe Cuccio, Vinnie Rosano (twice), Tommy Bell, Rocco Rossano, Douglas Radford, Roman Alvarez, Buster Tyler and Tony Pellone were all seen off. Though he suffered two defeats in this run, it ought to be noted they were against world champions (a 27 February decision against lightweight champion Ike Williams over ten rounds and a non-title fight on 23 September against Sugar Ray Robinson). He had reached the level he wanted to be at, a fact which fed his popularity in Havana, where he took the biggest purse of his career, more than he took home for eventually winning the world title, $6,064 for beating Ben Buker in Havana in front of a massive crowd at the old baseball arena.

It was 1949 that made Kid Gavilan. His first two fights were victories against Ike Williams (who had beaten him the previous year) in which he broke Williams's jaw. These two fights were key to his being regarded as meriting a shot at the world welterweight title. However, for the moment that title would have to be wrested from a real champion. The fight was made with Sugar Ray Robinson for 11 July in Philadelphia's Municipal Stadium. Gavilan started well and matched the champion in the early rounds. He even made Robinson wobble in round eight. But Gavilan finished the fight knowing he had not done enough to beat one of the greatest boxers of all time.

He still believed his time would come. He continued to waltz past opponents of any class lower than Robinson, until he was beaten in Detroit by Lester Felton, a sparring partner of his of mediocre quality who benefited partly from knowing Gavilan's style and partly from gangster connections which sparked an investigation after the fight. None the less the result stands as a peculiar blot on Gavilan's record. That sort of peculiarity would come around for Gavilan again and occasionally he himself would benefit from inexplicable verdicts.

1950 was different, however, with one win and three defeats threatening his stay at the peak of the sport. The rumours on the circuit at the time were that he was enjoying himself too much, drinking and partying, and that he was starting to pay the price physically. He heeded what he was hearing and turned himself around later that year, marrying his long-time girlfriend, an event which heralded a return to form and a succession of victories interrupted by one defeat, to Gene Hairston in Scranton NY, his last setback before he finally achieved his goal of winning the world title. That was to be in 1951.

'We met each other in Camaguey for the first time in 1951,' said Olga. 'I was fourteen and he was eleven years older than me and on the verge of being a world champion. He used to come to Camaguey to see some buildings he was having put up and I was always in his house. I thought he was so pretty and such a gentleman, but he was there with his first wife. I could see that even though I was very young he found me quite pretty and one day he caught me staring at him and he said, 'When you're grown up you're going to be my wife.' But then I never saw him until 1964 because he moved to Havana and I was stuck in Camaguey.

'Then years later, in 1964, I moved to Havana and I went to visit his mother at the farm. I didn't think he would be there, I just wanted to say hello to the family. His cousin answered the door and I explained who I was and asked him how Gavilan was, what country he was in and they said that he was still in Cuba and he would be back at the house any second. I was sitting in the kitchen when he arrived and as soon as he got in he said, "You're little Olga from Camaguey who I said I was going to marry." He had remembered me after fourteen years. I was twenty-seven then and I had married and divorced and I had a son. He had got divorced too. "Good timing," he said. Anyway, when I was having a bath in the house he slipped a note under the door saying; "Olga, if you feel like it, would you like to come out to the cinema with me some time?" I said yes, we went and you can imagine the rest. It was really beautiful and I loved him very much.'

When Sugar Ray Robinson decided to move up a division to middleweight in 1951 and give up the welterweight crown, the scramble to replace him began. Gavilan won his shot at the title with a defeat of Gene Hairston, the deaf fighter, at Madison Square Garden. Gavilan hardly stopped punching the whole night, the left bobbing permanently at Hairston's face, the right winding up into the by-now famous Bolo punch, a swinging uppercut that came from a long way back and which Gavilan claimed, slightly fancifully, he had developed from cutting sugarcane at the age of nine. Gavilan's stance, stooped with his head practically withdrawn into his shoulder, made him an impossible target to hit. Hairston fought hard, but Gavilan's tireless punching never left him a way into the fight.

He fought Johnny Bratton for the title in New York on 18 May. He broke Bratton's jaw inside the first five rounds and Bratton fractured his right hand in two places, which left him unable to throw punches in the last six or seven rounds. Gavilan was the unanimous winner and Cuba's second world champion.

By August he was defending against Billy Graham. It was a

tough fight and though Gavilan started well Graham got on top of him and ten out of twelve ringside journalists voted for Graham. Gavilan was judged the winner by those who counted, however. The referee and one judge voted seven rounds each and the other judge voted 9–6 for Gavilan. He held on to the title. The one suspicious element of the fight was the pre-match odds with Gavilan fighting as a 13/5-on favourite, a ridiculous price given that Graham had beaten him once in his career already (narrowly) and lost once (narrowly). However, Gavilan was still the champion. Graham had come close but not close enough.

Bobby Dykes was next, in February 1952. It was Florida's first mixed-race bout. Gavilan had Dykes down early before Dykes started to pick off Gavilan in the middle rounds. But a good last couple tipped it and by a split decision Gavilan held on to his title. Next up, 7 July 1952, in Philadelphia was Gil Turner, a young, undefeated thirty-one-win welterweight in front of his home crowd. Unusually an early flurry of punches from Turner brought the crowd roaring to its feet and Gavilan had to hang on. The fifth to tenth were Gavilan's though – Turner did not have Gavilan's skill at throwing his punches in spurts and resting. With Turner exhausted in the eleventh and with thirteen seconds left the referee stepped in to protect the defeated and dazed challenger.

It was the beginning of the end. The Turner win made American fight fans really sit up and notice Gavilan, but Gavilan's people had done a deal to get him the big fights which involved giving Frankie Carbo 10 per cent of their purses. They skipped town without paying after the Turner fight and headed for Argentina. Gavilan's camp claimed they couldn't return to the United States because they feared the Mafia, so his next defence was set up in Havana.

Billy Graham was the opponent in a packed Estadio de Cerro, which post-revolution was turned into the Estadio

Latinoamericano, where Havana's top baseball matches are held. This time there was none of the controversy of the previous bout. It was a unanimous and uncriticised win for Gavilan. However, the Mafia were in town at the Hotel Nacional a week before the fight and Frankie Carbo made it clear to Balido that it was time to settle accounts. Which meant that if he wanted to carry on living he would have to give up his contract with Gavilan. Balido announced his retirement as Gavilan's manager on the night of the fight in front of the capacity crowd because of 'illness'. The contract passed to Lopez. The deal meant Gavilan could go back to the United States and he did so with Lopez in charge and a Puerto Rican trainer called Mundito Medina in his corner.

As with other heroes of Cuban boxing, Gavilan was forced to take on fighters in their own backyards, but taking on Carmen Basilio, little-fancied Canastota onion farmer, in New York State at Syracuse in September 1953 seemed to pose little danger. Basilio dropped Gavilan to the floor in the second round and punished him for another four. Gavilan rallied for the second half of the fight, but the locals were sure they had seen a major upset. The split decision went to Gavilan with the referee of the contest voting for the Kid. He needed a police escort out of the arena. He then tried to move up a division to middleweight for a world title crack against Bobo Olson, but while he threw his usual flurry of punches he did little to hurt Olson and lost by a big margin.

The crown was lost and lost for good on 20 October 1954. Gavilan should never have taken the fight. First, he had only six weeks to recover from mumps before taking on Johnny Saxton. Doubts were also expressed about his mental state by Jess Losada, who had helped him make it in the States. Gavilan had spent most of the past year avoiding boxing in favour of a theatre tour which he produced and starred in. It was a commercial disaster and Losada estimated that he had lost the chance to earn $500,000 in purses that year. He wrote in *Carteles*, a Cuban social magazine of the time:

His fall from grace as a fighter is more than just mumps it is a psychosis, he believes his future is show-business, that he will be a famous director and producer and no one can tell him otherwise, not even his own manager who has been in that business for 20 years. He has broken contact with the Cuban press, doesn't listen to Angel Lopez any more, is dabbling in *santeria* and thinks the Cuban public all hate him. He needs to get rid of the people around him who are causing all this trouble and remember that love is not something that sportsmen have by right for all time. He needs to get back in touch with the shy kid from Camaguey who wanted to conquer the world and did it.

Apart from his own physical and mental state, the other reason Gavilan should have been wary of the fight was that Saxton was managed by a man called Blinky Palermo. Palermo had good 'contacts' in Philadelphia, where the fight was to take place, and that meant a points decision would be extremely difficult for Gavilan to achieve. Saxton was a tricky, slippery fighter, but that evening he did little of note apart from hold Gavilan at the first hint of any boxing actually breaking out. It was a terrible fight, with Saxton having done nothing to merit taking the title off Gavilan. 'What did they do to me?' said the headline in *Boxing and Wrestling* magazine the following week. An old man sold me the magazine when he heard I was interested in Gavilan. He'd nurtured a copy and a sense of injustice for forty years, but sold me the magazine for five bucks. Inside Gavilan gave his response to the defeat.

I wish I could tell this story with my fists [he wrote], and I could have Johnny Saxton in front of me to prove my point.

I need to explain what actually took place in the bitterest experience I have ever had.

The fight was a very bad one, no one knows that better than I, but it wasn't my fault. If you have a man in the ring with you who does not want to fight and whose main idea is to hold you and pin your arms to your sides there is nothing you can do. I talked to Saxton in the clinches and begged him to start fighting. When that didn't work I complained to the referee, but that was another stone wall. The people booed and threw things, they came to see a championship fight but all they got was a mambo contest. Maybe if something had hit Saxton on the head he would have come to life and started to fight like a man trying to win a title not like one who acted as if he couldn't lose no matter what he did.

I must have looked terrible when I cried after they gave Saxton the decision. But I couldn't help it, my heart was broken. As I stood there, my trainer Mundito said, 'You could not win here tonight unless you knocked him out and even then I'm not so sure.'

Blinky Palermo, Saxton's manager, ignored the clause in Gavilan's contract that guaranteed a return fight within sixty days in the event of defeat. Gavilan never fought for the world title again.

After the Saxton defeat, Gavilan's contract was sold to a Lebanese gangster called Jamil Chade, whose reputation was as a jewel smuggler. His career plummeted and despite claiming he had been robbed of fights on numerous occasions he never recovered from the Saxton decision. Destiny had deserted him.

In Gavilan's testament in the Boxing Hall of Fame it says that

Gavilan left Cuba to escape the Castro regime and Communism. That story is a long way from the truth.

'He gave the revolutionaries money,' said Olga as we sat in her house, a tidy dark terrace in Buena Vista, a Havana suburb made famous by the old musicians who named their group after the local social club. 'When he was boxing in Mexico in the early Fifties after he was world champion they came to him and asked him for money to help them make a landing in the east in a yacht, from where they would start a guerrilla war in the mountains. He helped pay for that yacht, *Granma*, on which Che and Castro and all of them landed before being captured or killed. He was a Cuban patriot and when they came and asked him for help in liberating the country he gave it. In 1959 when the revolution triumphed he came back to Cuba because he wanted to retire here. When he got back he came to stay at the farm and at first everything was normal. They were seizing certain private properties but not the farm. What they did do, however, was build a motorway right through the middle of it without asking permission. It split the farm in half and made it impossible to work. The government pension he was awarded was only $200 a year, which he thought was an insult to someone who had spent twenty years earning money and bringing it back to Cuba, so with three kids to bring up he found it very difficult. Anyway in 1963 some journalists came to look for him and find out how he was and he told them how unhappy he was and what had happened to the farm and the pension. When the article was published the Sports Minister, José Llanusa Gobel, came to the farm and apologised and asked him what they could do for him. It was too late, Gavilan told him. All he wanted now was that they let him leave the country. They told him he couldn't leave, but that he shouldn't worry: they would increase his pension to $1,000 and would give him a car, or two cars, and a house in Havana. He told them he wasn't interested, that he wanted to leave not for financial reasons but for self-respect because he felt cheated by the government. But they wouldn't allow it.

'His health began to deteriorate. He had back problems which caused him great pain and he was having problems with his eyesight which the doctors said would be too risky to cure with an operation. In 1964 we moved out of the farm and into the house that he had bought for his mother in Havana.'

There Olga and Kid Gavilan waited to get out of the country however they could. To get into the United States you had to be 'reclaimed' by someone who was living there legitimately as a citizen. Gavilan had two *reclamaciones* organised for him, one by his son Gerardito, who had been a decorated colonel in Vietnam for the US army, and the other by the World Sports Association, who had read about his plight in the press.

'But the Cubans just wouldn't let him go. They said that he had to be a boxing trainer here and he wouldn't do it. We survived. I was working as a teacher and Gavilan had his pension. And we waited for these *reclamaciones* to come through. At the end of August in 1968 we went to El Laguito, where you had to go to apply to leave the country, and they told us that we wouldn't be allowed to leave unless we did some work cutting sugarcane for six months first. Well, that was out of the question for Gavilan because of his back and eyesight. But we kept going and pleading with them. I remember one morning we turned up at five and they still hadn't given us a time for interview at one p.m. and the man came out and said that anyone who was still here should go because he wasn't seeing anyone else until tomorrow. We went back the next day at five and the same thing happened. The third day we went back and hid behind a bush in the courtyard until everyone else had been sent home at one p.m. We jumped out of the bushes when it was quiet and went into the office where the man was working. He told us to get lost, but I shouted at him and showed him all the property that Gavilan had, the deeds to the farm, the house in Havana, another big house that we had in Camaguey, two or three plots that we had in Marianao and a couple of apartments – I can't remember where they were. We were hoping that seeing as you had to give up your property when you left they might pay us some attention if they knew how much we had. But the man was just not interested. He could see Gavilan was ill because he had to wear dark glasses for his eye problems. He told us that we had to cut cane first or we weren't going anywhere and if it killed us that was our problem not his. He was flicking through our papers while he was talking and when he got to the deeds of the farm he just stopped dead. He looked quite shocked. "Las Margaritas Farm? That's in Bejucal, isn't it?" He paused and looked a little shocked. "Take your glasses off, Mr Gonzalez." Gavilan took them off. "My God. You're Kid Gavilan. What are you doing still in Cuba? I thought you left years ago." And the man started to talk to us about the past. "You used to give me food when I was a policeman near your farm. My beat was from your farm in Bejucal to Sanctuario and I used to come to your farm all the time because you always helped us out. And if you weren't there your mother would give us something. Your door was always open to anyone who needed help. She used to tell us that because her family had had it hard, but her son had been lucky and made lots of money, she wanted to share his luck with everyone." All this because he recognised the name of the farm.

'He said he was really grateful to Gavilan's family for the way they had treated him and that he would put us on a flight as soon as we wanted with one of the *reclamaciones*. This was on 29 August 1968. Three days later they came to the house asking for Gerardo Gonzalez, with a ticket for a flight on 16 September. He had to hand in all the deeds of his properties.

253

But when he asked them where my permission was, they said they only had permission for him to leave, not me. His papers were ready but mine weren't, nor were my son's. I didn't have a passport or anything because we didn't expect things to happen so fast. I just got on with the admin stuff without thinking. I went to Camaguey to renounce his claim to his property there and I did the same in Havana for the flats and his car. He had the first Dorado of anyone in Havana, but he never drove it because he knocked someone down once and after that he didn't like to use it. We had to do all this by 2 September and the police came back on 5 September to check it was all in order. They gave him the confirmation of his departure date and on 16 September he left.

'Gavilan told me to be patient and that as soon as he got to Miami he would organise for me to follow him. He had a millionaire friend there who had been a big fan back in the days when Gavilan was Kid Gavilan. This man spoke to Gavilan and told him not to worry, that I would be with him very shortly. And in seven days I had my permission to leave as well. They said I was on a plane in twenty-four hours and that I should pack my bags. The problem was that I couldn't organise it quickly enough. My son was a minor and his father wouldn't give permission for him to leave the country. We pleaded with him, but he just said that the boy had to stay if I was going. He was only six and he was my only child, so what could I do? So that was it.

'It was a bad time. He contacted me to ask when I was coming, but I kept telling him I wouldn't leave my son and he lost his temper and told me that it was just that I didn't want to leave and that he wasn't going to ask again. Then I fell out with his family, who told me to get out of the house I was in which belonged to them and in 1971 I was living in the street and in parks with a couple of days in a hotel if I could afford it here and there. Things were like that until 1973. I started picking up work at the embassies and eventually the Spanish ambassador found me an apartment and I lived there until 1980. Gavilan still had it in his head that I would leave Cuba and in 1980 when the Mariel boatlift happened and when people in Miami sent boats to pick up their families and take them to the United States, Gavilan sent me cable after cable saying that he would send one, two, three, four boats, that I could bring whoever I wanted but that he needed me to be with him. But I told him that I couldn't, that it was too late. My son had a life and had just graduated as an agronomist and I had re-established myself after he left. He said that if he couldn't be with me he didn't want to be with anyone. But I told him that I couldn't leave. It was so difficult, but I had made a new life for myself. In 1985 I asked him for a divorce. We'd been married seventeen years and there was no future. He admitted he wasn't coming back to Cuba again, even for a visit. I've tried to call him since then, quite recently to find out how he is, but the woman who answers won't let me speak to him. She says she is his daughter, but I don't believe her.

'Anyway, in 1985 I wanted to remarry and I got the divorce, though it wasn't easy. Because he had gone legally they said he could return and so they had to do an investigation into the reasons for the divorce and then they put me before a commission to see if I was pregnant by him. I mean, how stupid is that? He hadn't been in the country since 1968 and they were worried that I might be having his child. It took me three months to get the divorce. I've tried to go and see him. A couple of years ago I went to the American embassy to try and get a visa, but they turned me down. And you know what the biggest irony is? The father of my son, the one who stopped me going thirty years ago, left himself and lives in Miami now. Our story is a true love story, we really were made for each other, but Cuba got in the way.'

19 *How Much Is That Lada Tyre in the Window?: The 1997 World Championships*

By now I was starting to feel part of what was going on. I'd spoken to plenty of people, I could just about understand what a mumbling, slurring boxer was saying to me and where I couldn't I had, as you have to when you work abroad, perfected the art of laughing in the right places. Foreign languages are easy to fake. In Cuba you can disguise total bemusement with a smile and an exclamation – 'Nooooo. *Coño*'. (Which literally translated means 'No! Cunt,' but seems to lose pretty much everything in translation.) I could do it to order when I was expected to express some sort of surprise or disgust. I could even have a conversation with a taxi driver at almost Cuban speed – basically because I only ever had the one conversation with them the entire time I was there.

'Estas en vacaciones?' they'd start. That would be my cue.

'No. Soy periodista de deportes. Trabajo por el *Guardian*. Estoy escribiendo un libro sobre el boxeo. Si, m'encanta Cuba, pero la vida aqui no es facil. Eh.'

That was all the encouragement the driver ever needed to rabbit on about how he was really a brain surgeon or an engineer or a writer, but he was forced to humiliate himself by driving taxis around with rich wankers (for such a short, harmless-looking word, 'tourist' hides a lot of bitterness) like me in the back to earn just a little bit of money.

For most of them it was a fantasy. They would have been a cabbie back in Crouch End if they had been English and the nearest they had come to brain surgery was picking their noses. But as with a lot of things in Cuba, they repeated it as a fact so often that they almost believed it was true. In truth the taxi drivers were of exactly the same breed as they are all over the world, scruffy, hard-working, mainly unhappy at what the world dished out to them and, with the odd exception, unreliable.

When I first arrived I took pride in getting lifts off the street, just standing there and sticking my hand out at anything that came by. My Cuban friends laughed at me. 'He thinks all cars are taxis,' they would chuckle to each other. But to a foreigner they pretty much were. The overwhelming power of the market, however, was having a hard time with Havana taxi drivers who, perhaps as a legacy of gangsterism of the Fifties, or perhaps as a result of their own powerlessness in the face of state monopoly, favoured the forming of informal cartels to set prices. Few taxi drivers realised a basic fact of their profession that, given the choice between a ride with a smart driver from a state company in a Mercedes and a 'Maybe we get there, maybe not' lift in a battered Lada, in which the exhaust fumes occasionally seeped through the dashboard and there was a dead pig on the back seat (it only happened the once, but it happened), most people would go with the state car unless there was a decent price advantage. But there rarely was.

Weirdly as well, in a city which isn't that large, which is

257

based on a grid system and where passengers are only heading for a very small number of destinations, large numbers of them didn't even know where they were going. Taxis also had a very inflationary tendency, the theory being that if Miguel from the Hotel Nacional got ten bucks out of a guy for taking him to Miramar, that was now the going rate until at least five punters refused to pay. I occasionally got turned down for rides for asking them to charge less than the state taxis, but normally you name your destination, they umm and aahh, instantly taking into account your clothes, age, self-confidence, language ability, level of geographical disorientation – and then they name a sum. You knock a dollar off it or a dollar fifty if you're having a bad day and the guy starts walking to his car without saying a word. And you are supposed to follow. Then it would be into the conversation all over again.

'Where you from?' he would ask. 'Ahhh, England. Lady Deee. I have a cousin who was in Germany once. You like Cuba?'

And off I went. It was like a part of every day, a mantra to remind me what my story was. In a very Cuban way at times even I lost track of what was true and what I was making up to hide what was true. It was now time to assess what I was really doing in Cuba.

The fall of Tyson and Warren's problems had been a major blow to my enthusiasm. But what was I supposed to do? The year thus far had shown me graphically how quickly things turn from bleak to beautiful and back again in boxing. My part of the bargain was going OK. The 'research' was going well, Savon was back in shape, a couple of the boxers now knew who I was and the Cuban boxing journalists had adopted me as their odd cousin from England. I was skint, but it had to be done. I was going to Budapest, to the world amateur boxing championships. I was going to go with the journalists and the team and find out what it really was like to be part of a Cuban team abroad. And I was going to try and get to know a few of them well enough to ask them a few questions which had been bugging me for ten months. It ought to be easier to chat to them out there. My theory was that whereas in Cuba they held the upper hand, had their friends around them and were only inclined to talk if they thought they could do so without being noticed or there was a dollar at the end of it, in Hungary they wouldn't be quite so cautious about what they said because there was only one security guy with them (the bloke who wore his tracksuit limply everywhere except around his ample gut). In Hungary there wouldn't be many things for them to do other than chat to me. And we'd be there for a couple of weeks. It was as good a chance as I was going to get to really mingle with the boxers and find out what the truth was, who maybe wanted to leave and who didn't.

It would make an intriguing story in its own right. Into a grim former Communist country (if the most half-hearted of the Bloc), cold and wet and grey, and with all the ambiguity that accompanies the transition from one economy to another, poverty with enterprise, uncertainty with opportunity: into this step the self-appointed defenders of the faith, of old-style Communism. Actually I suspected the grim faces of the team at the airport were more likely to reflect the difference in temperature between Havana and Budapest in October than any political distaste. None of the boxers had ever worn more than a tracksuit in the entire time I knew them. To them, an overcoat was something you painted on your Lada after you'd put the undercoat on. I knew how cold it was going to be, that biting, dry, central European coldness that bone-chills you when you step into it for the first time. But when the boxers left José Marti airport they probably didn't and I doubt Adidas had supplied them with woolly jumpers. The team flew out to Spain a couple of weeks beforehand to prepare and I had work to do. I still had to buy my ticket, a process that might take days to recover from. I also had to find out where the team was staying, where the hacks would be and how much I would have to pay to get there.

My first stop was the house of Modesto Aguerro, the television anchorman and sports reporter who had helped me at the national championships back in February. Modesto was one of those men who ooze confidence in themselves, the guy who always makes jokes at other people's expense in the certain knowledge that his self-assuredness will prevent them retaliating. He lived close to Cerro, a suburb of Havana with a reputation as the nursery for all that was good about the Cuban working class, hard but fair, tough streets that bred fighters and revolutionaries and the odd thinker, like Liverpool or the East End of London. Modesto's house was on the fringes of Cerro in Buena Vista, set on a hill with a view over the city. Modesto presented the Sunday afternoon sports shows as well as the universally watched sports bulletin on the early evening news programme. He was a good journalist, attractive, well-informed, intelligent, liked by sports people and punters and in any other country would have lived very well indeed. In Havana, though, he lived on the fourth floor of a nondescript, dank apartment block in a clean flat with a television and a video recorder the size of the Space Shuttle which didn't work very well. And no telephone. Whenever you rang him his neighbour would have to call him to the phone in their apartment. Think about it for a moment. 'DEEEESSSSS. THERE'S A MR LINEKER ON THE PHONE FOR YOU!!!' I'd come on the bike and brought some seven-year-old rum in a water bottle. Modesto put it in the fridge and leaned the bike against his own in the front room. He was all bronzed white Latin charm, just tanned enough to look as if he permanently had his television make-up on, not so bronzed that anyone would make the error of thinking he wasn't white. Just smart enough in well-fitting cheap shirts to look a little above the ordinary.

'Yon Dooncaaan,' he said and shook my hand. I'd brought a couple of boxing magazines for him to look at. He did what every Cuban I ever showed them to did and looked through all of them for Cubans who defected and American boxers they had seen as amateurs. Occasionally he looked up and made a comment about some Pole I'd never heard of, or a Bulgarian light featherweight. And he'd tell me how this Cuban and that Cuban had always beaten them.

'Yeah, Modesto, but wouldn't it be great if Cubans could fight professionally and show the world what they can do?' Jesus, did I really just say that? After ten months of keeping my mouth shut I was starting to get cocky. It was a mischievous question, I suppose, so predictable that the response to it was almost automatic. I knew and he knew that he couldn't really say what he thought to a foreigner. 'Tsk, no, Yon. Professional boxing is inhuman, exploitative, barbaric. It is run by gangsters and the boxers all end up poor and with nothing.'

And he went back to poring over the *Ring* ratings for the previous month, as opinionated as every boxing nut I ever met, knowing that he can't give in, he can look but not touch, not admit to himself that he likes it, but enjoying the smell all the same. And maybe he's repeated it enough times himself by now to believe it's true. And, typically Cuban, it was an opinion based on the circumstances of the late 1950s, with no room to admit that the world might have changed since then.

He wasn't sure where the Cubans would be based, but gave me the name of the hotel where he thought he would be. Having got the information I needed, I settled down for a rum or two while he showed me a video that someone had sent from the United States – of Jorge Gonzalez, a big lummox of a super-heavyweight who had defected after the Barcelona

Olympics and got a fight as a plausible but easily knockdown-able challenger to Riddick Bowe, who was on his way to challenging for a world title. It was hard to see through the visual white noise and tracking problems of the video, which was Betamax, of course. Cuba shopped in the car-boot sale section of the world market for everything.

The American network coverage on the tape was stunning in its absurdity. It went something like this. Cue sad Mendelssohn-style violins. 'Jorge Gonzalez. Eight times amateur world champion.' (Pause button. Clunk. Modesto looked up over his glasses, tutted and pointed out, quite correctly, that Gonzalez would have to be as old as Joe Bugner's dad to have been world champion eight times – there have only been eight world championships since the first one in Havana in 1974.)

'He escaped the tyranny of Cuba and dreams of his homeland, back on the pearl of the Caribbean under the yoke of the hammer and sickle.'

Pictures of barbed-wire fences in the dusk, Gonzalez looking wistfully into the distance. In an attempt to give a man who was plainly not a brilliant pro boxer some sort of image they had put a ten-gallon hat on him. He was a good ol' boy now, you see, not a Commie, just in case anyone didn't get it. He had shaved his head except for a long ridiculous strand that trailed on to his shoulder.

'He wants to make someone pay for the sadness of his country and tonight he intends to take his anger out on . . .'

He got in the ring, didn't get a single shot in and got pulped by Bowe. In a few pointless rounds. It was a little scary.

'He was an idiot,' said Modesto. 'He was never a good fighter and as stupid as they come.'

Not that stupid obviously. Even for a mediocre thrashing as a soft touch for Bowe's world title challenge he earned more in two rounds than most Cubans will get in two lifetimes. It had to be said, though, that looking at his entourage he stood a good chance of having it removed from his wallet well before the end of this one.

We chatted about the team and who would be in and who out. There were doubts at middleweight, where there was talk of leaving out Ariel Hernandez and putting Jorge Gutierrez in his place. And Modesto, like most Cuban journalists, thought Alexis Rubalcaba should be left at home in favour of someone smaller who could box a bit, like Armando Campusano. He thought they would take Gutierrez and Campusano. I said they should take Hernandez and Rubalcaba. When they announced the team live on Modesto's programme the next day, I was 100 per cent right and he was 100 per cent wrong. Maybe I had picked up more knowledge than I thought. I had failed, however, to pick up the knowledge I had come for – where the Cubans were staying. I would have to play it by ear when I got to Hungary.

Next came the far less pleasant task of getting a plane ticket. Cubana has a system so mindless that it can only be deliberately obtuse. There are three entrances to the office, two of which are padlocked shut and none of which are marked ENTRANCE. You can't see that two are padlocked on the other side because the sun turns the glass doors into a one-way mirror, but everyone inside can watch you humiliate yourself for free. Once inside there is a reception desk with a queue. You might think this desk would direct customers to where they should go to buy the ticket they want. That would be useful because there are no signs to differentiate the four waiting areas with desks and assistants from one another.

The reception desk is where Cubana passengers have to reconfirm their flight arrangements, which everyone has to do at least forty-eight hours before their flight. Its other purpose is to hand out numbered tickets that tell you your place in the queue at the international inquiries desk. Experience had taught me by this point to do it the Cuban way, to go straight to the front of the queue and ask for a ticket, thus escaping twenty pointless extra minutes of wasted existence. Then you have to barge in on the nearest person at the international desk and ask what their number is. It's what a Cuban would do and you half-suspect that the gruff Cubana girls respect you for treating them with so little courtesy.

Anywhere else in the world, if you were twelve numbers away from being served, you'd probably settle down with the newspaper for a ten-minute wait. In the Cubana offices twelve numbers is the equivalent of about two hours. So I picked up my bag, left the office with the raffle ticket in my pocket and went shopping. I knew about the waiting, but most of the other people there were tourists and didn't. I knew that their mounting irritation would become contagious if I hung around. It is best to queue in Cuba with your eyes closed or at a safe distance. With twelve people in front of me I could have popped round the corner to see a film and got back in time. If there had been twenty to go I could have read and translated Fidel Castro's speech to the sixteenth congress. Just. If there had been thirty I could have read *War and Peace*. With forty I could have written it. I got my ticket eventually, although the assistant was unaware I knew there was a special offer on and she should be charging me half the price she'd quoted. She looked it up, found out I was right, grunted and issued the ticket.

When I arrived at the airport the Cuban press contingent was already there, looking nervous. If I thought my attempts (as usual futile) to get an emergency exit seat were frustrating, the three of them (Pacheco, Modesto and a guy called Roberto, who represented the entire TV and radio team being sent to one of Cuba's biggest international sporting dates) had more fundamental problems. They had to be there early to find out if they were even on the plane. Having got tickets for Cuban pesos via official sources they knew that if there were people paying dollars their comrades at Cubana wouldn't hesitate to chuck them off. Pacheco was wearing a heavy woollen/polyester suit and tie right out of a Fifties gangster film. He had been told by Modesto that everyone was wearing them for the flight and Modesto and Roberto then turned up in jeans and T-shirts. With his big black moustache and waistcoat, Pacheco looked as though he'd been waiting to get out of Cuba since 1959.

I sat with them in the departure area and bought a few beers. I was upbeat, knowing I was getting out of the country to somewhere cold and European, where even if I couldn't speak the local language English would get me through. Pacheco sat as usual fairly quietly, gesturing with his head at any overweight woman with dark hair and pursing his lips. I never grasped his taste in women. Modesto drank his beer and chatted to a Cuban friend he didn't appear to have seen for a while. Roberto talked about his work.

'I'm a technician at the television company,' he said, 'but normally I work with the satellites.'

'What satellites?'

'The American ones that broadcast films.'

'What do you mean you work with them?'

'I record the films for Cuban TV so that they can be shown here.'

'You mean you pirate films for the state?'

He shrugged his shoulders and smiled.

We got on the plane and took our seats. I was quite looking forward to the journey. It was a chance to get some useful information from the guys on which boxers were which. And a chance to gauge from people quite close to the state what was going on in the minds of officialdom about professional boxing. As we settled down, the chief steward made an announcement.

'Will Mr Modesto Aguerro please make himself known to

cabin staff?' Modesto's face drained. He got up and went forward. He came back smiling. He had been chatting to the pilot, who had been at school with him. There were three spaces in first class and he had been upgraded. The three of them picked up their bags, and grinning at me, went forward to first class, Pacheco in his suit looking now like a Communist dignitary promoted to his rightful place of luxury.

'No space for me, I suppose,' I said. Modesto did his best not to gloat and put on his best 'What-can-I-do?' face before disappearing behind the curtain. Here was a country that appeared at times to be run by the state for the benefit of foreigners, but in which everyone at a personal level did everything in their power for each other. And here was I in cattle class on Cubana for £750 while three Cubans who had paid $20 in local money for their seats were lording it in first because one of them went to school with the pilot. I chuckled out loud until the 6ft 2in Englishman with his socks off next to me started to stare.

'Sorry, mate.' Back to being English again.

The problem with the Cuban way of doing things is that if you take Cubans out of Cuba they're lost. No cousins, no family ties, no one they went to school with, and they are forced to rely on logic and on the evenhandedness of a system, which Cuba doesn't really prepare you for. When we landed at Heathrow they practically wanted me to hold their hands as we tried to find our way to the baggage reclaim. I was spending a day in London seeing a friend so I had to collect my luggage. The chaps told me that Cubana had told them their bags would be transferred directly from Heathrow to Gatwick, where their connecting flight took off in three hours. I explained to them where the bus was and, as my bags were taking a while to come through, they started to get nervous about the time and left me.

I learned later what happened to them. They made it in

time for the flight at Gatwick, only to find out that their clothes and equipment had been sitting on the carousel at Heathrow for the past few hours. They booked on to another flight the following morning and caught the first bus back to Heathrow, but they missed the last bus back to Gatwick and had to spend the night on a bench in Heathrow.

I didn't know this when I turned up in Budapest the next day. They'd given me the name of the hotel where they were staying. It was sure to be cheap if the Cubans could afford it and I wanted to be close to them to keep the relationship going, so I got a cab there. The Hotel Grot was a grim place near the centre of Budapest on a giant roundabout near the railway station. It was unkempt and uncomfortable, the doorway smelled of disinfectant, only one up from piss, and when you opened the door strong foreign cigarette smoke mingled with the smell of dust and cooking fat.

I paused for a moment. It was one of those places which gave off an overpowering sense of colour. Sadly, in this case, it was brown: from the stained walls to the peeling graffiti'd panels in the lobby and the oversized reception desk which allowed hotel staff to stand above you and look down. The lobby was empty apart from a couple of young, skinny, pasty-faced women in cheap tracksuits and an old bloke in a worn brown suit smoking a cigarette on a ripped leather sofa.

A scarred middle-aged woman in an off-white shirt and blue skirt mottled with cigarette ash was behind the desk. Her voice said, 'Welcome to the hotel, Mr Duncan.' Her eyes said, 'Fuck off, you annoying foreign wanker.'

'Can you tell me what room Mr Pacheco and Mr Aguerro are in?'

'We have no one of that name here.'

'They're Cuban friends of mine. They are booked here and I'm meeting them.'

'We have no Cubans here.'

'Could you just check again for me?'

'We have no Cubans. Here. Take keys. Room 425.'

'Well, has anyone left a message for me?'

'No message. Take keys.'

The lift was small and the doors scraped against each other as they closed. Ahhhhh. More tobacco-flavoured disinfectant. The lift wobbled from side to side as it heaved to the fourth floor. I dragged my bags out of the lift and on to the dark landing. All the rooms were set out on one side of the hall around an internal courtyard. Opposite each door was a peeling brownish wall. The lights barely worked. The door to room 425 was wooden and rattled when I put the keys in the lock. That was probably explained by the fact that marks next to the lock made it quite plain that the door had been crowbarred open at some point in the recent past. It was a narrow room about the length of a Volvo car and the width of a Ford Fiesta. There were two beds, one against the right-hand wall, the other against the left. In between them was a bedside table with an ashtray and that was it. The radiator was off because it had been disconnected. I hid my computer and complained to reception. A man came as I shivered on the bed.

'No working, move rooms. 525,' he said. And led me to room 525, which looked exactly the same but was about 2.5° C warmer. Maybe Hungary wasn't such a great idea.

A bright wintery sun shimmered into life over Budapest the next day. I was too busy shivering in the cold and dark of the Hotel Grot under the frayed edge of the single blanket that had been provided to notice. No one had stolen my computer while I slept or the cigars I had imported, so the day was already rich with promise. Breakfast was a glass of orange juice and a piece of toast you could have filed your nails on if there hadn't been a lump of pig fat sitting in the middle of it. The coffee tasted of soil, possibly nutrient rich but undrinkable. The hookers in shell suits were still sitting on the sofa. It seems they had organised themselves into shifts. How enterprising. I had to get out.

I packed everything that had the remotest value into my zip-broken leather bag and out of the stiff glass door I went. The hotel was directly above a concrete bull-ring housing a metro station, cheap pizza shops, a few newsagents' kiosks and a couple of scary-looking cheap fashion outlets. It was a fine example of Seventies horror architecture, with about fifteen exits, lots of arrows pointing to vandalised tunnels and no obvious sign of the metro entrance. I bought a local paper and asked.

The Cuban team, according to the front page of *Sport*, had landed the day before. There was a picture of Felix Savon in a suit, practically trailing the trophy on the tarmac and trying to raise a smile. I knew how he felt. The team at least had been advised to wear suits.

The stadium was a mere three stops away and I decided to avoid paying on the metro. That would teach them. I saved 20p. The teams were all staying at the hotel attached to the stadium, which meant that Miguel Hernandez from *Granma* would be based there too. They gave me his room number at reception. It perhaps showed how used I was to being paranoid that I felt they shouldn't have done. What about security? What about the enemies of socialism eager to disrupt the concentration of the representatives of our great nation? But I was too relieved to make a fuss.

The Cubans were all on the second floor and, by fate or coincidence, it turned out the Americans were too. I knocked on Miguel's door. He was lying on his bed talking to the *Granma* photographer, who surely had one of the most thankless tasks in sports journalism. Since the paper crisis had reduced *Granma* to eight pages, the chance of anything other than the minutest of ill-printed pictures appearing on the sports pages was zero unless nothing else happened in Cuba that day. And in a country where the unveiling of a new cane-cutting combine harvester made it as the lead item on the television news, that wasn't likely. The camera bag carried by most Western photographers contains huge phallic lenses and lots of tiny specialist compartments for all sorts of wide-lensed attachments. Paco's had a select few tatty lenses, possibly held together by the Festival of Youth stickers he had plonked on them and one not very technical-looking battered old 35mm body. He appeared to be constantly on the verge of apologising, not at all like the cocky snappers who inhabit sport in England. This was partly for the same reason they were lying on their hotel beds at eleven-thirty a.m. They didn't have any money to do anything else. They couldn't go to the bar. Or the café. And the stadium was as far away from the historic centre of anywhere worth looking at as you could be. Neither of them had seen Pacheco, Modesto or Roberto. I arranged to meet them in the hotel lobby for a coffee and went out of their tropically heated room into the charmless modern hallway, which was not, it has to be said, charmless enough to make anyone long for the Hotel Grot.

Up and down the hallway Alexis Rubalcaba was jogging and shadowboxing. Rubalcaba is a giant of a man, around 6ft 6in, with hands so muscled they feel as if someone has implanted his palms with rubber. He noticed me and vaguely recognised me, I think. But he had mastered the boxers' art of noticing, letting you know he had noticed and carrying on as if he hadn't noticed, letting you watch in awe without letting you know that he knew you were impressed. Rubalcaba would have made a moderate professional. His biggest plus from a pro point of view was his ability to inspire love or hatred in the public. He's one of those sporting figures on whom there is no middle ground, a fighter about whom people fight. He wasn't much loved in Cuba, mainly by virtue of not being a very technical fighter. He was slow around the ring and because he always towered over whoever was in front of him he looked like a big bully. He had also made the unforgivable error of losing in Atlanta to a Tongan, a hugely overweight Sumo merchant who wouldn't, reckoned the anti-Alexis crowd, have given a proper boxer any trouble at all. Rubalcaba underestimated him and the Tongan dropped him. It was humiliating for Cuban boxing. His style was dinosaurically slow, with his legs looking firm and rigid but his upper body ponderous, as if his body electricity just ran out of charge covering all that turf. Mainly he wasn't loved because he wasn't Teofilo Stevenson, whose inheritance as a super-heavyweight he had to try and live up to but was never going to match. But he annoyed the Cubans by beating almost every other Cuban they put in front of him. He would prod at them and prod again. They would duck and weave away from him, jolting one way and the other, his left hand stroking with the outstretched glove, his right coiled back. And then he would launch in. Not with any direction really, into the body, the gloves, anywhere. But it hurt even to watch. And if he caught your head you didn't get up. And you would hear a groan from the crowd and he would leap into the arms of Alcides Sagarra in his corner, wave his fist at the spectators, bow perfunctorily, put one leg over the top rope, then the other, and trot menacingly back to his dressing room. Personally I liked him.

I pressed the button for the lift. And when it arrived out stepped Felix Savon. He looked up and smiled and as he brushed past me he hit me in the back playfully. Between boxers playfully. 'Hey, English,' he smiled. The flattery of it lasted a half-second and then a little stinging pain in my lower back took over. Quickly into the lift.

The arena for the boxing world championship was a functional dome, dark in the upper reaches, seating about 7,000 when full, with ordinary plastic seats that managed to seem light and cheerful in comparison to the Cuban venues I'd sat in over the past year. There was a press seating area in the stands with small tables and television monitors lined up over four rows. There were two rings in the centre of the arena, darkened and glowering, purposeless for the moment, with a timekeeper's clock hanging above the centre of each ring. There was even a free bar in a sky-box above the press seats. And a press working area with computers and an Internet machine and a staff of about twenty people all buzzing around to try and help in whatever way they could. In other words, much like a normal international sporting event.

The strange thing was that even though this was all familiar territory I didn't really feel as if I had a role. This wasn't an important event journalistically for me, I hadn't been sent. No one back in England was remotely interested in what was going on. There were only three Brits there, Alex Arthur, a bright young bantamweight Scot, a cocky black kid called Ian Napa, whose hero was Naseem Hamed and who looked as if he couldn't wait to get out of the amateurs, and a heavyweight Londoner, Folando Okesola, who had done badly in Atlanta and wasn't expected to do much better here. He had, he said, been offered money to turn pro but wanted to carry on as an amateur until the right offer came along. Or maybe you don't turn pro after losing in the first round of the Olympics.

While the press operation seemed reasonable enough, anything involving the intervention of officials from the world of amateur boxing came with the emphasis on the amateur. The draw was a shambles. A giant plastic tombola was set up at the edge of the arena, with up to ninety ping-pong balls bobbing around inside, each with a team abbreviation felt-tipped on it. The tombola was supposed automatically to drop at least one ball into the selection holder, at which point the draw was filled in on a schoolroom-issue overhead projector. Predictably the tombola didn't work when there were fewer than ten balls in it, so a gormless bureaucrat had ostentatiously to turn his back, put one hand over his eyes and the other into the bowl, as if it were a lucky dip. It was all made more surreal by the Macedonians and the Greeks. Every time the Macedonian ball came out and the name was announced in English as Macedonia, one of the Greek journalists shouted out what he felt Macedonia should actually be called. The way that Iran (IRN) and Ireland (IRE) had been scribbled on the ping-pong ball also caused confusion, but after about an hour of sitting in the unlit arena with only the glow from the Mongolian tracksuits to write by it was all over and we went back to the hotel.

By this stage the Cuban journalists had decided to let me in on their food scam, possibly as a reward for helping them organise their television rights with a woman from Hungarian TV who spoke perfect English but no Spanish. The required fax and guarantee had not arrived from Havana and the day before the tournament there was still uncertainty as to what they were entitled to show. I had to do the deal for them there and then, convincing the Hungarians to give us (did I just write 'us'?) the pictures and get it sorted out with the authorities later. The food scam was small but touching. The food in the team hotel cost about a fiver for non-team members, but the team members had raffle tickets to get their food for free. The Cuban team officials were slipping the hacks the tickets not required by the team, who were being limited for weight reasons to one meal a day. So in amongst the world's finest amateur boxers in their shiny tracksuits that first night sat four blokes in jumpers enjoying high-protein fare, whilst enduring the sneers of the hotel staff, who could do nothing about it. There was something reassuring about being part of the con. I could have afforded the food – they knew it, I knew it – but I suppose they wanted me to be part of their gang, part of the Cuban team. And the best way to be inducted into the team was to learn how to survive on the grace of friends with no money and only your wits and contacts for help. It was as high a compliment as I could have been paid. The pasta was lovely. Even after the third helping.

It turned out that Pacheco, Modesto and Robertico had come to much the same conclusion as I had about the Hotel Grot, but had had the common sense not to even bother checking in. The next day I went to Tourist Information, where the woman said if I came back at closing time with $100 deposit she knew an apartment in a nice block of flats not too far away. After trying the keys she had given me in the wrong flat, much to the surprise of the occupants (the flats were all given letters rather than names and the woman's instructions were atrocious), I moved in. None of the Cubans wanted to move in with me and share the price of the flat, which had two beds, because they were in a modern hotel nearer to the stadium and next to a park in a nice part of town. They didn't fancy shifting to a tenement block next to a giant Ikea and the bus station and I didn't blame them.

At all major tournaments the pattern of life is very dull. You turn up to the venue early and catch up with any news. You wait for other people to arrive. You check the computers, scribble a few notes, think about lunch, have lunch and go to see what's going on. But I didn't have any reason to be there other than to get to know the Cubans. I couldn't check into the team hotel because it was taken by AIBA for the competing boxers and officials only. I wasn't staying with the Cuban hacks. There wasn't much point in taking notes because I wasn't working as a journalist. I got so bored that I rang up the *Scotsman* and the Scottish *Daily Herald* to file some stuff on Arthur as he fought. Just to give me a reason for being there. I needn't have worried. Once the Cubans started in earnest in the ring they found a role for me.

The scoring system in amateur boxing has changed over the years, largely as a result of a series of scandals involving home-town decisions that discredited the sport and nearly led to it being thrown out of the Olympics. There have always been rows about who did or didn't win amateur boxing bouts. In 1924 Harry Mallin of Great Britain was beaten by judge's decision by Roger Brousse, but the decision was reversed when Mallin protested and showed that Brousse had been biting him throughout the fight. In 1964 a Korean flyweight, Don Kih Choh, protested a decision by staying in the ring for an hour after the contest had finished and the Spanish featherweight Valentin Loren punched a referee in the face and was banned for life. In 1968 a dozen referees and judges were sacked for incompetence.

In an effort to make the whole thing seem less brutal, protective headgear was introduced for the 1984 Olympic Games. Controversial refereeing decisions and home bias, added to continuing allegations of bribery of judges in Seoul in 1988, forced the authorities to change the way contests were scored. Where previously three and, later, five judges were allowed to make their own judgements on who had won the fight, a system of computer scoring was devised for major events which required five judges to hit a button the moment they saw a scoring blow for one of the boxers. At least three of them had to hit the button within a certain length of time for the blow to be registered as a point by the computer. Given that judges could no longer co-ordinate with each other, it was thought it would be impossible to bribe them. Nice try. But if you've ever sat and watched a bout where one boxer rains blows in on the other and gets a point, only to see the other one cough and get five, you'll know it doesn't quite work out that way. But it's better than it was.

Anyway, the score of the contest is not usually revealed to the public in the stadium or to the fighters. However, in Budapest to those of us in the stands with access to the television feeds, the scores registered blow by blow in the top right-hand corner of our monitors. At the end of each round members of the Cuban entourage used to look over to where we were sitting and ask what the score was. Miguel and Pacheco were generally still commentating, so this became, unofficially, my job. Thumbs up for the Cuban winning. Then a number of fingers to indicate the score. Then a (usually smaller) number of fingers to indicate the opponent's score. The guy passing on my score to the corner was the team's psychologist, Jorge Luis Lopez, whom I remember mainly because he very nearly got into a fight over one decision later on in the tournament. I was cheating on behalf of Cuba. They needed me. It was fantastic.

Maikro Romero was the first Cuban to fight on the first day. He was one of my favourite boxers, a slippery, highly technical fighter whom it was impossible to lay a punch on. He was as much of a ducker and diver outside the ring as he was in it. After the fight Romero came up to me in the bar of his hotel, where I used to hang out and grab a coffee.

'Buy me a beer?'

'Yeah, sure.'

'No, no, not here. They're watching.' He pointed with his forefinger and index finger as if he was imitating a pair of scissors and tapped them on his shoulder quickly so no one could see what he was doing. I'd seen this before. It meant that someone from the team security services was around.

'In the press bar, tonight, after the boxing, yeah?'

'Yeah.'

So at the end of the evening's boxing he came over to where the Cuban television gang sat among the world's TV crews and motioned me with his eyes to meet him underneath the stadium. I followed. He was with another of the Cubans, Isael Alvarez, the light heavyweight, both of them in their immaculate Cuban national tracksuits. We got in the lift to the press bar, where I had not seen a boxer the entire time I was there.

276

They sat down in a corner looking nervous, hoping, I suppose, that no one would notice them. I queued up and got a couple of free beers from the Formica table that served as a bar. They took them, looked around and drank them in one – I, all the while, looking out for Cuban journalists who might take this the wrong way, as a corrupt Westerner leading the nation's athletic elite astray with the temptations of the flesh. Luckily no one saw. And with the beer downed they were gone as quickly as they had come.

'Thanks.'

'You're welcome.'

Gone.

The next day Maikro walked into the hotel lobby with the welterweight Juan Hernandez Sierra and came up to me.

'Can you come and help us?'

'Sure, what's going on?'

'In Budapest no one speaks Spanish.' I think he expected me to be shocked by this revelation. 'You speak English, don't you? Come and help us in the garage.'

We walked over to the petrol station across the road from the hotel, where there were two other boxers looking at wing-mirrors and locking petrol caps.

'Ask them if this wing-mirror is for a Lada,' he said.

I asked. It was. The attendant had one himself on his own Lada.

'Ask him how much it is in dollars.'

The attendant had no idea. So in my head I translated it from Hungarian currency into pounds, which I knew, and into dollars from there.

'It's about fifteen bucks,' I said.

'That's expensive,' said Maikro. 'Will this one fit a Lada?' He pointed to a cheaper, plastic one. It was one of those wing-mirrors that fits any car because you have to drill a hole in the bodywork and attach it. It was ten bucks.

'Yes.'

'Tell him we'll take one each.'

The attendant looked at them, amazed and slightly awe-struck. He knew who they were – those gleaming tracksuits gave them away – and he knew they were probably among the best boxers in the world. With the stories going around of million-dollar contracts for their own Hungarian local, Istvan Kovacs, the attendant knew these guys shouldn't be worrying about the price of a Lada wing-mirror. He didn't look old enough to remember that not long ago Hungarians were in much the same boat.

'Ask him whether they sell tyres here.'

They didn't. Not for Ladas. But there was a new tyre warehouse a hundred yards away. So off we went. I didn't quite see what they were up to. 'How on earth are you going to carry spare Lada tyres back with you to Havana? Surely Lada tyres are the one thing you could get for yourself back in Cuba?'

'Yes,' said Maikro, 'but in Cuba they are very expensive and there are not many good-quality tyres. We always come back with Lada tyres. There's no problem. Everyone does it.'

Juan Hernandez Sierra was happy with his wing-mirror, shook his head and left us to go to the tyre warehouse alone.

'Ask him how much these tyres are,' said Maikro when we got there. It was a standard Western tyre warehouse, clean, rubber-smelling, blokes in overalls.

'A hundred dollars for two,' said the man.

'Too much. Ask him if he has any secondhand.'

'No. We don't do them.'

He drew us a map of where a man he knew sold Lada retreads and off we went. It was a couple of miles and we could have got a tram or a taxi, but we walked because it was cheaper. We chatted along the way, but whenever I intro-duced boxing he didn't really want to talk about it. And when he did get animated I couldn't understand a word. He spoke quickly and in short bursts, fast even for a Cuban. His manner and even his look was of a quickfire Irish hustler, cheeky as hell, ducking and diving, ducking and diving, his words monotonal and quick, a few rounds of talk and then silence. We walked on the pavement along a busy six-lane highway into an industrial area of the city. When we reached a dark railway bridge with no footpath we balanced on the inch of kerb and made our way between the cars, which stopped abruptly as this tiny athlete in his Cuba tracksuit darted between them, accompanied by a tall skinny white boy in scruffy tracksuit bottoms and a cheap coat.

We walked down into a basement, where the man was playing around with some scruffy-looking tyres. He smiled.

'Ask him if he has any second-hand tyres for a Lada.'

He had a whole selection.

'These good, look at tread on them,' said the man, 'they practically new. Only twenty-five dollars each, look.'

He got a calculator out, worked out what they were in Hungarian currency and translated it into dollars. Well, you had to give it to Maikro, these tyres did look almost as good as the ones back at the warehouse and at twenty-five dollars I had to admit he was getting a bargain.

'Too expensive. Ask him if he'll accept ten dollars. Or ask him if he's got anything else.'

Was he serious? A practically new tyre for twenty-five bucks and he wanted me to haggle the guy down?

'Errr. It's a little expensive. Could you do it for ten?'

Maikro grabbed the calculator out of his hand and tapped in the number ten. And smiled as if butter wouldn't melt in his mouth. If the man had spat at us both I wouldn't have blamed him.

'He wants these tyres for ten dollars? He must be out of his mind.'

Maikro was already away ferreting at the back. 'What about these?' he said, pointing to a sorry-looking pair of tyres, one of them with some serious bald patches, the other one pretty good.

'They're Lada for sure. The bald one you can have for ten but not the other.'

Maikro smiled and looked doubtful. Then pleading. 'Boxing. World champion. Cuban.' This was obviously a well-practised end-game and he struck gold.

'My brother, he box tonight in stadium. OK, ten dollars each. You mad.'

And so out we went, one tyre each, and treated ourself to a tram ride back to the hotel which cost 10 per cent of what Maikro had just spent on two tyres. I paid. We arrived back at the hotel carrying our tyres and went casually upstairs as if we had just strolled in after buying a newspaper. People, suffice to say, stared. 'Bring it to the room,' said Maikro. We waited for the lift with the dirty tyres leaning against our legs. Maikro was totally oblivious to any attention we were attracting. We went up in the lift and walked briskly to his room.

Maikro put his tyre in the bathroom, while I went to put mine over by the chair that was next to the window. There were two beds in the room – the boxers each had to share – and as I passed the second bed I saw that lying on the pile of suits and gloves and plastic bags was a used syringe.

My heart stopped. There was probably an entirely innocent explanation for it but I didn't want to raise the issue with Maikro. I didn't even want to think about it. He was still in the bathroom. I turned instantly and headed for the door. 'See you later, Maikro.'

The Cuban boxing team have had drug 'problems' in the past. It is also worth remembering that many of the advances in Cuban sport came under the influence of East German sports advisers, who were often happy to provide steroids to their own athletes back home if they helped prove the superiority of Communism. The physical dominance of Cuban boxers is also noteworthy. I lost count of the number of times I saw them up against foreigners who were two or three inches shorter and smaller than they were because the Cuban simply had no fat where he didn't need it. Cuban boxers have legs like sticks, chests like sculptured stone and arms like sides of ham. You can get a body like that by unbelievably hard training. Or you can get it by hard training mixed with steroids and diuretics to flush out excess water.

Five of the elite of Cuban amateur boxing have been banned for using diuretics, drugs which fighters use to shed weight quickly before a fight, a dangerous practice that has been blamed for several of boxing's most serious injuries. But let's not get paranoid here. It could have been vitamins. Or a painkiller. Or one of umpteen innocent things. For all I knew Maikro was a diabetic, but I never asked.

The next day word seemed to have spread that there was an English press guy who understood Cuban Spanish and could get you a good deal on Lada tyres. I was summoned from my morning coffee by Maikro and a group of three other boxers, who wanted to visit the giant Chinese market in Budapest, but wanted to make sure they weren't ripped off because they didn't speak English. My other role was to pay for the cab because the market was a little too far to walk.

When we got to the entrance there were metal detectors at the gate and two giant white guys, with blond, short-cropped hair, goatee beards and Harringtons with a security company name emblazoned on them, who looked like neo-Nazis or northern nightclub bouncers. There had been occasional shooting incidents in the market, a vast shambles of cramped stalls so close together that it felt as if you were undercover. The market specialised in utterly fake gear of occasionally reasonable and occasionally joke quality. All very cheap. And there were watches (fake), perfumes (even faker), hooky videos, crisps (bootleg crisps!), a few CDs and household appliances. It was to this last section that the group headed instantly, competing against each other to buy a set of saucepans. We must have walked a mile around the stalls trying to save two dollars on a set of cheap pans until they were satisfied they had located the best price in the market and then haggled it down further, smiling innocently all the time and stretching out their hands in a downward motion to indicate that they wanted it cheaper. Occasionally one of the stallholders would pull out a calculator and tap in a price in dollars. At which point one of the group would enter another much lower number and point to it. If I had been interested in learning Hungarian, I could have picked up some useful expletives that day.

Communism was wasted on these boys – they were born marketeers. One of the group managed to locate a stall selling cheap booze and found the only half-bottle of rum in Budapest, which we snapped up for $2.50 and shared to keep out the cold. We got a cab back to the hotel and everyone was happy. I understood maybe a quarter of what they were saying and I still felt like the slightly weedy kid at school grateful for the attention of the rugby team hard boys who, temporarily, needed me. But I couldn't help feeling that all the hard (OK, not very hard) work was paying off and that I was closer to the team than I had ever had any right to expect when I had arrived in Havana ten months before. Most of the rest of the plan, which ought to have been the easy part, Warren and his backing, Tyson remaining world champion, that sort of stuff, had unravelled hopelessly and left me in a stew. But no one could complain that I hadn't done my bit. I'd promised to get inside the camp, to get to know people, to understand them well enough to be trusted. And indeed here I was with about

$5 million of boxing talent haggling over the price of saucepans.

In fact it surprised me how far I had managed to get into the team, although Sagarra was still refusing interviews. He still insisted that it all had to be organised through official channels, which meant in practice that I would have to pay some money to an official body for the privilege. Still, he was on fine form in the championships, which did not go entirely to plan for the Cubans. My favourite Sagarra moment came during one of Alexis Rubalcaba's early bouts. As he often did, Rubalcaba spent much of the early part of the bout half asleep, prodding and prodding, waiting for a chance to unleash one big hit. Except that this time he didn't unleash anything and got caught a couple of times. This was what had got him beaten by the fat Tongan in Atlanta. And when the bell went for the end of the first round Sagarra, who was fuming in the Cuban corner on the stool next to the trainer, stopped him from getting up and putting the stool in Rubalcaba's corner to give him some rest. Sagarra just sat there below the ring with his arms folded shouting at no one in particular as Rubalcaba came over. Rubalcaba had to stand with his back to the ropes watching the other guy rest and spit until the buzzer went for the next round. He got the message and knocked his opponent unconscious with one pulverising blow two rounds later. He came out of the ring screaming with aggressive adrenalin-fuelled pride. Sagarra simply walked ten yards behind him, impassive with his eyes to the ground.

The one problem Sagarra couldn't solve in Budapest was Savon. Felix had done just about enough here, beating a Swede, a Russian, a Canadian and a Dane without really getting into trouble, though the first bout against the Swedish lawyer, Kwamena Turkson, who had a tattoo of Che Guevara on one arm, was won only 4–2. He was surfing precariously on the fear of his opponents and hoping that his size and technique and record would intimidate the judges. But in only one fight did he look as if he could knock out his rival at will. In truth he looked tired and punchless again. None of Sagarra's encouragement worked. There just didn't seem to be anything left in that huge right hand. I found out why when I met him in the lobby one afternoon. I held out my hand in a fist and he held out his. It was horribly deformed, with a huge bulge just behind the knuckle the size of a knuckleduster, which must have been incredibly painful every time he used it in anger. One of my Cuban friends whispered to me that the fact he was fighting at all here was a miracle, that, as happens to many professional fighters, there comes a time when your fists just go, rebel at the constant battering you put them through, and you can't hit any more. And Savon's time had come.

The Cubans did not have a great championships. Partly it was because they were weaker than normal in three or four key divisions (Aldo Moreno, Rudinelson Hardy and Roberto Guerra were mediocre by Cuban standards and were well beaten early in the competition). Partly it was because the Russians were doing better than expected and getting the benefit of the referee's opinions (Waldemar Font was unlucky to lose to a Russian in his final); and partly thanks to a very home-town decision against Ariel Hernandez, who couldn't seem to get the scoreboard moving whatever he did against the Hungarian finalist.

Despite that, the team title came down to two finals. Savon against Chagaev and Rubalcaba against Kandelaki. If one of the two Cubans could win their final, then the team trophy, more valued by the collectivist Cubans than by other teams, it had to be said, would be theirs. The Cubans had won it on every occasion but one (1989) that the championship had been held and then the championships passed into Cuban boxing mythology as the disaster of Moscow – a four-gold-medal disaster, but a disaster none the less.

During the week the Cuban press corps became convinced that the tournament had been rigged against them all along and the number of dodgy-looking Russian geezers in sharp suits who were wandering around the hall with official passes did little to dispel their anger. They knew the Russians, Communist or capitalist, well enough not to trust them.

Savon looked tentative and uncomfortable. Every time he looked like getting on top of his opponent, the Uzbekhi Ruslan Chagaev, the referee moved in to disrupt the rhythm of the fight. But by then I was as hopelessly biased as the rest of the team. To my eyes, nothing that Savon landed registered a score and what looked like air shots from Chagaev scored points instantly. The referee even took two early points from Savon for mysterious low blows, which meant if one more was given against him he was disqualified. It left an injured Savon without a big punch unable to attack very much for fear of being thrown out. By the end he looked demoralised, helpless and beaten. Even so, the final score of 14–4 was an insult. Chagaev was remarkably sanguine afterwards. 'It wasn't a surprise for me, that the judges took two points from Savon,' he said, 'because he was warned before. It is a very pleasant feeling to beat a living legend, but to tell the truth Savon is not as good as he was three or four years ago. It seems he's getting older. I feel I didn't get any help from the judges despite what the Cubans say. I feel the point difference is correct.'

Rubalcaba was worse. He never got going and lost his bout genuinely, to few Cuban complaints. He was in tears afterwards, comforted by the same Sagarra who had shunned him a few days previously. The Russians won the world championship by 53 points to 52.

A week later it was revealed by an American newspaper that Chagaev had fought professionally a couple of times in

Chicago, strictly against AIBA's rules, and he was stripped of his heavyweight title. Savon, with no fanfare, no ceremony and no national anthem, was the world champion and therefore so were the Cuban team.

Despite the rows over that fight, Savon had not looked very good and sitting there in the stadium as the rings were being dismantled it struck me hard and firm in the gut that it was too late for him. He couldn't hope to have a proper career in professional boxing because he had probably now lost a crucial part of what made him great, his big right hand, and that if he was starting to be found out by moderate amateurs in Budapest he would get murdered very quickly in the pros. He was too old to have much time to adapt. It wasn't going to work. Strangely, I felt relieved. It gave me a reasonable sporting basis to add to the increasing moral and financial doubts that I now had over the whole project.

In fact I felt quite happy as I sat in the hotel lobby on the final evening of the championships. The teams were all going to the official closing dinner that night and no journalists were invited. As far as I could tell even my Cuban comrades had not managed to scam their way in. There was to be a team party at the embassy: the other journalists had mentioned it was happening, but I didn't want to put them in the awkward position of having to tell me I couldn't go. So I sat and listened to an Argentinian and an Iranian trying to commiserate with each other and chuckled as an AIBA official worriedly announced over a loudspeaker that several teams had not yet paid their bills. Several men in bright tracksuits smirked. I had had a good time.

'Excuse me, sir. Are you Mr Yon Dooncan?'

It was an elegant, portly Cuban who I hadn't met before. He wasn't part of the team as far as I knew. One of the hacks must have given him my name and he must be looking for some sort of help that required English. It was the least I could do.

'Yes,' I said. 'How can I help you?'

'I have been sent by the ambassador to take you to the team party. Mr Hernandez and Mr Pacheco are already there and waiting for you. I have to leave now.'

There wasn't time to go back to my own apartment and get changed, so I walked out in my tracksuit bottoms and T-shirt into the waiting black Mercedes and the Budapest night.

It only struck me halfway there that I was being driven through a town where no one knew me, by a driver I had never met, to a party that I wasn't invited to. If I were to disappear no one would ever know what had happened. Maybe I had been found out. Maybe my personal movie plot had changed in mid-reel from jolly old happy ending *Our Man in Havana* to dark and serious *Long Good Friday* and here I was stuck with the Bob Hoskins ending, sitting there alone in a car smiling at my unfortunate fate. This quaint world view that I had embarked upon was nonsense. There were seriously dangerous people in the world I had naively wandered into and like the typical silly hack on a trip I hadn't thought that anything could possibly happen to me. But maybe it could. We turned into a quiet suburban road and stopped. The driver got out and jogged urgently round to the passenger door. He opened it, reaching into his pocket.

'This is the ambassador's residence. I have to go and pick up a couple of other people. This is the invite you will need to get in. I'll see you later.'

As I went through the front door there was Pacheco sitting beside a small table in the hallway. There were only a few people there, all Cubans, sipping beer and chatting. After a while we ate a proper Cuban feast with pork and chicken and rice and beans and Pacheco told dirty jokes after dinner to entertain the guests as the plates were cleared away.

At about eleven p.m. the team turned up in their team blazers, an elegant grey with the Cuban boxing-team shield on

287

the left breast and shiny new stripy ties at varieties of half-mast. It made the smaller boxers like Maikro, who constantly had his hands in his pockets, look like naughty schoolboys. The surreal element was that each of the gold-medal-winning boxers had been given a dagger as his prize by the AIBA officials, which they were all carrying around the room with them. Perhaps the very same ones with which they stabbed us in the back, I muttered to Savon. He didn't understand me.

For the first time I had been involved with them, some serious team boozing went on and more than a couple of the boxers were pleasantly pissed. Savon let me have my picture taken with him playfully putting his fist against my jaw. I watched them all dance and chat up the ambassador's daughter. Savon asked if he could borrow fifty bucks off me to buy some souvenirs. I didn't have it. What surprised me most was the transformation in the normally quiet and cautious Sagarra. He was chatting enthusiastically and yelling with laughter. I realised that I was witnessing something revealed to few outside the immediate circle of the team. Sagarra was rat-arsed.

After a time as we stood around in the smallish front room of the official residence the ambassador called for silence. He welcomed the boxers, made a perfunctory speech of condolence to the team for not having won the world championship, and introduced Sagarra, who was standing next to me. As I turned to listen to him, I realised I was practically in his face.

As the room looked at him he stood there with a smile on his face, looking at the carpet, and said nothing. The stony captivated silence of a room that had been raucous and noisy a few seconds before never wavered. 'Comrades.' Pause. He picked out a face and stared. One second. Two seconds. Three seconds. Not a sound. 'We were not born to be losers.' One second, two seconds, three seconds. 'Does anybody here feel like a loser?' Silence. One second, two seconds, three seconds.

'No one in this room is a loser. Nobody.' He was shouting now. Stylistically it was pure bombastic vintage Fidel Castro and it was mesmerising. 'Let me talk to you about winners.' He put on his glasses and reached for a piece of paper. Pure demogogic genius, timed perfectly. And he reeled off a list of the boxing achievements of Cuba, of the medals and the champions and the statistics that showed how great Cuba was, is and always would be, never mind what had happened that day. He talked about the week and picked out the good things to be taken from the championships. He picked out Rubalcaba for special praise and ordered the group not to blame him for the loss of the team trophy. Rubalcaba had been trying to hide in the corner as best a 6ft 6in giant in a blazer and a stripy tie can. And as he said it, the group turned to Rubalcaba and their sympathy was almost palpable. He picked out Savon, who felt invincible again. Listening to Sagarra there was almost a religious moment, his control of the room was so powerful. And when he finished he stood and stared in silence and a voice shouted from behind me, 'Viva Cuba. Viva Fidel.' It was Felix Savon. And he said it with all his heart and at that moment I knew beyond any reasonable doubt that I would never be seeing Felix Savon in a professional boxing ring. And if the truth be told I was glad.

20 *The Total Boxer: Adolfo Horta*

According to popular myth, Camaguey was designed to be a confusing city. Its streets are not on a grid system like the majority of Cuban towns but more like the rambling chaos of urban England. Local tourist guides will tell you that the city was designed like this to disorientate the pirates who regularly worked the shipping routes of the Caribbean and who would also loot and pillage inland if there was little booty to be gained on the high seas at the time. Camaguey is inland, another in the line of cities on the central route from Havana in the west to Santiago de Cuba in the east. Confusing as the street patterns might have appeared to someone brought up with roads and avenues and relentless right angles, to anyone who has had to struggle with the cramped, smudged newsprint of a London *A to Z*, getting around Camaguey was pretty basic.

What made it genuinely perplexing to visit was a much more modern peril, a one-way system which led you round in circles unless you were very careful. By the time I went to Camaguey to meet Adolfo Horta, however, I had become somewhat loose in my adherence to traffic regulations and took an ambivalent Habanero approach to one-way signs, i.e. I ignored them unless there was a policeman standing in the middle of the one-way street I wanted to go up (if he was only on the pavement I just drove a bit more slowly).

Camaguey is unlike the rest of Cuba in more than mere street layout. Having gone round the city once, guided by an unhelpful series of blue arrows that led teasingly close to my desired hotel before diverting sharply at the last second in the opposite direction, I decided to cut across town down an admittedly narrow one-way street. At which point an old man on a street corner told me I couldn't go down it and pointed to the fairly obvious No Entry sign. Bizarre. Must be a nutter. Then the car behind started hooting at me, much as would have happened in any country where people have faith in road signs and the terrible things that can happen to you if you ignore their power. Had the Special Period ended and no one had told me? Just as I was wondering what to do, two young kids on bikes sidled up to the window and asked me where I wanted to go. I smelled a hustle – well, it isn't exactly an original hustling situation, lost tourist, badly lit city, all his belongings on the back seat, trying to go up a one-way street, I was asking for it. They told me to follow them and then they whistled through the streets, around corners without brakes, their feet scraping against the road to slow down until, without breaking any traffic regulations other than all of those which relate to cyclists and pavements and the protection of pedestrians, we arrived at the hotel. It wasn't so great and I went to another one. They showed me the way to that one too. And at the end of it they looked quite insulted when I offered them a dollar for their trouble. I chatted to them for a while and told them that I was here to see Adolfo Horta, 'el hombre de boxeo total' (the total boxer) as he had been christened by one of Cuba's boxing writers. Rather like the Dutch soccer team with Cruyff and Neeskens in the early seventies who could all do everything, Horta was called the total boxer because he could adapt in mid-fight to whatever tactic was required and was brilliant at all the three distances of boxing: short, medium and long. Horta would fight you up close, at arm's length and anywhere in between. And wherever you were least comfortable, that is where you would find yourself fighting him. It was a typically functional and descriptive nickname, but the world was already too full of Kids and Sugars and Babies. It was given him by TV journalist and senior boxing hack Rolando Crespo.

I wanted to meet Horta very much and assumed that the local sports authorities would be able to put me in touch. I had rung ahead to check with the local INDER that Horta was in town. Now I needed them to tell me where he lived.

'Do any of you know where the INDER offices are?'

'Sure. But if you want to meet Horta I know where he lives.' They gave me an address and told me to ask one of the neighbours. 'Everyone knows where he lives, you'll find it easily.'

Indeed everyone did. In a pitch-black back street I knocked on the grand wooden door of a ground-floor apartment in a solid row of colonial terraces. After I'd knocked twice a head appeared out of the window of a neighbouring flat and stared.

'Do you know where Adolfo Horta is, please?' I asked.

'He's at his mother's house eating, I should think. He spends most of his time there and only really sleeps here. It's near the television station. Go down there, turn left, carry straight on and then ask. Everyone knows it.' There was a blackout, an *apagon*. You don't know what a dark street is until you've tried to walk down one without any electrical aid.

I followed the instructions as best I could understand them and kept asking for the television station. It was pitch black but, next to the television station, which had a shopfront little bigger than a TV repair shop, a woman was sitting on the steps. When I asked her for directions she said nothing but pointed across the road. It was only when I got within five yards that I saw a middle-aged black man in a string vest sitting on his step. He was visible only because of the smouldering cigarette hanging from one side of his mouth.

'Excuse me, can you tell me if this is Adolfo Horta's house?'

'Yes.'

'And is he in? I've come from Havana to interview him.'

The man nodded. 'I'm Horta,' he said.

It was late and there was a power cut, so it wasn't really a good time to chat. We smoked a cigarette or two and I explained that I was writing about the history of Cuban boxing and wanted to interview him. We agreed to meet at a hotel in the centre of town next day.

The hotel was old colonial and we sat in the marble lobby at a cheap glass table with three wicker chairs placed round it. We ordered two beers. The traditional wailing ballads struggled out of the hotel PA system at a ridiculous volume and it was impossible to hear him. Very gently he asked the waiter to turn it down and it was done. They knew him, he didn't need to strut or shout. His power over the people around him came from respect, like a Mafia boss. Its source was never mentioned, but it was there.

'I was born in San Lorenzo, which is a part of Santiago de Cuba, in 1957. People who lived there basically worked on coffee plantations. Times were pretty hard and my parents had to move around to gather coffee to earn whatever they could get. My mother was pregnant with me and carried on working. Anyway, she was out gathering coffee one day when she saw a snake in a bush. It wasn't a poisonous snake or anything, but it gave her a real fright and she gave birth there and then. To be honest, I've never actually been to San Lorenzo; the only time I was ever there was when I was born. My parents spent most of my childhood moving around. In 1967 they moved here to

Camaguey and in 1970 I started boxing. I spent some of my childhood in Moron, with my brothers – there were twelve of us in all. We wandered all over the place.'

To understand this a little bit of geography is in order, just in case Horta's casual description of his early life gives you the impression the family were popping into the next-door village from time to time. San Lorenzo is a tiny place at the south-eastern tip of the island, seventy miles from Santiago. Moron is a good 350 miles away in the province of Ciego de Avila, at least a third of the island's length further west and north. Camaguey is not that close to either of them.

'I remember Moron reasonably well, growing up with the family. We were always having a laugh, messing around, normal boys' stuff, I suppose. I couldn't say I did sport. We fought amongst ourselves a bit, played a bit of baseball. Afterwards I came here to Camaguey and a couple of years later I started on the road to being a boxer. It was in a place called Floral, where all the kids got involved in sport in some form. There were all sorts of coaches. I didn't really like the idea of boxing. I just sat there watching people boxing, but all the time I was watching I was picking up stuff about how to do it. I was there every day for about three or four months. The trainer was saying to me every day, "Come on, kid, come and put on the gloves," and I just said, "No, thanks, I don't like boxing." And the next day there I would be sitting watching again. The trainer still lives here in Camaguey, Jorge Navarro. He lives close to here. Anyway one day he just came over and told me to put the gloves on. He insisted, so I did. I got in the ring, and having watched what everyone else was doing I boxed pretty well. He told me to come the next day and I did. And that was where it started. I trained every day after that until my first fight a couple of months on. I lost. I won the second and the third. And I got to the stage where I had fought seven times, lost five and won twice. I told the trainer I didn't want to do it any more because I wasn't any good. He told me to keep on training, that I would be OK once I had developed a bit and by the time I was able to compete in proper competitions I would be good. That time came in 1971 and I entered the national championships at 40kg and I won. The next year, in '72, I got the bronze in the 46kg. In '73 I did it again, another weight up at 51kg, and I won the title.'

This somehow didn't ring true. To be a good boxer in later life normally means starting out with something special and building on it. All the other histories of Cuban boxers had been stories where the boxer got into the ring and was an instant revelation even as a kid. Why was Horta different?

'Because from the moment I decided to do it I absolutely committed myself to it, you see. From then on I trained every single day. I looked after myself and I went to the local sports academy, where I work now. Normally in those days you just went there for the day, ate there, trained, but I used to live there and I only went home at weekends and went back to the training camp on Sunday nights. It really meant that I had to be disciplined. There were a lot of boxers from my part of town, but I was the only one who really made it because of that discipline and dedication. My attitude was that if I was going to box I was going to be someone in the sport.

'When I was fourteen I was already starting to box against men of twenty and over in weight categories above me because I'd got too good for people my own age and they didn't want me hurting anyone. I got called up to the national squad when I was sixteen years and two months old. I went to Hungary with the national team to take part in the Honved tournament. I lost my first fight at that level against a Korean. From there I came back to take part in the Copa Cardin, which that year was here in Camaguey. I fought a Russian, Victor Liminov, and in the first round I knocked him down twice. In the second he hit me with a low blow right here in the balls and, well, I lost the fight. Around this time we were preparing for the first world championships, which were to be hosted in Havana in 1974. I couldn't take part because I wasn't old enough. Anyway, they gave me a fight against the guy who had beaten me in the national championships who was going to represent Cuba at the worlds and I beat him. So Alcides Sagarra and Honorato Espinosa asked me to train with the world championship team anyway to get a bit more experience. That was where my success all started.'

In many ways Horta's accidental start in boxing should never have happened. For all the much vaunted skill of the Cubans in picking up and nurturing talent it was a white butcher Jorge Navarro, who had never boxed, who had kept Horta in the sport after those early setbacks, who went on pestering him to put on the gloves and give it a go and who had drawn him to the attention of the boxing bodies as a hopeful.

'Apart from being my first trainer, he was like a father figure to me. He came to the boxing academy every single day and talked to me about how to look after myself, how to behave, what to eat, how to sleep, the standards that were expected of me there. He brought me money as well, for treats and things. He always loved me like that. He wasn't ever a boxer, but he was a big influence. He was very proper, very calm, very respectable and as a trainer, as a revolutionary, as a person he was amazing. And, for me, like a father. I have to say that when my career was over I dedicated everything I achieved to him.

'My mum and dad are separated, my dad lives in Ciego and my mum here. My mum didn't want me boxing. She used to hit me until I promised her I wouldn't box any more. So I had to train in secret and fight in secret as well. I had to tell her that I was going to watch some other kids boxing and she let me go and I would get in the ring myself. I had to swear that I wasn't doing it. She realised that I was a boxer when I came back one night after they had offered me a place in the regional academy and I told her that I was going, that I was a boxer now and there was nothing she could do about it. But to this day my mum has never seen me fight. Eighteen years in the sport and she has never sat down to even one second of my 319 fights on the radio or on the television. When I was fighting she locked herself in the bedroom and put a pillow over her head. She was able to watch other people boxing, but when they announced my bout she would run to her bedroom. My brother would tell her at the end what the result was.'

It was Navarro who, despite having no experience in the ring himself, and thus possibly no prejudice about the 'right' style of boxing, taught Horta the skill which made him outstanding as a boxer. Most fighters have a favourite distance in which they prefer to work: either at close range, where they can work head to head on the body, breaking away for occasional uppercuts; at long distance, where they can wear down an opponent with jabs and enter and withdraw before their opponent can reply; or the middle distance, where both fighters remain in range and can brawl. Much of the skill of boxing comes in imposing your preferred distance on an opponent who might not be as good at that range. Horta, though, could fight from any distance and adapt his style to whoever was put in front of him. It would be similar to an athlete who was Olympic class at 100 metres, 400 metres and 1500 metres. It is that rare. And it made him exceptionally difficult to box against.

'It was Navarro who gave me that. He made me practise each distance equally every day. My speed might have made me more suited to box at long distance, but I didn't ask questions. And he taught me how to be good in all of them. So when I got to the national squad, Alcides Sagarra and Honorato Espinosa trained me in all three as well. I felt comfortable right from the beginning in all of them and I always enjoyed the intelligent side of the ring, the technical side, and because I was good in whatever distance I was able to play tactical games inside the ring, to think under fire.'

The man who really got to work on him when he arrived at national level with the seniors was Honorato Espinosa, who trained him for the fourteen years he was with the Cuban national team. He was remarkably young when he arrived in Havana in 1974, only sixteen years old. Cuban amateur boxing had found its feet with the help of the Russians and East Germans. Two years previously at the Munich Olympics Teofilo Stevenson, Orlando Martinez and Emilio Correa had won Cuba's first boxing gold medals, a feat so unexpected that the Russians immediately withdrew the trainer who had helped set up the Cuban National Boxing Academy, Andrei Chervorenko, against his will. The Cubans were to win five more golds at the inaugural world championships in Havana in 1974.

'I got the bus to Havana and arrived at the training camp. I was the youngest and smallest there. I saw all these people around me who were champions of Pan-American Games and the Olympics. It was great for me because I had something new to aim for. I could see what they had achieved and it made me want to get there too. Honorato Espinosa kept me on the straight and narrow, because sixteen is a dangerous age to be in Havana, when your body and your mind are changing and you're eager to try things out. I felt a bit strange at first in the Finca. Everyone was really close to each other, constantly taking the piss. I didn't dare laugh at anything at first and they used me as a butt of jokes quite a bit because I was so young. I didn't laugh. I couldn't really understand why they wanted to take the piss out of me. They used to call me "son" and ask me to fetch them things and I suppose gradually I got to know them well enough to answer back and we were fine. We never fought among ourselves and we shared everything with each other. It was really like a family.'

The head of the family was, of course, Alcides Sagarra, who, after 1972, had an even more important role following Chervorenko's departure.

'I'd heard of Alcides, of course, and I'd seen him, but I had never actually spoken to him. The first time I had come across him was my first Playa Giron [national championships] in Havana. At the championships there's always a meeting of boxers and trainers from all over the country and I remember sitting behind a post so that he wouldn't notice me and pull me out of the group and embarrass me. He was one of those people who you know deserves respect. They never found out that I used to smoke in secret. Even today I'm too embarrassed to smoke in front of Honorato Espinosa or Alcides Sagarra, even now when I can do what I like. That was the sort of respect we had at that time. Alcides Sagarra is like the father figure of all Cuban sport. He's been around since 1963 and he's always been like that, as a person and a trainer. As a man he is the best and as a trainer he has introduced a discipline into the Cuban set-up which I believe is unmatched anywhere else in the world. Don't get me wrong. He's not created this discipline merely by being a humourless straight up and down person, which is how he appears to the outside world. He has a laugh at the right time with the team. The secret is that he knows when to relax with the team and when to be firm.'

In 1974 Horta was in the national squad, a rise more rapid than any other of Cuba's boxing stars of the time. But he wasn't able to take part in the world championships because of his age. 'It wasn't all that disappointing because I was training with the team in Varadero for those championships and I felt part of what was going on. I was only a kid, what did I expect? I was already way ahead of where I should have been. My own eye was on 1976 and the Montreal Olympics because I was going to be eighteen by then and able to take part.'

But 1976 was a disappointment too, with Horta not going to Montreal. In his place went Orlando Martinez, who was the Olympic champion at Horta's weight of 54kg (bantamweight).

'There was a Copa Cardin in Pinar del Rio in 1976 and I fought Martinez in the final there. He got the decision, but it was a very close fight. When it came to pick the fighters who would go to Mexico to prepare for the Olympics, I was out. That defeat hurt me a lot. You know that was the last time I ever lost to a Cuban? Not one Cuban ever beat me from 1976 to the day I retired, not in bantamweight, featherweight or lightweight. If I had won, I would have gone to the Olympics. As it happens, in Montreal, Martinez went and lost to a Korean in the second round, who I had murdered in the Cinturon de Oro the previous year. But there you go.'

Horta's disappointment was soon eased when he won his first national championship in his home town of Camaguey in 1976. It was the first of eleven successive national championships won at three different weights. 'It was superb to win it in my own town. I remember I had to fight José Aguilar [later a 60kg fighter], who had beaten me the previous year. I toyed with the guy, ducking, diving, leaning back, dropping my guard, but not letting him lay a finger on me, and the crowd lapped it up. The fans always told me that I reminded them of Kid Chocolate and even Kid Chocolate said he could see it. He told me in Havana once that he wished he was a few years younger and could get in the ring with me to see who would have won. When I retired he used to pester me to come out so he could watch me again because he liked to see me so much.'

One of the reasons for Horta's flexibility was his ability to lose or gain weight with little apparent difference to his strength in the ring. When Horta fought Jackie Beard in New York in a USA versus Cuba contest he had arrived five days before the match 15kg overweight. He lost the weight by not eating for four days and then getting in the ring and trouncing the American. Horta took part in nine of these contests and won six times. 'I enjoyed those bouts because the Americans all fought in a professional style, in the middle distance. Seeing as I could fight in all three I used to take them on in the middle distance. I'm not a political animal at all, but when I was boxing like that I felt like I was fighting for Cuba and for Fidel, that Fidel was watching back in Cuba and I couldn't let anyone down. They are our enemies OK in politics and, well, they are our enemies in sport too, I suppose. We were competing for the prestige of the country, so . . .'

Horta's moment finally came at the world championships in Belgrade in 1978, when he won his first world title of three, all at different weights, an unprecedented achievement. He must have been good because he beat a Yugoslav home favourite in the final on the 3–2 decision of the judges. 'At a world championships you have five fights in the space of two weeks, but we were well prepared for that. When we were on our mini-tours of Europe to Poland and Bulgaria, sometimes we would fight every day for five days in a row. But when I saw that I had a Yugoslav in the final I knew I was going to have to really wallop him to get the decision because I was fighting him and the public. I made it my business after a fight, no matter how hard, to get straight back in the arena and watch my next opponent with the coaches so I could see how he boxed and how I could beat him. When I saw Sacirovic, I knew I had him. I beat him easily enough, but I saved something a little special for the last twenty seconds and I got quicker and quicker and he was saved by the bell at the end. I definitely won. But when they played our national anthem the crowd whistled and booed, and to be honest it made me cry. You couldn't argue that he had lost the fight, but still they booed the national anthem, which to me is as low as you can get.

'When we got back to Havana, though, I was so proud. Me and Teofilo were carrying the flag down the steps of the plane and Fidel was there waiting for us. I was really nervous, of course, because it was the first time I had been face to face with him and I was only twenty. It was amazing to think that Fidel knew who I was, knew all about me. It was such an honour.'

The year 1980 brought his greatest regret and one which he was never given the chance to erase. Rolando Crespo told me that Horta only ever lost his boxing brain once in his career and he did it at what should have been the crowning glory of his boxing life, the final of the Olympics in Moscow in 1980, against Rudi Fink.

'He was over-confident,' says Crespo. 'I remember he let Fink fight in the middle distance where he was most comfortable and no matter how much the corner screamed at him he wouldn't change. It was terrible.'

You can still see Horta's shame at being reminded of this. The words Rudi Fink bring a pained smile to Horta's normally confident face. 'Let me tell you, Fink was the worst boxer I ever lost to. Fink didn't win that medal. I wrapped it up and gave it to him as a present. I was so hot coming into the Olympics that it hurt. No one could touch me. We had this golden rule in the camp that you never took on liquids on the day of a fight, no matter how thirsty you were or what weight you lost. But Fink was so poor as a fighter that I broke the rule and really gulped water down. The first round I was fantastic. If they had had the scoring system they have now [where boxers amass points over all the rounds as opposed to the old system, where you simply won or lost a round at a time], I would have won the fight just on what I did in that first round because I must have scored fifteen blows and he didn't touch me. Sagarra was pleased and I went out for the second, thinking I would show him what a thrashing really was. I wanted to show him that even on his own turf, in the middle distance, he couldn't touch me. But suddenly I couldn't move and he was right on top of me. What the water had done was bloat me, I was like a water bomb sloshing around and I couldn't do what normally I would have been able to do in an instant. I couldn't move away and he picked me off a couple of times. He won the last two rounds, though not by half as much as I had won the first, but still I lost the fight.'

It was a bad moment for a boxer who, pound for pound, many well-informed Cubans regard as greater than Stevenson or Savon.

'You know what was worse? Fink retired after that Olympics and I never got a chance to avenge the defeat. I told Sagarra that I didn't care what it took, if I had to trail around Europe all summer I wanted to get myself a rematch. I have no idea what happened to him after that. But while I was sad at first, when I got back it just made me more determined not to make a stupid mistake again. I got stuck in and prepared for the Los Angeles Games, because we didn't know at that stage that we would boycott them. I prepared for four years and in those four years I didn't lose a single fight. And then we didn't go. Not getting an Olympic gold is my only regret in boxing because that is the absolute peak and I never made it.'

He was relentlessly good in the last six years of his career. He won the world championship, this time as a featherweight, in Munich in 1982. And he called it a day after 1986 in Reno, where he fought as a lightweight.

Crespo remembers a semi-final against Orzubek Nazarov in Reno as one of the finest moments of Horta's career. Nazarov had beaten Horta easily in the same year. According to Alcides Sagarra the reason was that Horta miscalculated at which distance he could get the best advantage. 'It was packed with real drama,' said Crespo. 'They both knew that this was really the gold medal bout, even though it was the semi-final. Horta also knew in himself that this tournament was his last and that the result of the Nazarov fight would decide how he would go out of boxing, even if his last punches would be thrown in the final. It was beautiful. He just oozed class, outboxed, outmanoeuvred, outpunched Nazarov to the point where there was little doubt about the result, though it was a 3–2 verdict in the end. Justice won the day for once! But the Russians couldn't see it and threatened to pull their team out of the tournament if the result wasn't reversed. It wasn't. I sat with him on the plane back and we were silent for a long time. He turned to me and said, "Will you announce my retirement, Crespo? The punches you saw in Reno were my last."'

Adolfo Horta finished with 319 wins and 27 losses. He won a pile of medals and cups. And but for a bottle of water he drank in Moscow in 1980 he would have won everything in the sport. You sense that the 'total boxer' senses that his title doesn't quite fit. He likes people to call him that. He enjoys the respect he gets in the street, the friends he has, the family who love him. But he would swap another 27 of those 319 wins to fight Rudi Fink for the Olympic gold medal just one more time. And you know that this time his victory would be truly total.

21 *Close but no Sagarra: To the Heart of the Cuban Team*

That evening in the Cuban embassy in Budapest, when Felix Savon waved his damaged fist in the air to shout 'Viva Fidel!', had shattered my remaining illusions that he was aching to get into the professional ranks. My only hope now was for a change of heart in the government and the Sports Ministry about professional boxing. At least I knew the Sports Minister, sort of, from my time at the Copa Cardin in Pinar del Rio.

Cubadeportes was the government department responsible for commercial transactions involving sportsmen and women. It dealt with everything from their contracts with foreign organisations, to sponsorship agreements, their work as rented-out coaches and players to foreign teams, right down to their plane travel. It also dealt with foreign press inquiries. In the year I had been in Cuba I had avoided all contact with Cubadeportes because I knew from anecdotal evidence that they would want me to pay them handsomely for every tiny scrap of freely available information which they could possibly assert some sort of ownership over. As an example, they once tried to charge a visiting BBC World Service team $100 for the right to record background noise in a public sports arena. Cubadeportes were basically sports pimps and having found out for myself by experience that most sports people were happy to talk for free (or for a few discreetly offered dollars for their kids), I had never really seen the point in giving them the chance to get their claws into me. But I was getting to the stage now where I needed them to set up the one interview I just wasn't going to get on my own – with Alcides Sagarra.

So when I got back from Budapest in November I rang Cubadeportes. I told them I was writing a book on Cuban boxers and that I needed an interview with Sagarra and a few other boxers who lived outside Havana, whom I wasn't able to track down. A couple of days later a man who had all the presence of a street-cleaner, the ubiquitous short, wiry bureaucrat, turned up at my flat on his moped. It was the very man who had tried to rip off the BBC, the man who Martha Gonzalez had warned me against, the man she simply called the Moron. He sat down and we chatted, very quietly and calmly, about what it was I wanted to do. He told me at every turn that he could organise everything I wanted. He was particularly keen that I should meet Pedro Roque, who coached the Cuban's national youth squad, which seemed fine by me. He promised as well to get in touch with INDER's regional offices and set up meetings with boxers in Holguin, Baracoa, Santiago and Camaguey. He seemed very friendly. Then gently he broached the subject of money and in came the sting.

'You see, John, if you want to write a book about boxing in this country then we are happy to help you, but our role must be recognised. It is up to us to protect the image of sport here and we own that image. Many people have profited by what Cubans have achieved in sport and we only want some of that to be put back. So before we do anything for you, you will have to sign a contract with us that gives us a percentage of everything that you earn on the book. This sort of arrangement would be normal in your country: that when someone writes a book about someone else than that person shares in the profits, yes? I think it's going to be a great book, John.'

At that moment all I could think about was bottled water. I wasn't thirsty, but here was a man whose job in life was to convince rational, intelligent people to pay for things that with a little effort they could get for nothing. I was getting mightily pissed off and I couldn't rustle up more than the faintest veneer of politeness in responding to his request.

'I can't do that, I'm afraid. The rights of the book are not mine to give away. They are already owned by the publishers.

'You must understand that I will make very little money from this book. The sort of percentage you want would leave me with nothing to show for a year's work here and so there wouldn't be any point in having done it, would there? I mean, I'll have a word with the publishers and see what they say, but I don't think they are likely to agree. Just let me make sure you understand, though, that this is not a bestseller. It's a book recording the history of Cuban boxing. It's almost finished and with the greatest respect you haven't contributed anything to it so far, so I don't really see why you should be entitled to share in the proceeds. If the only way I can get an interview with Sagarra is to pay some money then so be it, but I am not signing a contract that gives you money from sales of the book.'

'Yes, John, but with our ability to distribute the book in Cuba we could sell many copies here. You could arrange for us to be given some copies, couldn't you, John?'

I told him what a great idea it was and told him I would do it. It was an easy promise to make because I had no intention of keeping it. He was basically arguing that Cubadeportes had some sort of copyright on Cuban boxing history, despite the fact that the Cubans didn't have enough respect for their past even to fund a boxing historian to gather information on one of their national sports or pay for the upkeep of their tinny, leaking, shoddy sports museum, where the exhibits rotted in glass cases. The idea that I might have had to deal with them over organising an actual fight, something that required imagination, an intelligent appraisal of the value of what they had, an acceptance that someone else should make some money too, and the determination to deliver what they said they would, just seemed unimaginable.

Still. Keep going. I tried the usually successful technique of namedropping to get past our negotiating impasse. 'I do know all these people myself, you know,' I said. 'I know the commissioner of boxing from way back in January and I met the Sports Minister in Pinar del Rio at the Copa Cordoba Cardin. I'm sure he would be happy to help me.'

'I'm afraid the Sports Minister is no longer in the job, John. We are currently going through some reorganisation.' And indeed they were. What he failed to mention was that Cubadeportes had been targeted by the government as being corrupt and a whole wedge of people had been sacked. The word was that several people in the organisation had been creaming off dollars from foreigners and then – oh so hard to believe, no, no, comrade, not in Cuba – not passing them all on to the treasurer of Cubadeportes. But this meant I had no access to the Sports Ministry because my contacts had been sacked.

The Moron and I danced around one another for several weeks. First he said that Sagarra had agreed to an interview the following Wednesday and I would have to pay several hundred dollars in advance. I pointed out to him that Sagarra would not be in the country on that day – one of the boxers in the national team had told me they were all going to Mexico. He promised to check it out and didn't ring back with any sort of explanation for his error. Next he said that he personally had made a big fuss about how I was being messed around and that Sagarra would give me an interview at the Cubadeportes exhibition out in the Expocuba complex the following week. One of the Cuban journalists had already told me to go along because Sagarra was going to hold a press conference and there would be a couple of exhibition bouts. I told the Moron that I wasn't going to pay to attend an open press conference. He didn't seem to know that it was happening, but fizzed off on his moped assuring me that I would get a one-to-one with Sagarra. He can't have thought that I believed him.

I turned up to Expocuba not really expecting anything. The international exhibition was the usual farce. Adidas had a stall in one corner of a bright, modern exhibition hall. There were four or five smaller stalls around the edge belonging to Cuban state organisations like Batos, who make baseballs and boxing equipment, and a central stall of cheap-looking gymnasium products from a variety of countries. No one was looking around or negotiating deals. There were just a few bored young men and women in blazers sitting at the stalls flirting with whoever happened to be nearest.

Eventually the Cubans' team bus turned up with a group of about twenty youngsters in blazers and tracksuits. When they got into the hall some workers were still struggling to put up a temporary boxing ring in the corner, watched by a group of schoolchildren who had also been bussed in. Several of the hacks I knew were also there. It was a pleasant atmosphere, chatty. The boxers quickly found a stall to sit at and gossip. A couple of them cheekily asked if I would buy them a soft drink, which I did. Sagarra walked in, looked around and moved off to sit in a glass-walled office in the opposite corner of the hall with a man in a suit. It was the new Cubadeportes boss. Younger and leaner than his jolly, good-living predecessor, he didn't dress like an old Communist bureaucrat, but definitely looked like one of the younger breed who were starting to get to positions of power in Cuba.

After a while the Moron went into the room. He hung around, smiling and fawning like an obsequious manservant. Sagarra never looked him in the eye and seemed to stare, annoyed and silent, out at the empty exhibition hall as the Moron wittered on and smiled. There were to be no exhibition bouts (who would they be watched by?). And there was to be no press conference, a cancellation that the press who had turned up took stoically. In England they would have murdered him in the papers the following day for dragging them out on a wild-goose chase.

I'd come with an acquaintance, Rodolfo, who was the son of a famous baseball player, had played to a decent standard himself and was now the manager of the Bolero bar in posh Miramar, where I used to go for pizza. He knew Sagarra through his father and I thought that by association this might make Sagarra treat me more warmly. The pair greeted each other pleasantly when I was ushered in to see the official group by the Moron and Sagarra actually smiled and laughed as Rodolfo and he exchanged family pleasantries. Then Rodolfo left us to our own devices and the smiles disappeared with him. The new Cubadeportes guy spoke first.

'It is our responsibility to protect the image of Cuban sport and to make sure that it is not exploited by outsiders, John. I understand that you want to write a book and it is fair therefore that you should make a contract with us and we will offer you all the help you need in this book.' This was the same speech the Moron had made the first time I met him, but I had to be polite to this guy. I wasn't going to get any help from them if I didn't agree, so I changed tack.

'OK. I'll do it if you get a copy of the contract you want me to sign. Then I can let my publishers look at it and see what they think.'

If you can't beat them, use their weaknesses against them. I knew it would take them weeks to do anything so bold as draw up this contract of theirs. If I insisted that we do some interviews in the meantime, then I would have everything I needed before I had signed anything. Yes, it was a con. Yes, it was stooping to their level, but they started it. Sagarra sat silently through all of this, smiled faintly as he shook my hand, and then left to supervise the dismantling of the ring. I was no nearer to getting into a long conversation with the one man whose feelings might be the key to saving the project. I think I knew by now that he wouldn't be positive, but I had to find out for sure.

Out of boredom I coughed up $100 to the Moron and he took me to see Pedro Roque. The Cuban youth squad is based out near the Pan-American Stadium, a housing estate and outdoor arena constructed for the Pan-American Games of 1991, to which Cuba had been committed before the Special Period and which they still hosted despite the total collapse of their economy. The team was based in what had been the athlete's village for the 1991 games. Kids in tracksuits were wandering around the place. The youth boxing gym was pretty small, about the size of a basketball court, with one entire end taken up by a tatty ring. The roof was not high and if I had stood in the ring I could have jumped up and hit my head on the ceiling pretty easily. I could see now why the giant super-heavyweight Alexis Rubalcaba, who had passed through this gym, seemed to stoop so much in the ring. I sat down and chatted with the trainers, who were playing dominoes. Training had finished for the day.

'Tell me about Sagarra,' I asked the group.

'He's certainly a personality,' said one. His name was Waldo Santiago and he had, he said, gone to the first post-revolutionary Central American Games in 1962 and won gold. But on a tour round Europe he was injured and had to give up. He became a trainer and official: he was an AIBA central committee member and international referee at three Olympics (1968, 1972 and 1976). Eventually he became Cuba's commissioner of boxing, a post he held until 1980, when he stepped down and began training the youth team. 'I worked with Sagarra in the national team as an assistant. He only had one actual trainer, Gabriel Lopez Nunez, We We Barton.'

I had heard the name We We Barton before. It's not a name you forget easily. He was mentioned whenever I asked about the start of the Cuban system as the man who was there at the very beginning. As to his exact role and who was with him, that depended on who you were talking to. Barton was a professional trainer at one of Havana's most important gyms in Cerro when the revolution came along. He trained Sarvelio Fuentes, the giant grandfatherly man who had played nice cop to Sagarra's nasty cop in the Cuban team until he was mysteriously told to leave the plane for the 1992 Olympics while it was on the ground at Havana because, implausibly, there wasn't a seat for him.

Soon after that, Sarvelio and his family went to work in Argentina with their national team. No one ever talked about why. Back in 1960 Barton and Fuentes started up the Cuban amateur boxing association and went looking for a training camp with the help of the East German, Kurt Rosentrip, who had been sent to help the new comrades. Out running one day, Rosentrip found a derelict farm on the fringes of Havana, well away from the temptations of the centre and from prying eyes, which he thought would be perfect. At first all they did was construct a ring in the field next to the old farm building and train by running around under the trees – the area was further protected by being in the middle of a large wood. They started with nothing, most of the good amateurs wanted to turn professional and took the opportunity the government had offered to get out of the country and carry on as pros. The change in culture was also different for the public who used to pack out the Ciudad Deportiva, the arena still used today for Havana's biggest amateur fights.

The first step was to start a championship, so they came up with the Playa Giron, named after the victory in the Bay of Pigs. It was held at the Ciudad Deportiva, not, as now, over a concentrated couple of weeks but every Saturday night, mirroring what the professional pattern of programming had been. The first Playa Giron therefore took two months to complete.

'I boxed in the first round with a guy from Guantanamo whose name I forget because I don't think he ever boxed again,' said Santiago. 'The rest were three boxers from Havana. Anyway, instead of a straight knockout they told me I would have to face each one of them. There wasn't much of a crowd to start with, but gradually they started turning up and paying to get in, so we could afford to send a team to the Central American Games. In 1962 we won the boxing part of those games. It was a serious task from then on building the team up. The head of the trainers then was We We Barton. In 1963 there were the Pan-Americans in São Paulo. We only got one gold medal which was Roberto Caminero Perez, who they called Chocolatico. We carried on working.'

With help from the Soviet bloc and after a few years getting to grips with a new intake of talent the results started to come. The team management became tougher, more disciplined and more scientific in its approach. Whatever they did was based at the farm until eventually when anyone talked about the team they would just refer to them as the Finca, as royalty has become the Palace and Downing Street has become the centre of British political power. The Finca was where Sagarra worked. If there was a secret as to why Cuban boxers were so good I would find it there. I had to get out there and have a look.

That wasn't going to be easy. But flushed with success at having managed to screw money out of me for the visit to the youth team and the old men playing dominoes, the Moron believed there was cash to be made. He redoubled his pitiful efforts to get Sagarra to speak to me. Then one day he rang and said that it was on, he had got permission to take me to the Finca. He would come to the house the next day on his moped and I could organise a taxi to take us there. Maybe this guy wasn't such a moron after all.

It drizzled with rain the day I went to the Finca. I half-expected to be blindfolded to protect the location of this secretive place. There was no need – although I paid attention the whole way, I couldn't find my way back there again if I had ten years in which to do it. We went through little villages, up suburban streets, on to the main road, through a wood and along a straight small road, passing farmers all the way until we reached a fenced-off farm building with a guard on the gate. We stopped and the Moron went in. As I was standing there several of the people I knew from the team came running round the barely marked out three-foot-wide red Astroturf running track that ringed the borders of the farm. Several smiled at me as they charged past. Some were obviously running off injuries, others were desperately pushing them-selves, presumably to maintain their weight. I stood at the gate and waited for permission to be let in to talk to Sagarra. The Moron came back and said that Sagarra would see us soon. I should have expected what happened next.

As I waited and smoked, a Lada drove towards the gate from within the Finca. Inside was Sagarra. He was in a hurry. The Moron tried to talk to him again, but Sagarra didn't even stop the car as he gesticulated to the Moron and jabbered away. He had a central committee meeting booked in for exactly the time the Moron had said I was guaranteed an interview. He drove off at speed. The Moron shrugged his shoulders and tried to look upset on my behalf.

The guard gestured me into the Finca and we walked across a muddy path to a little committee room.

I wasn't too downhearted. Though the whole point of the day's exertions had been to talk to Sagarra, I had to admit that actually being at the Finca, this almost mythical building which has come to represent the discipline and pain of Cuba's boxers, made me feel pretty cocky about myself. Maybe I had set off with grandiose Quixotic ideas and maybe I had rather childishly enjoyed the idea of being a secret agent, a spy, a man with a secret mission. But standing here I realised that I had taken that mission just about as far as it was possible to go. I was at the Finca, the nerve centre of Cuban boxing, where they deeply disapprove of the presence of foreigners. Quite patently I wasn't going to achieve what I had come to achieve. But a lot of that had not been my fault. Tyson hadn't kept his part of the bargain. Warren wasn't in a position to keep his. Savon, unwittingly, hadn't kept his part of it either. But me, I had kept plugging away and I had got here. I had arrived at the inner sanctum of the Cuban team and I thought that somehow I was about to be let in on a secret.

Sadly, there doesn't seem to be one. If the Finca is the secret, then it isn't very impressive. The building is ramshackle, a long gym in what presumably was a hayshed, with several rings set up inside and various punching bags and weights. It's well lit and well maintained, but I've seen school sports halls with better equipment. Off the main hall are some offices and the medical and massage room, where the masseur I had met in Hungary was sitting at his desk puffing on a big cigar and reading a magazine.

The team doctor gave me the spiel, a load of dates and technical stuff I wasn't interested in. The coaches came in one

by one to a cramped classroom to run through the achievements of Cuban boxing, but there were no anecdotes. Just
dates and lists and shrugged shoulders and compliments to the
fine work of Alcides Sagarra. Some of it was interesting, but I
had heard most of it before. It ended and I went for lunch with
the Moron in the team canteen, a hut at the far end of the
complex about the size of a greasy spoon, where I ate rice and
beans and some sort of meat. The dinner ladies looked at me
as if I was from outer space.

The Moron left me alone and I walked around and thought.
I was never going to get to see Sagarra, my year's unpaid leave
was up and the *Guardian* had said that if I didn't come back
after the New Year I wasn't going to be coming back at all. I'd
had my adventure and I'd done as much as I could. Here I was,
I'd conquered what I could, but I wasn't going to get any
further than this and if I stayed here much longer I wouldn't
have anything to go back to. My sister had moved out of the
flat. I was running out of money. I'd loved what I'd done, but
it was over. The next day I went and booked my flight home. I
never spoke to the Moron again. And I never tried to get to
Sagarra again, though one day when I was bored and looking
through the phone book there was his home number right in
front of me. I never rang. It was none of my business.

22 Houston, 1999

You never quite leave something like that behind entirely, though. Several ex-boxers rang me up reverse charge at the *Guardian* over the next few months asking if I could find them work in England. And I programmed my computer to look for news on the Internet of Cuban sport. I even started taking a passing interest in the Pan-American Games. And each February I remembered playing softball at the national championships in February sunshine and wished I was back. But mostly I was glad I was on the outside looking in.

August 1999 was the real end of the road, I suppose. Not just for me, but possibly for Felix Savon, maybe for Cuban boxing.

I had spent my time since leaving Cuba gathering information and keeping contacts with my Cuban friends, as far as was possible from England. I only spoke to Frank Warren once in that time, fairly soon after my return from Cuba, when he invited the press to come to his Hertfordshire mansion, a grand country house decorated as befits a lord of the manor. He had called us there, oiks and all, to put his view across on the row he was having with Don King, with whom he had now split. Warren complained that King had tried to steal Naseem Hamed behind his back and that King wasn't delivering his side of the bargain in getting the big fights in the United States for Hamed. Warren said the contract ended on a certain date, but that King had added an extension in handwriting on the end which suggested it was continuing. Warren said this wouldn't stand up in court and that as far as he was concerned it was over. King took Warren to court in the UK, claiming that to dissolve the partnership meant that everything involved in the partnership had to be split equally right down the middle. Legally it turned out he was right and Warren lost millions. He was now forced to buy back 50 per cent of his own business or see King share in all his profits. King, ever the smart hustler, had isolated his own part of the partnership so that Warren only shared in King's European interests, which were not substantial.

Warren was his usual upbeat self, indiscriminately charming to all his guests. I finally grabbed thirty seconds alone with him at the end of the massive dining table which dominates the living room of the house.

'I'm sorry about what happened over the Cuba thing,' he said. I wasn't sure exactly what he meant. Was he sorry we hadn't succeeded or worried that I might feel pissed off because he hadn't coughed up all the money?

'Don't worry about it, Frank,' I said. 'I still think there is something in it. We can talk about it another time when there are fewer people around.'

We never did.

But I kept an eye on what was going on in Cuba because I genuinely believed something might happen there and that the knowledge and contacts I had gained were too valuable and unique to be thrown away and forgotten. Over those two years Savon had not been impressive. In fact, he had lost four times, suggesting that what I had felt at the end of the world championships in Hungary – that Savon was finished – was basically correct. But the word in the lead-up to the world championships in Houston in August 1999 was that he was back to his best, having won the Pan-American Games the previous month as part of a Cuban team which had some younger faces I knew nothing about. I decided to go and see for myself.

My arrival in Houston was delayed by a hurricane, which meant that I got stuck in Miami for three days. I decided to use the time to try and find Kid Gavilan. In a very Cuban way everyone I met claimed to know where he was, but every time I followed up their leads they turned out to be wrong. The hurricane cleared so I had to give up and go to Houston.

When I arrived I was, for once, booked into a proper hotel, the Holiday Inn Astrodome, which would have been very convenient if the tournament was being held in the Astrodome but it wasn't. It was taking place in an area of town they called the Medical Center, eight miles down the road. In any city, anywhere else in the world, eight miles is not a great distance. A bus, metro or cheap taxi would get you there in fifteen minutes, but this was America, where the words public transport were one up from bubonic plague in the lexicon of desirable things for a city to have lots of. However, the organisers had provided a shuttle bus, I suppose with the intention of easing transport problems.

The first morning I found the bus outside the Holiday Inn and, great, it was going to the George R. Brown Convention Center, where the boxing was being held and where the press accreditations were being dished out. I got on the bus.

'Excuse me, sir, can I see your accreditation?' The voice belonged to a fat, middle-aged black man whose blue shirt was at least one size too small for him.

'I'm going to the centre now to collect my accreditation. But here is my press card.'

'I'm sorry, sir, I'm going to have to ask you to leave the bus.'

'I'm sorry, I don't think you understand. I'm a journalist here to cover the boxing and I have to go to the George R. Brown to collect my badge. I'm not accredited yet, which is why I need to go there.'

'I'm sorry, sir, but if you don't have accreditation you can't come on the bus.'

'But I can't get accreditation until I get to the venue and I can only get to the venue from here on this bus. This is absurd.'

Two Lithuanians sitting in the front row looked at me blankly.

'You will have to speak to the police officer there. If they radio ahead and the man in the control centre says you can get on the bus then I will let you on the bus.'

I walked over to the police officers. Houston must be a great place to live if the city can spare two police officers to mind a bus queue and have a control centre especially to deal with problems that the bus queue might throw up. But that's the sort of system you get if no one has enough imagination to solve problems for themselves. I told them who I was. I showed them the press card. They could have told the driver just to let me on, but that was more than their jobs were worth, so a senior police officer was called upon to make the decision. After consulting one of the organisers of the tournament he decided to let me on the bus, which had by now left. I was going to ask when the next one came, but I suspected that only the US State Department would be authorised to reveal information at that level. So I got a cab.

The George R. Brown Convention Center is a vast two-floor building, a functional, no-frills cavern with high ceilings, one vast hall plonked on top of another. It is slapped down

320

next to a motorway viaduct on the fringe of downtown Houston and if it had had any windows they would have offered a fabulous view of the glassy majesty of Houston's jaw-dropping skyscrapers. They were an odd phenomenon for a city with so much space and so little restriction on growth that it was fast heading for being 100 miles from its most northerly point to most southerly (London to Leicester!). I could only assume that the skyscrapers were there because someone somewhere must have figured that a big city has to have skyscrapers to be taken seriously. They were in fact a modern American folly. Pointless but exceptionally beautiful.

The hall was soulless and empty of atmosphere, but you couldn't blame the Americans for that. The tournament had been due to be held in Manila in the Philippines, but the Filipinos had pulled out at the last minute. The Americans had stepped in with three months to go and, given the time, had done a pretty good job. There was no buzz around Houston about a world championships being in town and no one turned up except for finals night. Even then the crowd all seemed to be family or friends of one of the boxers. TV coverage was limited to ESPN2, who were preparing a package to be broadcast in a fortnight's time. The only people taking a live feed were the Cubans, who may have found their rights easier to negotiate this time around because it would, I suppose, be illegal to take their money under American law.

But they were all there. Pacheco, Robertico, Modesto Aguerro, Eddie Martin and a new face partnering Pacheco, who looked as if he hadn't been abroad much before. They were, as ever, staying at a better hotel than I was and paying less. It was just like being in Budapest except for the setting. Instead of a freezing Hungarian winter we had a boiling hot Texan desert August. And, of course, in Budapest they had pedestrians.

By the time I got there, two days into the tournament, there were already signs of what was to come. The double Olympic middleweight champion, Ariel Hernandez, had already lost his first-round bout to an unknown Romanian on points. There were no complaints, he had simply been sent home to Havana in disgrace the same night, because the team, or more precisely Alcides Sagarra, felt that he had not tried. They may, of course, have smelt a rat. The team had been pestered by sports agents in Winnipeg at the Pan-Ams to the point that even the American team officials issued a statement condemning the behaviour of their own countrymen in harassing the boxers. Maybe Ariel was going to defect. Or maybe he had finally lost his heart for boxing. It was reminiscent of Angel Espinosa's final fight, against a nothing Pole at the Barcelona Olympics whom he could have beaten in his sleep any day of this or any other week. He just did nothing and let the guy spoil the fight and sneak the win. Whatever the reason, Ariel wasn't around long enough for us to find out.

So from a boxing point of view Houston began exactly where Budapest had left off, with the Cubans being the victims of some weird and unwonderful judging. During the first few days the patience of the Cuban team was pushed and tested and pushed again by a series of decisions that ranged from the merely questionable through eyebrow-raising to the utterly inexplicable. Manuel Mantilla, the flyweight, lost. Judel Johnson, the new young featherweight whom I had not seen box before, lost. Waldemar Font, a world champion in 1997, lost. To be on the receiving end of one iffy decision in the early stages was part of the risk of amateur boxing. Referees and judges don't always see everything and if you leave it too close you take a risk. It was the nature of the sport. But for the Cubans it was rapidly becoming normal to be the victims of three or more decisions like this in international competitions.

Other teams, it has to be said, suffered too. The classy

French middleweight, Jean-Paul Mendy, lost incredibly to a Russian on points, 14–7. I spoke to the trainer Aldo Consentino afterwards and he was incandescent. 'It was robbery. The judges saw five scoring blows for the Russian in the first round that no one else in the arena saw.' He stormed off shouting to himself. The Italian European champion, Giacobbe Fragomeni, lost an admittedly lacklustre heavyweight bout on points to an inexperienced Welshman called Kevin Evans, who few observers thought did enough to beat him. But Fragomeni hadn't done enough to be 110 per cent sure, which meant that Evans went through to the semi-final. And he would be up against Felix Savon. In that semi Evans, to his credit, did OK, and was edging the first few minutes, but then he started to take a terrible hammering and had to be saved by his own corner throwing in the towel at the start of the final round.

The finals were to be held on the Thursday and Friday night. The Cubans were in an extraordinary position. They had a mere five finalists, four of whom were fighting on the Thursday. Even if they all were to win, it would equal their worst performance at a world championships. The evening started badly. Maikro Romero lost the decision against an American, Brian Viloria, a slight Hawaiian who boxed above expectations. Romero could hardly have expected to leave the ring with more than the knowledge that one of the world's great boxers had beaten him by only four or five points. Instead he left with a gold medal and a 9–2 points victory, which for Maikro, who can go through a whole tournament without conceding nine points, constituted a thrashing.

When the result was announced and the grey-haired man sitting at ringside in front of the computer held up the red ping-pong bat, to confirm to the referee the colour of the winning corner, Romero sank to his knees and shook his head. Not sad but angry, humiliated. An honest boxer, he composed himself quickly and went over to the American to shake hands and, he obviously hoped, to solicit some sort of acknowledgement from Viloria that the judges had got it wrong. But there was none. Not consciously anyway. But boxers can never truly hide it when they know they have lost. When Maikro tried to talk to him, Viloria shuffled away. He couldn't quite look Maikro in the eye. He knew he had been lucky.

Alcides Sagarra stood in the corner leaning on the corner post and looked across at Maikro with a smile tinged with mock horror and surprise. 'Maikro, don't worry about it,' shouted Sagarra, as Romero stalked around the ring, frustrated and shaking his head. Like a caged animal, he walked from one corner to another trying to catch someone's, anyone's, eye who might offer him a sympathetic glance. The AIBA officials seated on the podium, with Professor Chowdry, the President, in the centre, stared down at the forms littering their desk and talked self-consciously among themselves. Eventually Sagarra called Maikro out of the ring so that the medal ceremony could take place. The Cubans had got used to it by now. This had to be written off as just another bad decision. As the American anthem was played, Maikro stood respectfully and watched another man receive the medal that was his. He shook hands and was gone, still shaking his head and looking pleadingly at the crowd. Pacheco turned to me and held his hands up and open as if I could explain. His face was puzzlement tinged with anger. He looked as if someone had just told him his grandmother had once been forced to ride an elephant naked through the lobby of the Hotel Inglaterra.

The atmosphere at the Cuban press desk, where I had set up camp for the evening, calmed down when their next fighter went up. The lightweight Mario Kindelan won his gold-medal bout against a Russian, which disappointed the conspiracy theorists in the Cuban camp. The fact was that he had left no room for doubt. He had crushed Alexei Steponov. Maybe the Cubans were just being paranoid, maybe these were the sorts of error that you get in sport, part of the game. It had certainly happened plenty of times before.

It's true that ridiculous decisions are nothing new in amateur boxing. Probably the most infamous of recent times was when Roy Jones Jr, in the Seoul Olympics of 1988, was judged the loser of a fight that his opponent barely survived. Si Hun Park, who happened to be from the host nation, won gold instead. The scandalous refereeing of 1988, where the Koreans did exceptionally well but somehow disappeared as a major force in amateur boxing immediately afterwards, brought investigations and a change in the scoring system. But I had heard a story, from two good sources, of a Russian with envelopes of cash attempting to bribe an English judge in the world juniors.

By the time Juan Hernandez Sierra got into the ring the Maikro incident was practically forgotten. Juan Hernandez had had a fabulous tournament. I had always enjoyed watching him as a technical boxer, a stylist, but arguably he lacked real aggression and he was forever losing out to poor decisions, and one or two fair ones, in the finals and semi-finals of major competitions. He was what no boxer wanted to be, a double Olympic silver medallist, losing in 1996 to Oleg Saitov and in 1992 to Michael Carruth. Two years before in Budapest he had lost a semi-final 5–4 to Oleg Saitov: I remember watching the television monitor and thinking that somehow the button the judges were supposed to press for scoring points for Hernandez must be broken because nothing he did was making any difference. Maybe it was just my imagination because I wanted the guy to do well. Maybe it was his own fault. His occasional undeniable sleepy round in really big fights had cost him dear.

But this was a new Hernandez in Houston. Out of the ring he is a softly spoken man with a distant, weary sort of smile. He says very little and when he speaks he almost seems to apologise for it. But in Houston, for the gold that he was obviously determined was going to be his, he was pumped. He trotted over to the other corner and handed over a small gift, but he made it seem like he was handing over the address of his undertaker of choice. Perfunctory, polite, without warmth. I was pleased for him. He leapt in the air as he faced his opponent and banged his gloves together, stretched his mouth. It couldn't start quickly enough for him. For four rounds he gave a display of everything that is fine about Cuban boxing. Ooomph for Barcelona. Thhuuuud for Atlanta. Dooooossh for Budapest. He danced in front of his opponent, Timur Gaidalov, darting in with scoring punches and darting out before he could get anything in return. But he did more. He hammered away at his opponent's guard to open it up for blows to the head and he slammed blows into his guts. Bang, bang, bang, sshwooop, for everyone else's national anthem and their flag edging ahead of Cuba's to the top of the poles. Uuugghh-uuugghh-uuugghh, for every stinking piece of silver in the world. He was on top for the whole fight, no lazy rounds this time, nothing too technical. This was as comprehensive a master class in the art of amateur boxing as you would pay to see. It was worth the wait.

Hernandez deserved this moment. He, us, them, everyone, we all knew he had butchered Gaidalov for four two-minute rounds. He deserved the smile on his face, he had earned the satisfaction and relief. The referee stood between them holding their bandaged hands. What a great moment for a great boxer.

'Ladies and gentlemen,' slow and laboured, teasing us, teasing him.

'*Damas y caballeros*,' quicker, Latin, more urgent . . .

'The winner on points . . .' Where's the man with the ping-pong bat? Can't see him. Never mind.

'*El ganador por puntos* . . .'. What a great word *ganador* is. Much more triumphant and decisive than winner.

'Five to three . . .'. Are they joking? By two measly points? Where are these judges sitting?

'*Cinco a tres.*' Forget it, a gold's a gold. No one remembers the margin.

'In the blue corner . . .'. Who cares the colour of the corner? Except. Hang on.

'Timur Gaidalov of Russia.'

There was a moment of silence.

'You fucking pricks. Don't fucking do this to him,' I thought. Hernandez's face was contorted in real pain, anguish that hurt more than a gloved fist in an unprotected face, worse than the hours and hours spent running, lifting weights and sparring and eating the shit they give you at the Finca to get you to moments like this. This was the pain of a man whose life has been stolen from him by five men who have left their desks at ringside and disappeared, long gone. Hernandez pulled his hand away from the referee and the celebrating Russian a yard away and walked to a neutral corner. The irony was that all he wanted to do was hit something and hit it hard, but he had already done that and it hadn't got him anywhere. Here he was in a boxing ring that suddenly was stripped of its purpose. Five fights in ten days had been a waste of time. He was never going to win the gold medal here. It didn't matter what he had done.

Within two seconds the crowd started to boo. Not just the Cubans, not just the Latinos. The whole crowd began to boo. The boxers booed, the kids booed, the press booed. And Hernandez stalked around the ring forcefully but aimlessly like Maikro before him, a trapped animal. The head of the Cuban delegation, José Barrientos, stormed up to the raised desk where Mr (sorry) Professor Chowdry, the AIBA President, sat with a couple of colleagues. I walked briskly behind him to hear what he was about to say.

'That decision is an utter fucking disgrace,' said Barrientos. 'How can you sit there and humiliate a boxer and disgrace a sport by allowing a decision like that to stand? We protest that decision and we want the protest heard *now*.' Chowdry looked down at his papers as a translator went to work.

The normal timescale for a protest to AIBA was simple. An appeals committee meeting had to be convened, sometimes the same evening, sometimes the next day, and the decision would be reached as soon as the appeals committee saw fit. That would now be tomorrow on the last day of the tournament. Or it could, if AIBA wanted, be later. There would then be the chance for an appeal by the Russians.

The problem for the Cubans was simple. The next-but-one fight was Savon against an American. If they didn't make a stand now, the appeal wouldn't be heard before that fight. As they saw it, Savon was being set up for the same treatment and they weren't going to have a national hero humiliated by these motherfuckers. AIBA had to climb down now before the Savon fight, lose the battle and then Savon might have a fair crack at the gold medal. If they postponed it until after the Savon fight the tournament would already be over for the Cubans and they could make as much noise as they liked and it would not have any impact. After the Savon fight they would be out of bargaining chips.

'We cannot have the appeal immediately. There is no time,' said Chowdry quietly, but his voice wavered. This was an unexpected and unpleasant development for him. The booing of the crowd, the cameras, the press. Meanwhile, with Juan Hernandez Sierra still in the ring, Sagarra had moved close to the podium where the AIBA mob were seated. He looked out of control.

'You people have no respect,' he yelled in Spanish. He was

328

being held back by another team member. 'You people have no respect for the sport.'

He turned his back and muttered and swore to himself. Teofilo Stevenson was next to him, oddly calm, like a naughty boy who knows he shouldn't be where he is but knows that it is the place to be and maybe they will let him stay. He didn't hurry, in his tan safari suit perfectly tailored for his tall, lean upright body. He didn't look angry. He was shrugging his shoulders a lot.

Barrientos had walked away in disgust. The police were starting to move in to clear the area around the Cubans when Barrientos came striding back.

He pulled Alcides and Teofilo two yards in the other direction into a corner four yards away. I moved over and could just about hear what they were saying because Barrientos was so angry he couldn't keep his voice under control.

'I've spoken to the *commandante*.'

That meant that he had spoken to Fidel Castro, whose official title is *commandante en jefe* or commander-in-chief.

'*El commandante* says that if they [AIBA] don't change the decision immediately we are to leave the stadium and go back to Havana. Get the flag. If we go, we go behind the flag.'

This was no longer just another angry protest at a bad decision. It was one thrown punch short of an international incident. The President of Cuba was involved. The three men moved away to talk privately and I went to see what was happening among the Cuban journalists. They were screaming their heads off at anyone who would listen. Robertico was red-faced with anger.

'Teofilo told me before the fight that this was going to happen,' he said.

Pacheco thrust the microphone under my face.

'Mr Yon Dooncan from England. What is your opinion on what we have seen?'

I couldn't lie. I thought it was a disgrace.

'That was a robbery, a total robbery. We've seen it happen in Budapest, at other championships, but now this is too much. The problem is that amateur boxing is not run by good people and there are a group of people who have too much influence over what is supposed to be a noble and clean sport. I think the Cubans should walk out now. If someone steals your watch, you don't stay there in their house for a cup of tea until they've got your wallet as well.'

I sat down and the same member of the Cuban delegation now rushed over to the television commentator Eddie Martin, who was sitting three seats away from me. Martin is a veteran and respected anchorman and analyst who has been doing boxing for Tele Rebelde (Rebel TV) since the Sixties. He is Cuba's David Coleman.

'It's the *commandante*,' said the official. 'He wants to speak to you.'

Martin dropped his microphone and headset hurriedly and reached over for the mobile phone. Like many people unfamiliar with mobile phones, he held it to his ear tentatively and when he couldn't hear anything looked at the keyboard quizzically before putting it back to his ear. He couldn't work out what was wrong and handed the phone back to the official with an apologetic shrug. In the hand-over he must have pressed one of the buttons accidentally and put Fidel Castro on hold. The official apologised to *el commandante* and returned the phone, which Martin then pressed hard against his ear. But he couldn't hear what Castro was saying above the booing and shouting. He left the press area to seek a quieter part of the stadium. He came back briefed, I assumed, to take the firmest possible line against AIBA and to prepare television viewers for the walkout.

Castro has always taken an interest in sport and the sporting achievements of the country. He used to drag members of the

330

national basketball team out to the presidential palace for late-night games in the early days of the revolution. I'd spoken at an embassy party to someone who had played in one. Castro would want to keep going until his team won. There are also photos of a baseball match played in the national stadium in the early days of the revolution when Castro and Camilo Cienfuegos put together a team of top revolutionaries called the Barbudos (the Beards) for a well-publicised match. Castro claims to have been offered a professional baseball contract, but there is no evidence to confirm or refute this. His interest in boxing is less clear, though in the Eighties he once famously greeted a group of boxers returning from the Berlin world championships with a two-hour dissertation at the airport when they arrived after a twelve-hour flight.

Teofilo Stevenson was back in the huddle of bodies around the AIBA podium. The atmosphere was getting more flammable by the minute. A police officer asked Stevenson to move. Stevenson merely glared down at him, like that giant guy with the metal teeth in the Bond films. With a faint smile that would have sent me screaming back to my hotel in terror, he told the officer politely and in broken English that he was in no one's way.

'Don't worry. Be happy. Everything is all right,' he said. Very scary.

Barrientos rushed back to the desk. The Cubans made one last attempt at a compromise.

'If you don't have time to see the video before the end of tonight we suggest you postpone the Savon fight until tomorrow, have the appeal tonight and we will stay to hear what you have to say. If you do not postpone the Savon fight or do not reach a decision before it, then we are walking out of the door.'

Chowdry should have grabbed the offer with both hands. This was a way, a messy way, but a way none the less, to save the world championships from ignominy. But he just sat there and tried to say that they didn't have enough time, that normal procedures would have to be followed.

'Right, that's it. Get the flag,' said Barrientos.

The flag was found and the Cubans gathered by the corner of the ring just to one side of the press desk. Three boxers held the flag at waist height while the team, in their tracksuits, gathered behind it. Rubalcaba was there, Stevenson was there, and Savon, gloved up and ready for his fight in his dressing gown and headguard, was there too. Sadly the flag wasn't very big, so it took some time for those around who didn't understand Spanish to realise what was happening. As the fighters were called to the ring for the heavyweight final, the group tried to push into the ringside area but were held back by police. They couldn't stop Savon, Sagarra and another trainer, who all had a right to be there for the next bout. As they got through the cordon the rest of the Cubans began to sing the national anthem as loudly as they could. It was too sophisticated for the Americans in the audience, whose only instinct when faced with anyone else's national pride is to try and shout it down.

'Uuuu – Esssss – Aiii,' they started to chant, oblivious I suppose to the protests that had gone on and unaware of what was happening. They probably just thought this was the build-up to the main event, the Cubans backing their boy, them backing theirs. But it spoiled what could have been a poignant moment. Savon and Sagarra marched once around the ring, back to where the other boxers had gathered, and then carried on marching, out of the arena.

A press conference was called hurriedly. Barrientos made a statement. AIBA tried to get in on the conference as well, but Barrientos wouldn't let them speak. When he had finished, he thanked the press, put down the microphone, and said audibly, before the AIBA official could speak, 'Y ahora nos vamos pa' la pinga.'

I can only translate it as, 'Now we are fucking off.'

And they did. I never saw any of them again. They went back to the hotel, locked themselves in their rooms and in the early hours headed to the airport for flights to Cancun, from where they connected to Havana.

They were met at the airport by Castro, who greeted them as heroes who had stood up to AIBA.

The appeal was heard that night and the decision was reversed. The AIBA statement read:

Last night after receiving a protest from the Cuban delegation, the five-person jury for bout No. 258 between Timur Gaidalov, Russia; and Juan Hernandez, Cuba; found irregularities in the judges' scoring and reversed the decision of the judges. The gold medal will be awarded to Hernandez and the silver medal to Gaidalov in ceremonies at the competition tonight. Today President Anwar Chowdry of Pakistan convened AIBA's Vice President's bureau and at his request the members took the following action. 1. They endorsed the decision of the [appeals] jury. 2. Four judges from the bout were suspended immediately, pending a decision of AIBA's 34-person executive committee at its next meeting next March/April. The suspended judges are: Doitchev (Bulgaria), Primakov (Estonia), Batbileg (Mongolia), Zelikowiez (Argentina). Cases of this type carry a minimum of four years and a maximum of life suspension. 3. Alcides Sagarra, head coach, and José Barrientos, chief of the Cuban delegation and president of Cuba's boxing federation, are suspended immediately pending the next meeting of the executive committee. Whether or not to take sanctions against the Cuban Federation will be decided by AIBA's Executive Committee at its next meeting. 4. The investigation is ongoing. The scoring papers of each bout in the world championship will be reviewed and serious irregularities in judging, if any, will be dealt with in an appropriate manner. 5. AIBA will restructure the duties of its referees'/judges' commission; the most notable changes will be appointing a panel of two or more persons to review each bout at its conclusion and report any recommendations to the jury immediately. AIBA reaffirms its position of intolerance and firm, swift action against anyone found to be biased, incompetent or corrupt in the conduct of its competitions or in the operation of the federation's other activities.

All very nice. But they could start by selecting judges whose geographical neutrality was a little more obvious. The panel for the controversial Hernandez bout, between a Russian and a Cuban, remember, had included a Bulgarian, an Estonian and a Mongolian (all very much within the political orbit of the old Soviet Union and the corrupt influence of the new Russia) and an Argentinian with a Polish name (which may mean nothing, but certainly catches the eye). From the outside, they looked like a geographically and politically unbalanced panel. But I'm sure the Bulgarian in charge of the referees' and judges' commission (which according to the AIBA web-site doesn't yet have any other members) knew what he was doing.

Beyond the AIBA rhetoric about fighting corruption, it was the Cubans, the injured party, who were left with the roughest end of the stick. Sagarra and Barrientos were suspended until March at least and the team was under threat of a ban after that. If the executive takes action against individual boxers in March, then even a six-month suspension would put them out of the 2000 Olympics in Sydney. Such a ban would most likely be attracted by the boxers who had failed to turn up for their bouts. That would hit Jorge Gutierrez (who was already back

334

in Havana when his name was called for the gold-medal bout in Houston) and Felix Savon. So the meat of this press release was that Houston could have witnessed Felix Savon's last bout in a major competition – against a little-known Welshman called Kevin Evans.

The affair had turned full circle on the Cubans. Their aversion to professional boxing, the aversion that I had been unable to see much weakness in during my year there, had been almost entirely based on pro-boxing's image as corrupt and exploitative, where money did the talking and boxers were just its brutal currency. Amateur boxing was preferable because it was pure sport. There was no money involved, so there would be no corruption and no exploitation. Simple. The boxers did it for pride, because they wanted to compete, to test themselves, not because it was the only way they knew of earning a living. Therefore they were better than the pros.

The flaws in this argument were pretty evident before Houston. First, the professionalisation of a number of Olympic sports had left Cuba in a strange position. Professional sport in general had been made illegal in Cuba in 1962, but several of the country's major sports stars now earn money – on the Grand Prix athletics circuit, for example. The Cuban national team also compete regularly for the $1 million prize money in the world volleyball league. The only sense in which these sports are not professional in Cuba is that the government rather than the sportsman takes the most money. Of course, the cash gets ploughed back into Cuban sport. But once the idea of strict amateurism as the only basis for participation in international sport is gone, then the question becomes why should boxing be specifically excluded?

Because of the dangers? Not really. Boxing is dangerous in both codes. As many of the Cubans told me, they feel that amateur structures mean that they fight more and harder than the pros. The headguards that amateurs wear are considered

335

by some scientists to make amateur boxing more rather than less dangerous: they protect the boxer from cuts, perhaps, but allow them to take more jarring blows to the head than maybe they would without it. The one undeniable additional advantage in amateur fights is that the referees have a more protective obligation to the boxer. But the corner can throw in the towel whenever they want. And the doctor can stop fights too.

Exploitation, then? I don't think so. Cuban boxers are already exploited by the state to provide mass entertainment, generate international prestige for their country and to build a foundation for foreign currency earnings. Cubadeportes makes money out of interviews, out of sponsorship deals, and supplies a number of other countries with Cuban boxing coaches. Many Cuban ex-amateurs feel just as 'spat out' by boxing and the people within it as any washed-up penniless professional. The difference is that the rewards for submitting to exploitation in Cuba are pretty small. The best are rewarded with cars, houses and extra food or jobs for their relatives. The amateurs get to keep a private life, but then so do all but a handful of pros. At least as a professional, if you are even a little bit smart, the potential prize for allowing yourself to be exploited is the financial security of your family. For ever.

Corruption? Well, the pro game has its dirty tricks and its fiddles, for sure. But the corruption of professional boxing as a sport is much more subtle than in the past. It is corrupt now mainly in the sense that the best boxers somehow never seem to fight each other, that there are cartels in several countries or that mediocre fighters seem to be better ranked with one organisation than another depending on who their promoter or manager is. There are still some seriously unscrupulous people involved, but once you get the fighters into the ring, it's a tolerably clean sport. The world championships had suggested this was not universally considered to be true of the amateurs. At the very least there was little to choose between the two.

In Houston the Cubans ran out of arguments. The problem they were facing was that amateur boxing, as they themselves stated so clearly when they stormed out of the George R. Brown Convention Center, stank to its exceedingly high rafters. For all that I had been seduced by amateurism in Cuba, for all the warm glow that seeing Savon chatting to the crowd without any hangers-on had given me in Holguin, for all the almost naive enthusiasm for the sport that the Cuban boxers themselves exuded, the truth was that, once you ventured outside Cuba, amateur boxing was as cynically manipulated as the professional code. And too few other teams seemed to care or want things to change. Partly that was because they weren't going to be hanging around for too long. Many of the boxers were only there to get some practice before turning professional: the French team in Houston was financially 'assisted' by the brothers who control French professional boxing.

The pressure for the Cubans to get out of amateur boxing and take part in the pros in some form was now greater than it had ever been since 1961. They faced the real possibility of an Olympic ban in 2000 for what had happened in Houston. Worse than that the debacle had been witnessed by an IOC delegate, whose report must have been sweet music to the vocal lobby who wanted to see boxing and its annoying controversies kicked out of the games. If the Cubans were banned in 2000 and the sport itself excluded sometime later there would not even be an internal reason for the Cubans to persist in the amateurs. Cuban sport is geared entirely to the Olympic Games. Non-Olympic sports get nothing from INDER. If boxing lost its Olympic status then it would have to find a way to fund itself and there would only be one way to do that. In Houston the Cubans had reached the end of their

337

tether. The irony for me personally was that the goalposts had suddenly moved of their own accord not two years after I had given up pushing against them with Frank Warren's money.

If finally this was all going to happen, however, where were the Cubans going to start? They would have to change their law, manage their own boxers, train them for the pros, do their own deals, promote their own fights. Of course, to do that on the international stage they would need someone who knows his way around the business a little, someone who they're familiar with, someone who knows a bit about boxing, someone with good contacts outside the island. Someone who, when it comes down to it, loves Cuba and Cubans.

In fact, pass me that beer mat. I've just had a great idea . . .